The Moral Psychology of Admiration

Moral Psychology of the Emotions

Series Editor: Mark Alfano, Associate Professor, Department of Philosophy, Delft University of Technology

How do our emotions influence our other mental states (perceptions, beliefs, motivations, intentions) and our behavior? How are they influenced by our other mental states, our environments, and our cultures? What is the moral value of a particular emotion in a particular context? This series explores the causes, consequences, and value of the emotions from an interdisciplinary perspective. Emotions are diverse, with components at various levels (biological, neural, psychological, social), so each book in this series is devoted to a distinct emotion. This focus allows the author and reader to delve into a specific mental state, rather than trying to sum up emotions en masse. Authors approach a particular emotion from their own disciplinary angle (e.g., conceptual analysis, feminist philosophy, critical race theory, phenomenology, social psychology, personality psychology, neuroscience) while connecting with other fields. In so doing, they build a mosaic for each emotion, evaluating both its nature and its moral properties.

Other Titles in the Series

The Moral Psychology of Forgiveness, edited by Kathryn J. Norlock
The Moral Psychology of Pride, edited by Adam J. Carter and Emma C. Gordon
The Moral Psychology of Sadness, edited by Anna Gotlib
The Moral Psychology of Anger, edited by Myisha Cherry and Owen Flanagan
The Moral Psychology of Contempt, edited by Michelle Mason
The Moral Psychology of Compassion, edited by Justin Caouette and Carolyn Price
The Moral Psychology of Disgust, edited by Nina Strohminger and Victor Kumar
The Moral Psychology of Gratitude, edited by Robert Roberts and Daniel Telech
The Moral Psychology of Admiration, edited by Alfred Archer and André Grahle

Forthcoming Titles in the Series

The Moral Psychology of Regret, edited by Anna Gotlib
The Moral Psychology of Guilt, edited by Corey J. Maley and Bradford Cokelet
The Moral Psychology of Hope, edited by Claudia Blöser and Titus Stahl

The Moral Psychology of Admiration

Edited by Alfred Archer and André Grahle

ROWMAN &
LITTLEFIELD
———— INTERNATIONAL
London • New York

Published by Rowman & Littlefield International, Ltd.
6 Tinworth Street, London SE11 5AL
www.rowmaninternational.com

Rowman & Littlefield International, Ltd. is an affiliate of
Rowman & Littlefield
4501 Forbes Boulevard, Suite 200, Lanham, Maryland 20706, USA
With additional offices in Boulder, New York, Toronto (Canada), and London (UK)
www.rowman.com

Selection and editorial matter © 2019 by Alfred Archer and André Grahle
Copyright in individual chapters is held by the respective chapter authors.

All rights reserved. No part of this book may be reproduced in any form or by any electronic or mechanical means, including information storage and retrieval systems, without written permission from the publisher, except by a reviewer who may quote passages in a review.

British Library Cataloguing in Publication Information
A catalogue record for this book is available from the British Library

ISBN: HB 978-1-78660-768-3

Library of Congress Cataloging-in-Publication Data Available

ISBN: 978-1-78660-768-3 (cloth)
ISBN: 978-1-5381-5882-1 (pbk)
ISBN: 978-1-78660-769-0 (electronic)

Contents

Introduction *Alfred Archer and André Grahle*	1
Part I: The Nature of Admiration	**9**
1 No More Heroes Any More? *Sophie-Grace Chappell*	11
2 Ideals and Idols: On the Nature and Appropriateness of Agential Admiration *Antti Kauppinen*	29
3 Happy Self-Surrender and Unhappy Self-Assertion: A Comparison between Admiration and Emulative Envy *Sara Protasi*	45
4 Admiration and Self-Respect *Jan-Willem van der Rijt*	61
Part II: History	**77**
5 Gazing Upwards to the Stage: Mendelssohn's Notion of Admiration and Its Consequences *Anne Pollok*	79
6 Nietzsche on Admiration and Admirableness *Simon Robertson*	95
Part III: Social and Political Dimensions of Admiration	**111**
7 Towards a Concept of Revolutionary Admiration: Marx and the Commune *Vanessa Wills*	113

8 Judging in Times of Crisis: Wonder, Admiration, and Emulation 129
   Marguerite La Caze

 9 Admiration as Normative Support 149
   André Grahle

 10 Admiring Animals 165
   Amanda Cawston

Part IV: Admiration and Moral Education 179

 11 Is It Morally Good to Admire?: Psychological Perspectives on the Potentials and Limits of Admiration and Elevation 181
   Ines Schindler

 12 Admiration and the Development of Moral Virtue 201
   Alan T. Wilson

 13 Obstacles to the Admiration of Moral People 217
   Florien M. Cramwinckel and Benoît Monin

 14 How Admiring Moral Exemplars Can Ruin Your Life: The Case of Conrad's *Lord Jim* 233
   Alan Thomas, Alfred Archer, and Bart Engelen

Index 249

About the Contributors 255

Introduction

Alfred Archer and André Grahle

Wesley Autrey became famous when he jumped onto the subway tracks in front of an oncoming train to save the life of a fellow passenger. Autrey was called "The Harlem Hero," awarded a Bronze Medallion for exceptional citizenship, and received special recognition in the annual State of the Union address. Admiring those who perform extraordinary acts such as Autrey's is a natural part of everyday life. We feel admiration for heroes and saints, sports and film stars, as well as those close to us who excel in a more modest way. But what is admiration and what role does it play in our lives?

Despite the important role admiration seems to play in our lives, it is an emotion that has received little attention from contemporary philosophers (we will discuss the exceptions to this below). This stands in contrast to the recent surge in philosophical interest in emotions such as shame, contempt, guilt, and anger. Perhaps, this displays a preference among contemporary philosophers to focus on the negative rather than the positive, to focus on explaining when people deserve to be subjected to blame rather than when they deserve to be praised. Perhaps it tells us something about the emotions most commonly experienced by contemporary philosophers, or those they are encouraged to feel by the philosophical community. Whatever the reason, this lack of attention amongst philosophers stands in contrast to the significant work on admiration carried out by psychologists (for recent overviews of psychological work on admiration see Schindler et al. [2013] and Onu et al. [2016]).

The purpose of this volume is to make a first step towards investigating the nature of admiration and its role in moral psychology. By bringing the work of philosophers and psychologists together, this volume provides an interdisciplinary, though predominantly philosophical, exploration of an often-discussed but rarely researched emotion: admiration. By exploring the moral psychology of admiration, the volume examines the nature of this emotion; how it relates to other emotions such as wonder, envy, and pride; and what role admiration plays in our moral lives. In the remainder of this introduction, we situate the contributions in this volume in the existing philosophical literature on admiration.

PART I: THE NATURE OF ADMIRATION

The first section of this volume will explore the nature of admiration. Emotions are complex phenomena and are typically taken to have a number of different features. First, emotions have a *phenomenology*. In other words, there is something that it feels like to experience that emotion. The contemporary philosophical literature has very little to say about the phenomenology of admiration. If we look elsewhere though, a claim that frequently occurs about the phenomenology of admiration is that it involves feelings of wonder and surprise. Schindler et al. (2013), for example, note that dictionary definitions of admiration often make this link. We can find this link in the work of Adam Smith (1759/2007, I.i.4.3) who claims that "[a]pprobation heightened by wonder and surprise, constitutes the sentiment which is properly called admiration." Similarly, Charles Darwin (1872/1998, p. 269) claimed that admiration consists in "surprise associated with some pleasure and a sense of approval." Sophie-Grace Chappell's contribution to this volume, "No More Heroes Anymore?," also makes this link as part of its investigation into the phenomenology of admiration. Chappell then draws on this investigation of the nature of admiration to develop a fascinating exploration of different ways in which we admire sporting or musical heroes on the one hand and the way we admire moral and political heroes on the other.

Emotions also involve an evaluation of an object. Uncontroversially, admiration involves a positive evaluation of its object. This, though, does little to distinguish it from other positive evaluations such as respect. There are a number of claims to be found in the literature as to the distinctive form of positive evaluation involved in admiration. One is that the value possessed by the object of admiration is *rare* (Forrester 1982, p. 102). Another suggestion is that admiration involves a judgement of the object's *superiority* in relation to the subject (Schindler et al. 2013, p. 89). Finally, we might follow Macalester Bell (2013, p. 64) in thinking that admiration is a *globalist* attitude, one that takes a whole person as its object.

In his "Ideals and Idols: On the Nature and Appropriateness of Agential Admiration," Antti Kauppinen contributes to this discussion by developing an account of the fittingness conditions for admiration. On his account, admiration is a construal of its target as realizing a worthwhile ideal of the person to a greater degree than either the admirer or the normal level. On this view, admiration is an emotion that targets *people* rather than the acts they perform or the traits they possess. Kauppinen then develops this view by exploring the issue of the appropriateness of admiring people who realize one important ideal whilst falling well short in relation to other ideals.

In addition, emotions involve motivations to act in certain ways. In the philosophical literature, discussions of the motivational profile of admiration have focused on the claim that admiration is linked with a desire to emulate (see Zagzebski 2017). While this view has been criticized (Archer, forthcoming; Compaijen 2017), it is nevertheless the most commonly discussed feature of admiration in the literature. In "Happy Self-Surrender and Unhappy Self-Assertion: A Comparison between Admiration and Emulative Envy," Sara Protasi provides a fuller and more nuanced account of the motivational profile of admiration by comparing it to that of emulative envy. Protasi draws on this account to explain the different valuable roles each might play in our ethical and political lives and in particular to defend the value of emulative envy.

Finally, we may ask whether the nature of admiration makes it a valuable emotion to experience. Jan-Willem van der Rijt argues that there is something inherently objectionable to the idea of cultivating moral admiration for other people's moral excellence. He argues that such admiration undermines the admirer's self-respect, insofar as it asserts a higher moral standard for the exemplar than for oneself. This, in turn, establishes two classes of moral agents, related to each other on unequal terms, which is why van der Rijt believes the assertion violates self-respect.

PART II: HISTORY

When it comes to the history of philosophy, admiration was not always neglected. Yet it cannot be said that it was ever really at the forefront of ethical reflection. As Linda Zagzebski (2015) points out, Plato and Aristotle have little to say about admiration.[1] Later then, in Descartes's (1649) *Les Passions de l'âme*, what the philosopher calls "l'admiration" is being discussed, but the analysis is, strictly speaking, one of wonder, which correspondingly is also the term used in the English translation.[2]

We are getting much closer to accounts of admiration as we use the term today when looking at the work of two eminent Enlightenment philosophers, Adam Smith and Moses Mendelssohn. Both can be credited with having formulated a version of the view that contemporary philosophers thinking about admiration as well as relevant empirical psychologists have been paying a lot of attention to: the idea that admiration includes or gives rise to a desire to emulate the admired object.

In *The Theory of Moral Sentiments* (1759/2007, p. 132), Smith, who throughout his book does not show much interest in distinguishing love from admiration, argues that "love and admiration which we naturally conceive for those whose character and conduct we approve of, necessarily dispose us to desire to become ourselves the objects of the like agreeable sentiments, and to be as amiable and as admirable as those whom we love and admire the most."

Moses Mendelssohn, in turn, has made a similar claim only three years before the publication of Smith's book, in a letter exchange with Gotthold Ephraim Lessing and Friedrich Nicolai, in which the three discuss the role of the Bourgeois Tragedy (*Bürgerliches Trauerspiel*) for the moral education of the people.[3] The main question is whether theatre should continue to aim at provoking its audience's sympathy (*Mitleid*), or whether it should stage moral heroes for the purpose of eliciting the audience's admiration (*Bewunderung*). Mendelssohn proposes the latter and justifies his opinion by way of arguing that admiration cannot be reduced to a simple "pleasurable affect" that we experience in recognition of another person's extraordinary qualities, but must be understood as a complex emotion that includes or gives rise to a "desire to emulate the admired hero where possible." According to Mendelssohn, such a desire was "inextricably linked" to the emotion of admiration and is the reason why admiration can facilitate the moral education of the audience.[4]

In her contribution to this volume, Anne Pollok introduces the reader to the complexities of Mendelssohn's view on admiration, while situating it in the intellectual context of its time. According to Pollok, the latter was marked by a "clear tendency towards an anthropological perspective," with empirical psychology and medical theories receiving an increasing amount of attention, and with aesthetics emerging as a serious field of philosophical research into the non-discursive, sensory nature of human life. Moreover, as Pollok elaborates in detail, there was a widespread interest in understanding the "vocation of humankind" that for Mendelssohn admiration could help us to detect.

Finally, Simon Robertson has a close look at Friedrich Nietzsche's perfectionist ethics, asking if it has a place for admiration and admirableness. While Nietzsche ethics attributes great significance to a certain category of excellences, the answer to this question might seem to be very likely positive. As it turns out, however, things are much more difficult. Robertson uses Nietzsche to argue that the admirable is agent-relative, while the value of excellence is non-relational. This alone implies that a person manifesting a certain excellence does not necessarily provide reasons for one to admire that person. Moreover, Robertson argues that admiring something is generally bad, even disadmirable, and can impose a threat to one's prospects of living the life that is good for one.

PART III: SOCIAL AND POLITICAL DIMENSIONS OF ADMIRATION

The third section is concerned with admiration's potential to facilitate progressive social and political change. Here prospects might seem rather dim. So for instance, Adam Smith (1759/2007, pp. 63–64) argued that "our obsequiousness to our superiors" can partly be explained by reference to "admiration for the advantages of their situation." According to Smith, the admirers would "desire to serve [their superiors] for their own sake, without any other recompense but the vanity or the honour of obliging them." If Smith was right, then admiration, far from being a force for change, comes with the potential to foster social inequalities. Much worse even, uncritical admiration could be seen as a crucial ingredient of worship and cult surrounding fascist leaders. The way fascist ideologies fetishize the idea of strength while preaching contempt for the weak has led some philosophers to reject admiration in contexts of sports events that many would be inclined to think of as politically innocent (Tännsjö 1998).

While it is important to critique social phenomena of admiration that are essentially harmful, it is important to see that most emotions can be abused in some way. Anger can be a direct expression of racism, while in other cases turn out to be an appropriate response to injustice, finally moving a certain oppressed group towards making their voices heard. Even love might be good or bad. It can ground healthy forms of solidarity among members of a certain group. However, it can also turn out to be destructive, such as when love for one's country turns into a destructive form of nationalism.

Both Vanessa Wills's and Marguerite La Caze's chapters can therefore be read as contributing to a more balanced picture of the political significances of admiration, by showing that admiration can also play a positive role. It can unleash motivation to overcome one's obsequiousness to superiors and even prompt individuals to resist immorality in times of crisis, where moral behaviour cannot be based on what has developed into inherently immoral social norms.

More precisely, Wills develops a notion of "revolutionary admiration," by which she means a form of admiration that "links together feeling, judgement, and action in such a manner as to make a better world more possible." Wills develops her account by way of productively engaging with remarks by Karl Marx expressing his admiration for the Paris Commune and presents it as a social project to be emulated in the future. She argues that revolutionary admiration has a normative basis, reflecting on the achievements of individuals whose choices have been difficult and who are now involved in producing the Commune. Admiration for them would be justified, given freely and wholeheartedly. Moreover, it figures as a reminder for us of what human existence could be, while inspiring us to decide to act in similar ways to those that we admire.

La Caze looks at the complex ways wonder, admiration, and emulation can lead individuals to do what is right, in times where a majority of people have begun to treat what is actually immoral as moral in ways that Hannah Arendt described. She argues that wonder can help us recognize the unfamiliar and that in times of crisis the moral act might be so unfamiliar that it provokes wonder. However, La Caze also argues that wonder does not include a judgement. Admiration, by contrast, does include a judgement about those being admired having valuable traits, which is why it is needed as well. Admiration, moreover, can include a desire to emulate the admired object. This said, Le Caze also admits that these three emotions and attitudes are not completely trustworthy.

The other two chapters of this section are rather different in nature. André Grahle argues that second-personal expressions of admiration such as "I admire you for being such a great dancer!" can amount to normative support. They can endow the admired person with extra reason for her to continue with her admirable projects. Having such support is often a good thing, but the choices we make in providing it for some people are subject to considerations of justice.

Finally, Amanda Cawston argues that admiration can play a positive role in determining the moral status of animals and in promoting morally acceptable treatment of animals. In doing this, Cawston ask whether admiration is a more interesting emotion for animal ethicists to focus on than empathy for suffering, as the latter has recently received a fair bit of criticism among philosophers.

PART IV: ADMIRATION AND MORAL EDUCATION

The final section of the volume investigates the role that admiration ought to play in moral education. The link between admiration and education has been a significant focus of the recent philosophical literature on admiration. Most prominently, Zagzebski (2017) claims that admiration for moral exemplars has a key role to play in moral education. According to Zagzebski, our admiration for exemplars brings about a desire to emulate those exemplars, which leads us to become morally better people. This claim about the important role admiration may play in moral education can be seen as the starting point for all of the papers in this section.

Ines Schindler's "Is It Morally Good to Admire?" investigates the ways in which admiration may facilitate learning from more skilled, knowledgeable, or virtuous others. However, Schindler also urges caution about the extent of admiration's ability to improve behaviour, warning that admiration is most likely to be effective through small cumulative steps rather than leading to an instant transformation of behaviour. Moreover, it is likely to be difficult to devise educational techniques that can reliably both generate the right emotions and transform them into emulative behaviour.[5]

The remaining papers in this section investigate a number of other difficulties that may prevent admiration for moral exemplars from playing a useful role in moral education. Alan T. Wilson's "Admiration and the Development of Moral Virtue" outlines three potential problems that may prevent admiration from leading to moral virtue. First, admiration may be directed towards inappropriate targets, towards people or traits that are not admirable. Second, admiration may fail to lead to a desire to emulate. Finally, admiration may lead to a desire to emulate but this may fail to translate into habitual virtuous action. Wilson finishes by exploring how an awareness of the various ways in which admiration can fail to translate into moral virtue can inform Aristotelian approaches to the use of role models in character education.

Similarly, Florien M. Cramwinckel and Benoît Monin's "Obstacles to the Admiration of Moral People" outlines a number of psychological processes that may block the admiration of morally exemplary people. First, people may feel threatened by the morally laudable behaviour of others and this feeling of being under threat may hinder their admiration. Second, people may feel that the moral excellence displayed by others may not be easily achievable for them, which again can serve as a block on moral admiration. Finally, admiration may be blocked if the morally worthy behaviour is performed by someone who does not rank highly in a formal hierarchy.

Finally, Alan Thomas, Alfred Archer, and Bart Engelen's contribution "How Admiring Moral Exemplars Can Ruin Your Life: The Case of Conrad's *Lord Jim*" explores how admiration may not only fail to lead to moral virtue but can also ground a distinctive form of moral error. Through a detailed discussion of Joseph Conrad's novel *Lord Jim*, Thomas et al. explain how the desire to emulate moral exemplars can lead people to moral error and failure. Their diagnosis of the error made by Conrad's eponymous hero consists in two parts: (1) Jim's focus on superficial aspects of his admired heroes and (2) the fact that he does not attend to those heroes' specific moral psychology. This leads to his mistaken belief that heroism will be easy for him to accomplish. Based on this discussion, Thomas et al. argue that there is an important role for narratives of moral failure in moral education.

NOTES

1. However, in a reply to Zagzebski, Terrence Irwin (2015) points out that reflections on *thaumazein*, which he argues is the Greek concept that comes at least close to the meaning of "admiration," can occasionally be found in both Aristotle and Plato.

2. See, for example, Descartes (1649/1989) translated by Stephen Voss.

3. The letter exchange has, to our knowledge, not yet been translated to English. The quotes that follow have been translated by us (A. G.). For the German original, see Mendelssohn's letter from 1756 (November 23) published in Lessing (1973, 167–70).

4. See Lessing (1973, 168).

5. See Engelen et al. (2018) for some suggestions of the kinds of strategies such techniques might employ.

REFERENCES

Archer, A. Forthcoming. "Admiration and Motivation." *Emotion Review*.

Bell, Macalaster. 2013. *Hard Feelings: The Moral Psychology of Contempt*. Oxford: Oxford University Press.

Compaijen, R. 2017. "Recognizing and Emulating Exemplars." *Ethical Perspectives* 24 (4): 569–93. DOI:10.2143/EP.24.4.3269043.

Darwin, C. 1872/1998. *The Expression of the Emotions in Man and Animals*. Oxford: Oxford University Press.

Descartes, René. 1649/1989. *The Passions of the Soul*. Translated and annotated by Stephen Voss. Indianapolis/Cambridge: Hackett Publishing.

Engelen, B., A. Thomas, A. Archer, and N. van de Ven. 2018. "Exemplars and Nudges: Two Strategies for Moral Education." *Journal of Moral Education* 47 (3): 346–65.

Forrester, M. G. 1982. *Moral Language*. Madison: University of Wisconsin Press.

Irwin, T. H. 2015. "Nil Admirari? Uses and Abuses of Admiration." *Proceedings of the Aristotelian Society Supplementary* 89 (1): 223–48.

Lessing, G. E. 1973. *Kleinere Dramaturgische Schriften*. Edited by Karl Eibl. Munich: Carl Hanser Verlag.

Onu, D., T. Kessler, and J. R. Smith. 2016. "Admiration: A Conceptual Review." *Emotion Review* 8 (3): 218–30.

Schindler, I., V. Zink, J. Windrich, and W. Menninghaus. 2013. "Admiration and Adoration: Their Different Ways of Showing and Shaping Who We Are." *Cognition & Emotion* 27 (1): 85–118.

Smith, A. 1759/2007. *The Theory of Moral Sentiments*. New York: Cosimo.

Tännsjö, T. 1998. "Is Our Admiration for Sports Heroes Fascistoid?" *Journal of the Philosophy of Sport*, 25 (1): 23–34.

Zagzebski, L. T. 2015. "Admiration and the Admirable." *Proceedings of the Aristotelian Society Supplementary* 89 (1): 205–21.

Zagzebski, L. T. 2017. *Exemplarist Moral Theory*. Oxford: Oxford University Press.

Part I

The Nature of Admiration

Chapter One

No More Heroes Any More?[1]

Sophie-Grace Chappell

I

Who are your heroes? Intelligent sceptical grown-up modern people like us have two discrete ways of responding to this question. Either we will take the question with full seriousness—but then we will respond with guardedness and suspicion, perhaps with disdain for the naivety of asking such a thing; or else we will take the question to be in some sense a *jeu d'esprit*, a "light-hearted" question. And then we will give correspondingly "light-hearted" answers: Venus Williams, perhaps, or Wayne Rooney, or Ella Fitzgerald or Frank Sinatra or Bob Dylan.

On the one side, a perfectly unbuttoned readiness to name as many heroes as you like; on the other side, a sceptical and measured resistance to the idea that there are any heroes at all. Try naming political heroes, without being partisan: let them be political heroes whose status is unchallenged more or less all the way across the political spectrum. You won't find many. To describe Margaret Thatcher or Jeremy Corbyn or Nicola Sturgeon or Clement Attlee as a hero is of course possible—but not without an open declaration of political partisanship. Such claims will run instantly into a barrage of counterevidence, and a wall of incredulity, from the other side of the political divide; in Tony Blair's case, from both sides. In British politics, the nearest one can get to a surefire supra-partisan hero is Churchill. But in truth Churchill's career was far from heroic, and far from lacking in partisanship, for much of its highly contested extent before World War II—and afterwards too. And moving from political heroes to moral heroes, something similar is true about them as well. Mother Teresa, for instance, is a moral hero[2] whom it is not possible to endorse without taking a stand on some fairly sharp controversies.

It says something interesting about us that we have this fissure in our thinking about heroes. The line of the fissure divides, at least roughly, most other kinds of heroes from two kinds in particular—sporting heroes and pop/rock heroes. (We might put sport and music together with each other, and with some connected phenomena such as Hollywood, TV, and related forms of celebrity, and call this subkind of heroes *stars*.) It is interesting too that the line of the fissure divides, at least roughly, what we take fully seriously as life from what we take less seriously as fun or leisure or entertainment. At some level our society *looks down its nose* at the subkind of heroes whom I call stars. Sometimes stars themselves are self-deprecating about their own celebrity status—most famously, perhaps, an Australian cricketer who also flew Spitfires in the World War II:

> MICHAEL PARKINSON: So, Keith Miller, as a batsman for Australia for all those years, you must have found yourself under a huge amount of pressure?
> KEITH MILLER: Mate, pressure is when you've got a Messerschmidt on your arse. Cricket is not.

Notoriously, stars are often objects of fanatical devotion. All the same, there is an intuition that this devotion is criticisable, because stars don't really count for as much as other kinds of heroes. Perhaps stars are not really full-blown *heroes* at all: so some kind of condescension is merited towards stars as such, in a way that it most certainly isn't towards, for example, war heroes.

My main project here is to develop an understanding of the nature of admiration. That question is bigger and more interesting than the question that I have been raising so far, why there is this division between our attitudes to saints, the heroically brave, and sages on the one hand, and on the other, to sports stars and rock stars and similar people (mountaineers, explorers, geniuses, etc.). The smaller question can be used to shed light on the larger—but also conversely. So I begin with some remarks about how to understand admiration.

II

We may start by describing admiration simply as the "Wow!"-response. More exactly, and more clunkily, we might say that admiration is that positive fusedly emotional-and-cognitive response whose characteristic expression, in English, is an unironic "Wow!" (And to stress the point about positivity, admiration does have to be a happy "Wow!": it can't be the kind of "Wow!" that can be evoked by a traffic accident, even if this latter is not at all ironic, as I suspect it usually is.[3])

"Fusedly emotional-and-cognitive": the admiration response is both emotional and cognitive. To say that it is fusedly so is to say that the emotional and cognitive "sides" are thoroughly entangled, not cleanly distinguishable. I take phenomena like admiration, and indeed a whole range of other human responses, to furnish us with *prima facie* evidence against the modern, neo-Humean, orthodoxies that the normative is the emotional, and that the normative and the cognitive are separable even in principle.

Happy "Wow!" has clear equivalents in other languages, most of them phonetically similar: "Wah!" in Persian and Urdu, "Eu eu" in ancient Greek, "Euge" in Latin (presumably on loan from Greek *eu ge*, literally "Well, yes"), "Oh la la!," apparently, in French, "Wow" as a loan-word or loan-noise from English in modern Greek and Hungarian and Spanish, various *English* swear words in Finnish, and "Yoho" in the language of the Cree First Nation of Canada—whence the name of the national park in Alberta. Not that anything I want to say stands or falls with translinguistic evidence, but such evidence is always amusing, and sometimes instructive too.

Admiration of X is a strongly positive attitude to X. (It is an attitude—strictly a reactive attitude—not an emotion, though it does have emotional and affective concomitants.) But admiration in the sense that interests me here is not *just* positivity towards X. We can if we like use "admiration" as a word for any positive attitude or "sentiment of approbation" towards X; the main objection to doing so, I think, is just that it's boring. It is more interesting and gives us something more definite and focused to think about—and something more real-life—to take it that admiration is not just high-intensity approval or approbation or "reinforcement" of X, that admiration of X is more than an emphatic form of the judgement "It is good that X exists." Nor should we be content to say that expressions of admiration for X are merely an instrumental ploy intended to encourage and promote the existence or production of X and X-like things. In fact admiration—of the kind that interests me; hereafter I'll stop repeating this restriction—is a rather complex and specific reactive attitude. Here is a brief phenomenology of admiration.

First, while my focus here will be on admiring persons, the thing admired can fall into any metaphysical category. You can admire primary substances, such as individual human beings; secondary substances, such as the species *elephant, musk ox,* or *dung-beetle*; quantities, such as the height of Mont Blanc or the depth of the Firth of Clyde; qualities, such as the sheen on a kingfisher's wing; relations, such as friendships; places, such as Pisa; times, such as Eric Morecambe's comic timing; positions, such as pawn structures; habitus, such as virtues; actions, such as Horatius's defence of the bridge; affections (ways of being affected), such as a spectator's response to a play; and indefinitely many other kinds of things that have no obvious primary place in Aristotle's list of categories. One such further kind is adverbials, which includes as yet further sub-kinds as qualities of actions (e.g., reproving someone *gracefully*), qualities of quantities (e.g., the *mind-numbing* hugeness of Mont Blanc), and indeed qualities of qualities (such as the *shimmery* frilliness of a petticoat).

Admiration differentiates to all sorts of kinds. There are moral, intellectual, aesthetic, religious, technical, sporting, and sexual admiration, and other kinds as well. Perhaps there is a distinct kind of admiration for every distinct kind of human endeavour. That's a lot of kinds. The difference between these kinds of admiration will be underplayed if we think of it merely as a matter of differences in the *reasons* for a unitary state, admiration. For though admiration is recognisably a single set of experiences—grouped, as suggested above, around the aptness of a "Wow!"-response—still experiencing (e.g.) moral admiration, say of Socrates's rigorous integrity, is a very different experience from experiencing sexual admiration, say of Alcibiades's cheekbones, and both are also very different from experiencing technical admiration, say of a deft piece of welding.

Now I will list three feelings that admiration *can* involve but does not essentially involve, and five feelings that it *must* involve, essentially. First the three nonessential but common concomitants of admiration of X: (a) We try to imitate or reproduce X; (b) We regret not having had X in our experience before; and (c) We are jealous or envious of X.

Perhaps the most important of these is (a). It matters to our understanding of admiration that we should see that, *pace* Zagzebski (see section V), there is no *essential* link between admiring something/someone and trying to imitate it/her. Sometimes admiring someone's strenuous performance will make me want to try and copy it. But—ironically enough for those who hope to use sports TV as a way to improve the nation's health, and inconveniently enough for those philosophers who think the motivation to imitate is essentially part of admiration—it is just as possible for it to have the opposite effect on me: as couch potatoes say, "Just watching them makes me feel tired."

As for (b) and (c), these are second-order negative responses to something first-order positive. Such higher-order negativity is quite common among those who "think too much." But there is nothing inevitable about either of these two negative responses, nor about various others at the second or higher orders that can also be imagined, such as feeling bad about yourself because you feel regret or envy. They too are common concomitants of admiration, but not essential parts of it.

On to the emotions that essentially accompany admiration:

(1) Admiration of X essentially involves a hope for *more like this*: given X, which justifies a wow-reaction, we would like to see *more* of X—whatever that may come to in context. Quite likely, for instance, we will hope that X will turn out to be part of a larger pattern, with more to it than the isolated

epiphanic flash or one-off experience or single route of thought whereby we came to admire X.

(2) Admiration also essentially involves something like surprise, perhaps even wonder, that X is possible; X strikes us as remarkable, extraordinary, perhaps miraculous even.

(3) Connectedly, and also essentially, admiration involves something like humility: roughly, the thought that *X is beyond me*—that X is something I could not do or reach or attain to, or at least not easily.

This feature explains both why there is something odd and perhaps even comic in the idea of admiring oneself, or one's own doings and also why it is nonetheless possible to do so. I cannot coherently think, from my own first-personal standpoint, that *I* am beyond myself, or that what *I* have done is something that I could not do. But I can, and sometimes do, take a third-personal stance on myself, just as I do on other people; I look at myself and my own deeds from what I suppose to be some observer's viewpoint. From that viewpoint I can perfectly well be impressed by achievements, even though they are *my own* achievements. Thus an athlete can reasonably acknowledge that what she did in setting a new world record for the 800 meter was, quite simply, awesome: just as awesome as it would have been if someone else had run that 800 meter. Her attitude to that run can be exactly as just described, an attitude of gratitude, hope, wonder, and humility—even though it was she herself who ran it.

Because admiration involves gratitude, hope, wonder, and humility, it also (4) involves something further that we can call *vulnerability* or *openness*. To admire is to admit that something else is bigger or better or more impressive than yourself, or not something you could have achieved, or not easily; it is to admit that the world has surprised you, caught you off your guard, left you in a state of wonder. As Thomas Carlyle says, it is undoubtedly good for us to undergo this kind of experience, and to admit that we undergo it; and bad for us to refuse to be vulnerable in these ways: "Is there not, in reverence for what is better than we, an indestructible sacredness?"[4] Or as Carlyle's contemporary Kierkegaard nicely puts it, contrasting admiration with envy, "Admiration is happy self-surrender. Envy is unhappy self-assertion."[5]

So to allow yourself to experience and express admiration is to expose yourself to two connected risks. One is that you should be duped: should mistakenly admire something that does not *deserve* to be admired, either because it is good but not good enough to merit admiration or else because it is no good at all. The other is that you should seem a dupe to others: that those around you should take you to be naïve, gullible, gushing, simple, easily impressed, wide-eyed and childish and credulous; over-prone, indeed, to happy but deluded surrender.

I think it is a virtue in us to be open or vulnerable in this way to wonder and admiration—to be childlike. The Jesus of the Gospels seems to think the same: "Whosoever shall not receive the kingdom of God as a little child, he shall not enter therein" (Mark 10.15). Of course, child*like* is one thing, child*ish* is another: there is certainly a fault of naivety, of over-openness, of too-ready admiration. But that fault is hardly our society's *besetting* fault. We as a society seem more set upon leaving both childishness and childlikeness behind us as fast as possible—and very often not so much for maturity, as for pubescent nihilism: "Not the wondering gaze of childhood but the cold, angry stare of the adolescent."[6]

Post-1960s western society has idolised adolescence rather in the way that Wordsworth idolised childhood. Perhaps it is unsurprising, then, that one of our society's most prized qualities is the decidedly adolescent ideal of *Cool*, and that a key part of Cool is the ability not to be impressed too easily (or at all?) by anything too slight (or anything whatsoever?). Or if you *are* impressed, at the very least to hide it well. Cool itself can be impressive too, of course, and then people watchers like me get the amusing spectacle of Cool people trying to be Cool about how Cool other Cool people are.

So admiration involves an openness, a willingness to be unguarded, a vulnerability. Insofar as Cool involves a rejection of this openness, I think we should question the value of Cool; maybe Cool is a thick property that is better banished by reflection.

(5) What I shall focus on most of all here is this: admiration of X is a species of the genus *positive attitude to X* that responds to what I shall call *spontaneity* in X.

To see spontaneity in X is to see X as something the existence of which is *surprising, wonderful,* perhaps even miraculous(-looking); that is, "X is spontaneous" implies "X is not predictable or to-be-expected from X's preconditions." We should take seriously the etymological connection between "admiration" and "miracle" in English (both words are built on Latin *mirari*, "to wonder"), and the cognate connections in other languages (e.g., between *thaumazein* and *thauma* in classical Greek). Admiration goes with productions or performances (or other sorts of things) about which there is something at least slightly *mysterious*, or perhaps, in slightly weaker but still cognate terms, something *marvellous* or *wonderful*: namely, how they come to be at all given their originating conditions.

Kant writes (*Critique of Judgement*, 50–151; cp. 151–152):

> Genius is a *talent* for producing that for which no definite rule can be given; it is not a mere aptitude for what can be learned by a rule. Hence *originality* must be its first property. . . . It cannot describe or indicate scientifically how it brings about its product, but it gives the rule just as nature does. Hence the author of a product for which he is indebted to his genius does not know

himself how he has come by his ideas; and he has not the power to devise the like at pleasure or in accordance with a plan, and to communicate it to others in precepts that will enable them to produce similar products.

Since Kant was both a professional academic and a deeply learned man, he surely intended these words to allude to Plato's famous claims that poets do not understand what they themselves are doing, and that poetry comes by divine inspiration (*Apology* 22a–c, *Ion* 534b–c). What Kant and Plato's Socrates note about poets, I want to apply more widely. Quite generally, I claim, to see something as admirable, in the interestingly specific sense of the word that does not just mean to be approved, is to see it as having something mysterious about its causal origins. We can approve something without finding it surprising, or original, or seeing a kind of saltation between the approved thing and its causal background. Not so with what we admire. What we admire stands out against, and away from, its background and its origins in precisely these ways. And that is what makes the admirable look something like a *miracle* or to use a word that I am rather fond of using, an *epiphany*.

In the case of artistic creativity, the mysteriousness of the process of production that both Plato and Kant note is a real and familiar phenomenon. Of course, it is an exaggeration on Kant's and Plato's part to say that writing poetry involves no degree of rule-governed technical mastery *at all*, of a kind that could in principle be taught to others; in practice, as poets discover by trying to write, being a poet involves *both* of what Locke separates as "Wit" and "Judgement" (see below), *both* the synthesising ability to see giddying connections, *and* the analysing ability to see sobering differences.

Yet even a humble amateur (and, damn it, largely unpublished) poet like myself sometimes finds that there is something inexplicable about how I arrive at a given poetic result. And often these results are the ones that I am most pleased about. Philip Larkin at any rate had no hesitation about the right name for this mysteriously inarticulate aptitude:

> *PARIS MATCH* INTERVIEWER: How did you arrive at the image of a toad for work?
> LARKIN: Sheer genius.
> (Larkin, 1983, 57–76)

This sense of a separation of a deed from its background is noticeable, too, in other cases of admirability of very different kinds. It seems, for instance, to be part of what makes Raimond Gaita (1991, p. xvii) write about an act of tenderness shown in a Nazi death-camp that "Charles's behaviour showed a goodness to marvel at." Charles's deed in caring for the dying Ladmaker is "to marvel at" precisely because it is underdetermined by its causal background. It is a kind of moral miracle because it is not a following of rules or an imitation of the way others are behaving in the context. It is an *original* deed, and a daring and creative one.

I think we might suggest that any admirably good deed at all will be wonderful in this sort of background-transcending—and rule-transcending—way; anything really morally admirable will have this kind of surprising creativity about it. (And yes, wicked deeds might be surprisingly creative too, though Arendt's study of Eichmann in Jerusalem perhaps suggests, *inter alia*, that creativity in wickedness is less common.) This reconception of *morally* good action as a kind of genius-like creativity is plainly at odds with the letter of Kant's writing, with its familiar emphasis not on one-off creativity but on rule-following generalisability. That does not put *me* off it, of course, since I feel no duty to adhere closely to Kantian orthodoxy; though it may well also be true that such a reconception is not at odds with the deeper spirit of Kant's ethics. I am hardly the first to suggest that Kant's *Third Critique*, and in particular its account of *Urteil*, judgement, should be taken as a guide to how we read his *Second Critique*; or that if Kantian agency starts in the ironly deterministic conditions of scientific nature and animal inclination, then something like a saltation is needed to get the agent out of those conditions and into operation instead, according to the rational laws of freedom.

III

The thesis that I have been developing is that to admire something, in the full and distinctive sense of "admire," is to see it as not reductively explicable relative to its background conditions; as involving an element of originality or creativity that eludes explanation, that is mysterious and evokes a degree of wonder—almost—that is *miraculous.* We have seen how this thesis can be supported by evidence from those who reflect on admiration as it shows up in various places of our culture. We may now add that the thesis clearly has some explanatory value.

For one thing, it is a familiar thought—compare section II on Cool—that at least some admiration comes from naivety and ignorance. What surprises, what seems inexplicable given its preconditions, is relative to the understanding of the person who is surprised or called upon to explain. Hence it is possible to think that *all* admiration is misplaced and would be eliminated by a fuller understanding of a fuller explanation; that since She is omniscient, "there are no surprises for God"; that science works by reducing everything to the "principle of least astonishment." On this picture admiration is *never* really appropriate—precisely because everything is exactly as it has no choice but to be. The world is flattened out to a determinist nexus all of which is objectively speaking at the same grade of surprisingness—the zero grade; only our subjective illusions can raise any part of it to any higher grade. In this world there is no surprise, no wonder, no spontaneity, nothing to admire, and no admiration; all of this has been *explained away*. The abolition of admirability, the abolition of heroes, thus looks like an achievement of the March of Science. Once we finally have that chimerical thing, "a complete physics" and with it the completion of the rest of science, on that day of destiny—so the idea goes—there really will be no more heroes any more.

This dismal possibility, explaining away determinism, is a familiar bugbear. It comes back again and again in one new guise or another; the contemporary "fundamental attribution error" literature, the point of which is to deny that there are really any virtues, is just its latest manifestation. That bugbear seems pretty clearly to have bugged Thomas Carlyle: "To the mean eye all things are trivial, as certainly as to the jaundiced they are yellow" (Carlyle 1841, Lecture 3). Very likely Carlyle knew of the traditional remark, found for instance in Montaigne's *Essays*, that "[n]o man is a hero to his valet"; also of Hegel's retort, "Not because the hero is no hero, but because the valet is a valet."

Thus explaining away determinism may well be connected with the familiar general idea that everything's gone to the dogs these days, and so that there aren't any heroes left. That is one of humanity's oldest and commonest clichés of thought. It's there in Homer's Nestor in Book 1 of the *Iliad*, and, as in my title, it's there in the Stranglers, though they seem to be mocking the cliché rather than endorsing it. Part of the attractiveness of this untruism comes no doubt from its close alliance with a rather similar recurring thought, that the age of miracles is past. In truth the age of miracles is *always* past, because, like the British Royal Family in Bagehot's studiedly obscurantist account of them, everything depends on the mystique of distance, and on the ignorance consequent upon that distance. And so—we might say—with heroes too. Our awe for them, like the belief in a past age of wonders, is essentially naïve, essentially dependent upon a less than complete acquaintance with the people we dub heroes as they actually were.

I draw attention to explaining away determinism not because I think it is an actuality as well as a possibility, but because the thought of the possibility is, culturally, an important one. To understand it is to see how determinism has so often seemed, in debates in our culture, to be the natural accompaniment of a sophisticated understanding, and the natural opposite to naivety, credulousness, and ignorance. To understand this possibility, and the cynicism and indeed nihilism that naturally accompany it, is a necessary preliminary to understanding what an alternative to it needs to be like.

Briefly, it needs to be an Aristotelian mean between naivety and cynicism. And it can earn the right to occupy this mean, if it shows how causation and explanation in some process can be as complete as science can make them, and still leave the outcome of that process not uniquely and inexorably determined by its antecedents.

I deny determinism because I think it is quite unproblematic to show this—to show that, as Aquinas would put it, only some causation is necessary, while other causation is contingent. Other less extreme and more reasonable positions than determinism are no less justified: for example and in particular, the position that says that *only some* admiration is based on naivety and ignorance, whereas other admiration is based on encounter with the genuinely admirable. But to argue in full for such a view is a task for another occasion.

Another thing we can now explain, I think, is the phenomenon we started with: the puzzling gap between sporting or rock heroes and the other kinds of heroes that we recognise. (In what I say here I will concentrate on the case of sport; what there is to say about rock heroes, and about some other similar cases such as Hollywood stars, will perhaps go analogously.)

Thus restricted, my question is this: Why do we look down our noses at sporting heroes relative to other kinds? Why do we not take sporting heroism *seriously,* at least in the way that we take, for example, war heroism seriously?

Two answers to this question that in my view do not pass muster are offered, respectively, by C. L. R. James (explicitly) and by Linda Zagzebski (implicitly). I say something about each of these in turn (James in section IV, Zagzebski in section V) before, to close, I briefly give my own answer.

IV

C. L. R. James's answer is a thesis that he develops, among other places, in his marvellous book on cricket, *Beyond a Boundary*. His answer is that cricket—like all mass-participation sports—is a working-class game, flourishing only in times of democracy, and that philosophers, critics, and aesthetes ignore it and other games because of class prejudice. Thus James writes, as follows, of the unique Gloucestershire and England cricketer W. G. Grace (1848–1915):

> A famous liberal historian can write the history of England in the nineteenth century, and two famous socialists can write what they declared to be the history of the common people of England, and between them never once mention the man who was the best-known Englishman of his time. I can no longer accept the system of values which could not find in these books a place for W. G. Grace. . . . Between those who, writing about social life in Britain, can leave him out, and myself, there yawns a gulf deep and wide. (James 1963, 208)

James's "liberal historian" is G. M. Trevelyan; his "famous socialists" are Raymond Postgate and G. D. H. Cole. With slightly different chronology, James might have added a fourth historian of the left of arguably even greater eminence. If it had been published only slightly earlier, James might have cited that paradigm of Open University set books, E. P. Thompson's *The Making of the English Working Class* (which also appeared in 1963). For Thompson too contrives to spend nearly 950 pages on his magisterial social, political, and economic analysis of the very timespan that concerns James, 1780–1832, without generating a single index entry on either "sport" or "games."

James is indignant at his fellow leftists' apparent uninterest in sport partly because he takes sport, and especially cricket, to have had a crucial formative place in the life of the English working class during and after the industrial revolution—so that a complete history of that class then cannot sensibly omit it. He is indignant also because he takes Trevelyan, Postgate, and Cole to be acquiescing in a class prejudice. This—and whatever else we may think admiration is, surely this is an epitome of admiration—is how James closes his beautiful tribute to W. G. Grace:

> He had enriched the depleted lives of two generations and millions yet to be born. He had extended our conception of human capacity[7] and in doing all this he had done no harm to anyone. He is excluded from the history books of his country. No statue of him exists.[8] Yet he continues warm in the hearts of those who never knew him. There he is safe until the whole crumbling edifice of obeisance to Mammon, contempt for Demos, and categorising intellectualism finally falls apart. (James, 1963, 244–45)

So for James disdain for cricket is "contempt for Demos," "obeisance to Mammon," and "categorising intellectualism."

How did this contempt arise? James wants to follow E. P. Thompson in pointing to the way that the Industrial Revolution broke the mediaeval patterns. It destroyed village life, the immemorial locus of the games and sports of old England. And anyone who tried to retain or restore those games and sports in the full heat of the Industrial Revolution in England, in Manchester in 1790 say, would have had Thomas Gradgrind (or Jeremy Bentham) preaching industry in his one ear, and John Wesley preaching frugality, sobriety, and the Sabbath in his other.

The mass-labour factory fundamentally divorced from each other the integral skills of the cottage-based artisan. It turned craftsmen, and craftswomen, into tools. It took whole human beings and made them into parts of a larger machine. Factory operatives were, by explicit intention, to become machine parts of whom, typically, one or only a few repetitive production-line movements were required, and those were movements that could be made without either thought or skill, all day long, from the dawn hooter to the dusk.

A different ideal, which James far prefers, is epitomised by William Hazlitt:

> W. G. Grace was a Victorian, but the game he transformed into a national institution was not Victorian either in origin or in essence. It was a creation of pre-Victorian England . . . the England of the early Dickens and William Hazlitt. . . . Hazlitt was an intellectual to his fingertips, and a militant, an extreme democrat who suffered martyrdom for his opinions. Yet he is not a divided man, he has no acute consciousness either of class or of divided culture. . . . He takes his whole self wherever he goes; he is ready to go everywhere; every new experience renews and expands him. He writes as freely and as publicly of a most degrading love-affair as of Elizabethan literature. The possibility of such completeness of expression ended with him and has not yet returned. (James, 1963, 208–9)

Modern cricket, James argues, was founded by people who, like Hazlitt, "took their whole selves wherever they went," the noble artisans, "men of hand and eye," who were the truest inheritors of the "undivided" age that Hazlitt represented.

James adds that Victorians like Dr Thomas Arnold of Rugby (1795–1842) and Thomas Hughes (1822–1896, the author of *Tom Brown's Schooldays*, 1857) recognised the value of Hazlitt's and the artisans' kind of undividedness, their taking your whole self everywhere. They saw it as threatened by the kind of change that is symbolised, in Hughes's book, by Tom Brown's dislocation—roughly in the year of the Great Reform Act—from the feudal life of his Berkshire village, to the very different and very new conditions of a Victorian public school. And they tried very hard to fashion a mini-society in such schools, and a macro-society in Britain at large, that would preserve and promote this sort of integrity, among other things by making sports like cricket and rugby central to the life of those societies. But—James's narrative concludes—they failed. In the hands of the Victorians, or at any rate in their time, cricket became, along with other sports, something that was placed on the Play side of the specific form of the Play / Real Life division that we still suffer from today. And hence a genuine hero like W. G. Grace is now not taken seriously enough even to be thought worth discussing in social histories.

Against this background, as against so many others, the Victorians were both unparalleled innovators, but also—albeit often with completely new technology—restorers of the older patterns. They could not bring back the life of the seventeenth-century village, and would (rightly, of course) have insisted that there was plenty about it that was highly undesirable anyway. Nor could the Victorians, from Thomas Carlyle via Matthew Arnold to Walter Pater and Rudyard Kipling, entirely see past their own inclination to (what James apparently takes to have been) high-minded neo-Puritan disdain about "idleness," and about the "vain and childish pursuits" of "the flannelled fools at the wicket, and the muddied oafs at the goals."[9] The most effective antidote to this disdain, for many of them, was to get even more high-minded, and remind themselves of *Iliad* Book XXIII, *Aeneid* Book V, and Pindar. But naturally, this did not always work, since the exact inflection of their disdain varied; sometimes it was Carlyle's and Kipling's hearty suspicion of anything that diverts youth's energies from war and the readiness for war, other times it was Arnold's and Pater's more aesthetic inclination towards arts that they took to be "higher" than all sports. Nonetheless the Victorians did their best, under unprecedented economic, social, and political conditions, to re-create the games of old England. To say, as James seems to want to, that they somehow *failed* in this seems absurd, given the worldwide importance today of the sports that the Victorians canonised.

Yet there remains the phenomenon that I've been pointing to all along, the sense that games, and success in games, is still somehow less important, less valuable, less *real* than success in some other fields; and so less admirable. To my mind C. L. R. James's suggestion, that the roots of this division lie in our society's divisions of class, is at best a half truth. It is not as if the popularisers of cricket and other sports in the Victorian era were all or even typically working class (though certainly those sports brought into Victorian society a kind of class-free-ness that many contemporaries found profoundly threatening); and it is not as if no one before the Industrial Revolution had ever had the thought that sporting success, sporting admirability, and sporting heroism are all less important than their non-sporting analogues "in real life." Quite aside from any kind of narrative of class analysis such as James offers—and no matter how valuable that kind of narrative may be in its own right—that simple thought about relative importance was always available and would have been endorsed at all times by sportsmen of all classes, including, no doubt, W. G. Grace himself. This is why C. L. R. James's account of our division between sporting heroes and admirability, and other kinds of heroes and admirability, is not in the end successful.

V

I turn to Linda Zagzebski, the most interesting and creative recent author on admiration that I have read. Her book does not explicitly answer my question, why we take sporting admirability and sporting heroes less seriously than we do other kinds of admirability and heroism. But she does answer it implicitly. Implicitly her answer is that the central cases of admirability and heroism are *moral* admirability and heroism; and that sporting admirability and heroism are less important because they are not moral.

I think this answer fails, because Zagzebski's account of the moral is ultimately unconvincing. In Zagzebski's thinking, the moral is what is admirable, and for what is admirable we should look, not to some abstract theory of welfare or goodness or perfection, but to concrete exemplars, particular people who are foci of others' admiration. From her very first page, Zagzebski divides these exemplars into three subkinds—heroes, saints, and sages; she later adds the intriguing "conjecture" that these three subkinds are distinguished by their "dominant virtues" (courage for heroes, charity/love for saints, [speculative] wisdom for sages). These are of course not the only virtues possessed by people in these three subkinds, but they are the virtues that are most salient in such people, and most emblematic of the subkinds.

As Zagzebski sees, her conjecture raises the intriguing possibility that there might be exemplars corresponding to other virtues too, though she does not explore this possibility at all exhaustively. She does (Zagzebski 2017, 126–28) have an interesting discussion of Abraham Lincoln as an exemplar of "magnanimity" (in the sense in which we say, for example, "You should be big enough to put up with their backchat," which is something rather different from Aristotle's *megalopsychia* in *Nichomachean Ethics* 2, 1107b23 ff). However, she does not, for example, ask what an exemplar of the Platonic virtues of temperance or justice might look like (see *Republic* Books 3–4, *passim*), or the Aristotelian virtues of magnificence or liberality (*Nichomachean Ethics* 1107b18–22, *Rhetoric* 1366b2–5). And some lack of one-to-one-ness in the correspondences of kinds of exemplar and dominant virtues is suggested by her remarks about "spiritual exemplars," whose dominant virtues may be, for example, reverence or faith. These remarks are puzzling inasmuch as it is hard to see what a "spiritual exemplar" is, if not a saint, whose dominant virtue is supposed to be charity. (A supposition that also seems questionable, by the way: by no means are *all* the saints in the Catholic calendar conspicuously loving or even charitable.)

By this point a rather bigger puzzle is also looming. Zagzebski says that exemplarity is determined by admirability, and rightly allows that we may admire all sorts of exemplars who aren't strictly speaking either heroes or saints or sages. Now two particularly obvious kinds of exemplars of this sort, people who in Zagzebski's terms aren't heroes or saints or sages, but whom we still often find preeminently admirable, are *stars*, people like Bob Dylan and Venus Williams; also *geniuses*, a kind that clearly includes, for instance, Michelangelo, Isaac Newton, Jane Austen, George Eliot, Albert Einstein, Virginia Woolf, and Marie Curie. If geniuses and stars are preeminently admirable in their own distinctive ways, then they are kinds of exemplar. But if they are kinds of exemplar, then why doesn't Zagzebski discuss them? To repeat, it is not because she has closed the door on the possibility that there might be other kinds of exemplar besides heroes, saints, and sages—on the contrary, she explicitly leaves that door open.

One hint at part of the answer appears right at the beginning of Zagzebski's book, where she says (2017, 1–2) that the genius and the sports star are excluded from her project because, while she is happy to be inclusive in her account of what counts as moral, still she does aim to build a moral theory. And the kind of admiration that we direct at geniuses and sports stars is "non-moral," as are their achievements. Also, and this looks to be connected, the genius's and the sports star's achievements are not "something that others can adopt for themselves," not imitable in other lives—though if the stars pursue their achievements and develop their talents with resolve and fortitude, *those* characteristics will be imitable.

But this answer makes trouble for Zagzebski. First, she also makes it very clear that the moral theory she hopes to build is "structur[ed] around a motivating emotion, the emotion of admiration" (2017, 3). Overall, it sounds very much like Zagzebski wants to say that the emotion of admiration can equip us with an *analysis out* of the category of the moral: that is to say, a definitional explanation of "the moral" that captures more or less completely what the moral is, but can itself go all the way without ever needing to use terms such as "the moral." But if that is right, then she surely can't also exclude certain kinds of admiration from her theory on the grounds that they are non-moral. If admiration is the explanans and "the moral" the explanandum, then it must be illegitimately circular to build into our notion of admiration then specification that we are concerned with specifically *moral* admiration.

The fix for this, presumably, is to find a non-circular way of excluding the genius and the sports star from being morally admirable. This brings us to Zagzebski's suggestion that the difference between saints, heroes, and sages on the one hand, and geniuses and stars on the other, has to do with *imitation*: we admire all five of these kinds of exemplars, but we don't try to imitate stars or geniuses—whereas we do seek to imitate saints, heroes, and sages. But this distinction seems hopeless on both sides. As is perfectly obvious from watching have-a-go TV shows like *Britain's Got Talent*, *Mastermind*, and anything involving Bear Grylls, lots of people most certainly do seek to imitate rock stars, geniuses, and sports/athletics stars; so it is mistaken to say that we don't try to imitate stars or geniuses. Conversely, there is at least a serious risk of a pretty familiar kind of fatuity and presumption about my going around trying to act like Jesus, or Confucius, or the Lone Ranger. Very often when people do that sort of thing, the three most reasonable responses are "Get a grip," "Get real," and "Get some humility." There really are some humans who are morally exalted, and many of them are exalted way above *our* scope or ken. To admire them, to be in awe of them, is entirely appropriate. To try—directly and immediately—to imitate them is, very often, no better than foolhardy.

It seems unlikely, anyway, that exemplarism's own purposes are well served by thinking about the relation between the exemplar and the follower simply as one of imitation. (I don't mean that Zagzebski is bound to think of it that way; this is meant as a helpful suggestion for future work.) All sorts of other possibilities are available that might be equally effective, or even more, as ways of spreading virtue from a given exemplar to her follower. Christians, it is true, are often urged in the New Testament to be like Jesus; but they are also urged at least as frequently to *follow* Jesus, or to be Jesus's disciples. The role of a first-century rabbi's disciple is a very specific one—and it is not *like* the rabbi's role, but rather correspondent to it. There are countless ways that dwelling with an exemplar might be morally inspiring, elevating, educative, and so on that have very little to do with imitation.

I thus see little prospect of success for Zagzebski's idea that the key to isolating a specifically *moral* kind of admirability depends on its link with our motivation to imitate. Admirability is admirability *whether or not* it prompts emulation or imitation; but it can prompt or fail to prompt either, both in the cases that Zagzebski wants to call specifically moral, and those to which she wants to deny this classification.

VI

I conclude with my own answer to this question. It is extremely simple. It is that the whole point of sport—and something analogous is true elsewhere, for example with drama—is that it is a response to the kind of problem for admirability, about cynical explaining-away, that I outlined in section III. "In real life" we are constantly confronted by the possibility of the debunking of anyone we attempt to set up as a hero; it is genuinely difficult to evade criticism that explains away or denies whatever we find admirable in, for example, politicians. Yet as Carlyle points out, and as I have been arguing myself, we long for heroes. We long to see people and deeds of which it can truly be said that they are admirable in the precise sense that I outlined above—they stand above and outside the normal conditions of predictable routine and causal laws; they bring something extra, something creative and original and wonderful, into our lives.

The point of sport is to supply this need for wonder; what it is designed to give us is, if you like, a "theatre of dreams." Sport can and does satisfy this need. (Though of course, there is plenty of humdrum mediocrity in sport too.) But sport satisfies this need *at the cost of artificiality.* It is a realm where "honour is flashed off exploit" particularly easily: where the original flash of creative genius is particularly frequent, particularly readily sparked, precisely because that is what it is *designed* to be; precisely because it isn't the real world with all its messy and cynicism-stoking ambiguities. (Again, yes, of course there can be such ambiguities in sport as well.)

There can be no rational objection to giving no more than a secondary importance to a world that is deliberately set up so as not to be the real world. And that is why taking sport and sporting heroism to be fundamentally less important than at least some other kinds of heroism needs be neither snobbery of the kind that C. L. R. James decries, nor moralism of the kind that Linda Zagzebski at times seems close to advocating. Taking sporting heroism and sporting admirability to be less important than some other kinds of heroism and admirability is defensible, I suggest, for the simplest reason of all: because it is.

NOTES

1. Thanks for their comments to all those at the Munich conference where this paper was originally presented, especially André Grahle, Alfred Archer, and Marguerite La Caze.
2. I avoid the word "heroine" here. For my purposes, heroes can be of any or indeed no gender.
3. In older English "admiration" did not necessarily refer only to a happy reaction: see, for example, Shakespeare's "most admired disorder" (caused by the king's response to the ghost at the banquet). *Macbeth*, Act 3, Scene 4.
4. Thomas Carlyle, *The French Revolution* (1.1.2).
5. Søren Kierkegaard, *The Sickness unto Death* (1849), 217. Quoted by Linda Zagzebski, *Exemplarist Moral Theory*, 56.
6. Gavin Maxwell, *The House of Elrig,* 202. It is a Kingsley Amis quotation, but I can't place it.
7. Perhaps Alasdair MacIntyre, who writes warmly about C. L. R. James in *Ethics in the Conflicts of Modernity*, had this phrase in mind when he offered his famous definition of "practice": *After Virtue*, 187.
8. True in 1963; false after 2000, when a statue of him by Louis Laumen was unveiled at Lord's.
9. Kipling, "The Islanders," *The London Weekly Times*, 3 January 1902.

REFERENCES

Carlyle, Thomas. 1837. *The French Revolution*. London: Chapman and Hall.
Carlyle, Thomas. 1841 (2008). *On Heroes, Hero-Worship, & the Heroic in History: Six Lectures; Reported, with Emendations and Additions*. Urbana, IL: Project Gutenberg. Retrieved February 26, 2019. Available at: http://www.gutenberg.org/ebooks/1091?msg=welcome_stranger.
Chappell, Timothy [Sophie-Grace]. 2012. "Climbing Which Mountain?" *Philosophical Investigations* 35 (2): 167–81.
Gaita, Raimond. 1991. *Good and Evil: An Absolute Conception*. London: Routledge.
James, C. L. R. 1963. *Beyond a Boundary*. London: Yellow Jersey.
Kant, Immanuel. 1914. *Critique of Judgement* (1790). Translated by J. H. Bernard. London: Macmillan.
Kierkegaard, Søren. 1954. *The Sickness unto Death* (1849). Translated by Walter Lowry. New York: Doubleday.
Larkin, Philip. 1983. *Required Writing*. London: Faber.
MacIntyre, Alasdair. 1981. *After Virtue*. London: Duckworth.
MacIntyre, Alasdair. 2016. *Ethics in the Conflicts of Modernity*. Cambridge: Cambridge University Press.
Maxwell, Gavin. 1965. *The House of Elrig*. London: Penguin.

Parfit, Derek. 2011. *On What Matters*. Oxford: Oxford University Press.
Thompson, E. P. 1963. *The Making of the English Working Class*. London: Penguin Books.
Zagzebski, Linda. 2017. *Exemplarist Moral Theory*. Oxford: Oxford University Press.

Chapter Two

Ideals and Idols

On the Nature and Appropriateness of Agential Admiration

Antti Kauppinen

When I was a beginning graduate student, I once attended a public lecture by Martha Nussbaum on the capabilities approach. At the beginning of the Q&A session, a gentleman—probably a professor—raised what he clearly thought was a devastating objection. Nussbaum started her reply by saying, "There are six reasons why that's not right." For the next five to ten minutes, she presented those reasons in long and beautiful English sentences, all speaking directly to the point. Each was individually convincing; together, they amounted to a decisive rebuttal of the challenge. The rest of the session proceeded along the same lines. I, for my part, was awestruck. I had never seen anything quite like that. There was no obfuscation, misunderstanding, changing the topic, or appeal to authority, just calm, lucid reasoning in response to a somewhat hostile charge. I thought that was the way a philosopher or indeed an academic in general should conduct herself, and I thought "I hope that one day I'll be like that myself." I went back to work with new energy.

Clearly, my attitude towards Nussbaum was (and is) one of admiration. What I'll try to do in this chapter is clarify the nature, function, and appropriateness of the kind of admiration we can feel towards agents, rather than nature or inanimate objects. I'll pay particular attention to commonalities and differences between admiration and related attitudes like pride, contempt, and shame. I label such attitudes *exhortative*, since they all in different ways serve to guide us towards realizing ideals of the person in our lives by developing or maintaining the right kind of characteristics and shedding problematic ones. Admiration, in particular, fixes on a perceived exemplar of an ideal we endorse, focusing on the whole person rather than a particular act. Given its person-focus, I argue, it is not always all-things-considered appropriate even when it's fitting in the sense that the person is in some way admirable—though at the same time, it is not inherently ethically problematic, unlike pride that focuses on oneself as a person rather than as the author of particular acts.

ATTITUDES AND IDEALS OF THE PERSON

My discussion does not presuppose any particular theory of emotion or attitudes, but I do assume that they have two important features: they are both intentional and motivational. More precisely, they have a double intentionality: they have an intentional object or target, such as a person, and they construe that target as being in a particular way, for example dangerous. The feature that the target is construed as having is often called the emotion's formal object. Equally importantly, emotions inherently motivate us to act in a way that makes sense in light of the construal—for example, anger, which construes someone as violating or having violated a norm we endorse, motivates us to act in a way that makes it more likely for them to conform to the norm in the future, other things being equal. Finally, the intentionality of attitudes yields conditions for their fittingness or warrant or correctness. I'll say that an attitude is fitting if the target really has the evaluative features it is construed to have. I think that this amounts to the same as saying that the target's features are reasons to act as the attitude motivates, but my arguments here won't rely on this assumption.

We have many different evaluative attitudes that can be classified in different ways. One fundamental division is based on the different social functions of the attitudes. Consider, first, that some possible choices make living together impossible, difficult, or a nuisance, while other possible choices spread joy and wealth. To discourage the former and encourage the latter, in other words to *regulate* what people do, we endorse and enforce *norms* for actions. It is such normative expectations that are manifest in act-focused responses like guilt, anger, and indignation. We also have attitudes like gratitude that respond to meeting or exceeding such expectations.

But besides particular actions, we also know that there are some people whose choices form a pattern across different situations that results in their thriving and the thriving of others around them, promoting or realizing important values, while others consistently cause misery, ugliness, and disappointment. The former may serve as *exemplars*, giving content to *ideals of the person* that we have, and the latter fall dramatically short of them. While normative expectations concern *doing* specific kinds of things, ideals of the person concern *being* and *living* in a certain way. We may have such ideals in the abstract—we might want to be fair and brave, say—but given our cognitive and imaginative limitations, coming to understand how to actually realize them in our lives typically requires attending to those who appear to have already succeeded. The role of what I'll call *exhortative attitudes* (for want of a better term) is thus to give direction to personal growth and change. They do so by motivating us to push ourselves or others in the direction of developing or maintaining the right kind of characteristics, and getting rid of the wrong kind of ones.

Below is a table of the key exhortative attitudes that shows how they relate to ideals of the person (see Table 2.1).

Roughly, pride is the first-personal response to living in accordance with or approaching an ideal we endorse (Fischer 2012) and shame to falling short (Tangney and Dearing 2002), while admiration is a third-personal response to another's living in accordance with an ideal (Shoemaker 2015) to a higher degree than the norm or oneself, and contempt to falling short (Mason 2003). Note that in saying that these attitudes are responses to living in accordance with approaching or falling short of an ideal, I don't mean to suggest that we first have some articulated conception of an ideal of the person in mind and then judge that someone approaches or falls short of it. More plausibly, our ideals are manifest in our reactions: it is what we admire or feel contempt for that shows what our ideals are, and as long as we have such responses, we have ideals, even if we have no explicit belief or conception of them.

I want to begin examining admiration more closely by looking at its commonalities with pride. First, I'll set aside their non-agential forms, which have nothing to do with the person's activity. Clearly, I could be non-agentially proud of my thick hair or long legs, if I had such. In taking pride in such things, I take them to reflect myself—to show that I meet some aesthetic ideal I endorse. Something similar is true of admiring someone's brown eyes or smooth skin—though it seems to me that in this case, our attitude might not be person-directed at all, in that we might not take meeting the aesthetic ideal to redound to the subject's credit. That is, I can admire your *features* without admiring *you*, like I can admire the shiny fur of a capybara without admiring the capybara itself.

Non-agential admiration or awe is a kind of "wow-response," to borrow Sophie-Grace Chappell's term (this volume), but it isn't admiration in the

Table 2.1.

	First-personal	*Third-personal*
Conspicuously close to ideal	Pride	Admiration
Conspicuously far from ideal	Shame	Contempt

sense that interests me. The reason we use the same term is probably the phenomenal similarity in the feelings aroused by exemplary people, on the one hand, and objects or characteristics that are in some way excellent tokens of a type, on the other. But beyond the feeling aspect, non-agential admiration differs from agential admiration both in its intentional and motivational content, which strongly suggests it's really a distinct attitude. When it comes to intentional or representational content, non-agential admiration involves no attribution of responsibility to the target. It may be perfectly fitting to admire a beautiful sunset or a butterfly in this sense. And in terms of motivation, it involves no tendency to emulate the target, nor other motivations characteristic of admiring agents. Its function might be primarily social—after all, what it does motivate us to do is often to invite others to attend to its target as well ("Check out that sunset/riff/math genius!"). Insofar as attitudes are centrally individuated by their intentional and motivational content as well as phenomenal feel, there are thus good grounds for thinking that the awe-like response towards non-agential objects or features is a different emotion from admiration proper. This is to be expected from a functionalist perspective: after all, as I've already suggested, admiration proper has a distinctive function of identifying those who give concrete shape to our ideals and guiding us towards realizing them.

My focus, then, is on *agential* forms of admiration and pride. As I've suggested, their target is a person, who is construed as leading a life manifesting (or approximating) an ideal of the person we endorse. The intentional content of admiration and pride is thus Janus-faced: on one side, there's a pattern of excellent performances, on the other, something excellent about the agent that is made manifest by the performances, in virtue of which they are attributable to the agent (so that she is in a sense responsible for them).[1] I think both are necessary. It's not sufficient that someone possesses a virtue to a high degree, for example—in that respect, talk of ideals of the person might be somewhat misleading. As Hume observed, bad luck, such as being stuck in "a dungeon or desert," might prevent a virtuous person from ever exercising their virtue (Hume 1739–1740 [1978], 584). We may still esteem or approve of such a person, but they're not an object of great admiration but rather something like pity. If you're inclined to think otherwise, consider whether you'd admire Nelson Mandela as much, had he never been released from Robben Island, which might of course have happened.

At the same time, merely *doing* something excellent doesn't as such merit admiration or pride. This is clearest when someone *accidentally* or *unintentionally* accomplishes something. Imagine that Donald Trump places a call to what he takes to be a Japanese businessman with the intention of getting him to invest in a chain of casinos and ends up bragging about his popularity and intelligence. Unbeknownst to him, however, he is in fact talking to Kim Jong-un, who consequently has an epiphany: just like Trump, he has deluded himself about how his people feel about him and decides to step down and dismantle the North Korean dictatorship. This would no doubt be a great accomplishment for Trump, but it would not be to his credit (though he would probably *take* credit for it).

Similarly, it is possible to do something great *intentionally but for the wrong reasons*. This is obvious in moral cases, but not limited to them. Imagine it turns out that Bruce Springsteen felt no compassion for people of colour facing deadly official prejudice when he wrote and performed "American Skin (41 Shots)," his moving take on the shooting of unarmed immigrant Amadou Diallo by New York City police, but instead put on a calculated display to manipulate an emotionally vulnerable audience in the hopes of amassing even more money than he already has. Since a crucial part of what makes his actual performance praiseworthy is that it gives audible form to a deep concern and compassion in a way that enables listeners to empathize with mistreated members of society, there is little to admire in the hypothetical alternative.

Let me try to be a little more precise. Here's my first thesis: admiration construes its target as leading a life characterized by praiseworthy achievements that are to a significant degree explained by their meeting a worthwhile ideal of the person—for short, as *realizing* a worthwhile ideal—and doing so to a notably higher degree than the norm or oneself. Consequently, it is *fitting* when the target indeed leads such a life in virtue of realizing the ideal to such an extent. We might also say it is *justified* when the evidence available to the subject warrants thinking that the target has done the things and has the features she is construed as having, and that the ideal in question is worthwhile—even if the evidence happens to be misleading, so that admiration is not in fact fitting.

I'll return to the implications of this thesis in what follows, but I'll first explicate it a bit. I've argued in the past that for something to be a praiseworthy achievement, it must be a competent performance that meets or exceeds a contextually relevant, authoritative, and challenging standard without excessive opportunity cost (Kauppinen 2017a). A standard is authoritative in the relevant sense when it derives from a system of rules, practice, or aim that promotes, honours, or realizes a sufficient amount of some genuine value. Moral standards are an obvious example of authoritative standards, but there are many different kinds of value that can be realized by a variety of different practices with internal standards, such as sports or even participation in a market economy. Consequently, many kinds of performance, such as executing a perfect pirouette, improving a microchip, or clinching a trade deal, can be praiseworthy, even if they don't directly promote or realize value. I emphasize, however, that exhortative attitudes are appropriate on holistic grounds. While we might take an individual achievement to be indicative of realizing an ideal (as well as partly constitutive of it), admiration is rightly reduced by subsequent failures. (I'll return to this soon.)

At the same time, as I've just argued, it is not enough that a performance is praiseworthy. To warrant an attitude toward the agent herself, the performance must be explained by something deep about the agent—by their meeting or approximating a worthwhile ideal of the person in virtue of having the right commitments and character traits.[2] Typically, having such characteristics goes hand in hand with realizing them in action. Consider a non-moral ideal, being a good scholar. If you ask me, it involves something like coming to understand some complex subject matter(s) ever more deeply, and conveying one's insights to others in talks, writings, and teaching. It takes more than, say, intelligence and systematic knowledge to *be* a good scholar—you also need to *do* things like write and teach. It is an ideal I endorse and have chosen to try to realize in my own life, unlike many other ideals I also endorse. I admire people like Nussbaum or Parfit, who seem to me to live up to such an ideal. Indeed, as exemplars, they *shape* the ideal: they show how the relevant values can be promoted or realized. Conversely, I'm still ashamed of a couple of bad talks I've given in high profile conferences, because they are not only evidence of but partly constitutive of my conspicuous failure to live up to the scholarly ideal.

Next, I acknowledged that admiration construes its target in comparative terms, as realizing the relevant ideal to a higher degree than oneself or at least the norm. As Simon Robertson points out (this volume), there is a Nietzschean case to be made against admiration on the grounds that it involves a kind of self-abasement relative to the target. However, I think it does make good sense to admire someone for conspicuously exceeding the norm with respect to an ideal, even if one takes pride in doing so oneself as well—why couldn't Bob Dylan admire Robert Johnson without false modesty? And when someone else really is superior to me with respect to a genuine virtue, looking up to them isn't servile, but an honest acknowledgement of having work left to do.

Let's suppose, then, that the positive exhortative attitudes of pride and admiration present their target as at least approximately realizing an ideal in their lives to an unusually high degree. Insofar as the motivational aspect of an attitude makes sense considering its intentional content, we'd expect similarities on that side as well. And indeed they can be found. Roughly speaking, pride motivates us to *keep* doing what we're doing even if it's hard (Williams and DeSteno 2008)—to keep living in a way that approaches an ideal we endorse. Admiration, it is often said, motivates us to *emulate* the person we admire—that is, to try to *start* living in a way that approaches the ideal they realize in their lives. This is related to its comparative nature, the sense of looking up to the target that it involves, or at least regarding them as better than most. This action tendency is presumably why the emotion evolved in the first place: there are benefits to be had by identifying successful people and doing the sort of things they do. Nonetheless, this claim about motivation must be qualified. I don't have to adopt every ideal of a person that I endorse as my own. I admire Zinedine Zidane, but this doesn't motivate me to execute clever breakthrough passes in the midfield. But watching him does inspire me to try to do better at my own chosen métier, and to recommend aspiring footballers to emulate him. (I don't think this exhausts admiration's motivational impact; I'll come back to this later.)

I do think that some kind of motivational aspect pertaining to realizing ideals we endorse is essential to admiration as an *attitude*. This may be obscured by the fact that we can often say that we admire someone without feeling any motivation (or indeed having any introspectively discernible feeling). But that's because such talk can express not only an attitude, but also a judgement to the effect that the target approximates some ideal, or that admiration is warranted. The difference between thinking that someone is *admirable* and occurrently *admiring* them comes out most clearly in the motivational aspect.

IDEALS, FOCUS, AND FIT

I've given an initial sketch of how thoughts about ideals and exemplars enter into the content of admiration. But matters turn out to be somewhat complicated. Looking more carefully at how our evaluative attitudes are focused reveals that among commonalities, there are important differences between pride and admiration, and that it is somewhat puzzling why admiration is fitting toward the kind of imperfect creatures we all are.

Let me first try to distinguish between two aspects of the intentionality of an attitude, target and focus. The *target*, as I've already said, is the object that the attitude is directed towards, such as a person or a chair or an idea. *Focus*, in contrast, is the feature of the target that it has to have for the attitude to be fitting. I emphasize that having the focus isn't sufficient for fit, since there may be and typically are other conditions, such as those relating to what the target does. For example, anger construes an action as a violation of a normative expectation, and an agent (the target of anger) as the author of the action. We can say its focus is authorship of the action—for short, I'll say it's act-focused—but for it to be fitting, authorship doesn't suffice, since the action must also violate a legitimate normative expectation. Importantly, focus can be seen in the way in which the attitude moves us to relate to the target. An attitude that focuses on someone merely as the author of a particular act leaves other modes of relating to the person intact, or nearly so. But not all attitudes are like that, as we'll soon see.

When it comes to focus, the basic distinction that matters for my purposes is between what I will call *act-focused* and *person-focused* attitudes. I'll say that an attitude is act-focused when it is directed towards oneself or another as the author of a particular action and person-focused when it is directed towards oneself or another as the bearer of an enduring constellation of traits and attitudes (as the kind of person one is). Person-focused attitudes may be and often are based on particular choices, but in that case the choice is taken to reveal something deep and lasting about who the agent is. Between these two there's also a third class of what we might call *trait-focused* attitudes, which are akin to person-focused attitudes in that they target a lasting feature of the person, but it is not taken to reflect something about the person as a whole.

Below is a tentative classification of some evaluative attitudes in terms of this distinction (see Table 2.2).

Guilt is the paradigm act-focused attitude.[3] If I treated you harshly because, as I finally realize, I was trying to prop up my own fragile ego, I may feel guilty for what I did. It is the particular choice I'm responsible for that I wish I could unmake, and for which I feel like I must make amends. Guilt thus involves thoughts regarding a specific action and motivates attempts at reparation and acting otherwise in the future. Anger and indignation are second-personal parallels. Shame, as many psychologists emphasize, is quite different. Famously, we need not take ourselves to be responsible for something to be ashamed of it. But even when we're ashamed of something we did, it is because we see it as deeply implicating who we are. We are defective, unfit to enjoy the regard of others. As June Tangney and Jessica Tracy (2013) put it, it involves feeling small and exposed and unworthy. Acute shame permeates our self-relation—we don't just feel bad about a particular thing we did, but regard everything about ourselves in a negative light. So it is natural that shame motivates us to hide ourselves or hide what we did by denying it, and often shifting the blame to others to escape the burden of self-hatred.

Table 2.2.

Act-focused	Trait-focused	Person-focused
Guilt	Localized shame?	Shame
Anger, indignation		
		Love
		Contempt
Authentic pride	Hubristic pride	Hubristic pride
		Admiration

Love and contempt further illustrate the distinctions in focus. They are characteristically person-focused. While we do sometimes say things like "I love your sense of humour" or "I feel contempt for your weakness," I think these sentences either express some sort of evaluation rather than attitude (I might have said, "You have a great sense of humour"), or are used to indicate the grounds of our attitudes towards the person as a whole (I might have said, "The reason I have contempt for you is your weakness"). These attitudes, too, permeate the way we relate to their target, which makes them hard to fit together, given their contrasting polarity. While anger is quite easily compatible with love—after all, it may even reflect our high expectations towards someone we care about (see Kauppinen 2017b)—contempt isn't, because it is hard to find someone wonderful and worth cherishing at the same time as regarding them falling far short of being the kind of person they should be, and being motivated to avoid their company as far as possible. (It is no surprise that Gottman and Levenson [2000] found contempt to be the best predictor of divorce.)

For my purposes, the most important issue concerns the bottom two lines of the table. The salient difference here is that there's a choice-focused form of pride, which I've labeled "authentic pride," in accordance with terminology in use in psychology. In contrast, admiration, I'm claiming, is never choice-focused, but always targets the person. The second difference that I'll come to soon is that while hubristic pride is ethically problematic, person-focused admiration is not.

I adopt the distinction between authentic and hubristic pride from recent psychological literature. Jessica Tracy and Richard Robins characterize the distinction as follows: in the case of authentic pride, we "attribute . . . success to internal, unstable, and controllable causes," while in the case of hubristic pride we "attribute success to internal, stable, and uncontrollable causes" (Tracy and Robins 2007, 522). What they mean is that when I'm authentically proud of something, I think that my praiseworthy achievement results from a specific effort or choice that I made that I might not have made, and that was up to me to make. Authentic pride is thus the counterpart of guilt, which similarly focuses on specific choices that were up to me. Hubristic pride, in contrast, involves thinking that I'm successful because of something inherent in me, a talent or trait that is superior to that of others, which is not up to me in the same way.

The labels "authentic" and "hubristic" might well be thought to be tendentious. The rationale for them is that findings suggest they have different consequences for individuals. Studies by Jessica Tracy and Richard Robins (2007) suggest that authentic pride motivates further effort to repeat a status-enhancing success that one doesn't take for granted, and is linked with personality traits such as agreeableness, conscientiousness, emotional stability, and self-esteem. Hubristic pride, in contrast, promotes seeking social status by domination, intimidation, and manipulation—if you think you're special, it's no surprise if you demand special treatment. Crudely, the difference between authentic and hubristic pride is the difference between thinking "What I did is great" and thinking "I'm so great." The former construes the self *thinly*, as the responsible author of an act who might well do something different the next time in the absence of renewed effort, while the latter construes the self *thickly*, as the bearer of enduring traits and talents that are responsible for one's achievement. It is plausibly ethically problematic to regard oneself in the latter way—*even if* it's true that one has met some ideal in virtue of talent or an enduring trait. I've suggested in earlier work (Kauppinen 2017a) that such thoughts involve something akin to Sartrean bad faith, namely thinking of oneself as existing in the manner of a thing, when in fact the existence of our traits and exercise of our talents requires ever renewed choice. When it comes to virtue, we can't rest on our laurels, since no virtue guides or constrains our future choices without our continued active involvement.

FITTINGNESS AND APPROPRIATENESS OF ADMIRATION

Assuming that pride indeed has two facets and that admiration is its third-personal sister attitude, we're left with two important questions. If pride can be act-focused, why not admiration? And why isn't person-focused admiration ethically problematic, if hubristic pride is? Let's start with the first one. I think there's a number of reasons to think that agential admiration must be person-focused, rather than act- or trait-focused. (We can, of course, have a kind of wow-response towards actions like juggling seven burning swords, but as I've argued, that's a different attitude.) This is one respect in which my view differs from Linda Zagzebski's (2017) well-known account, since she holds that admiration is directed towards particular traits, whether native talents or acquired excellences.

The first reason to think admiration is person-focused is that any bad behaviour, or more generally falling conspicuously short of any important ideal we endorse, is properly a strike against admiring someone. When it came out that the comedian Louis CK had sexually harassed a number of female colleagues by exposing himself to them, it didn't make him any less funny, but it did appropriately reduce the admiration that many had felt for him. Further, isolated acts simply don't make admiration fitting—though we may of course say that we admire someone *because of* a tough choice, when we take it to reflect commitments or character traits apt to lead to a life of praiseworthy achievement. Focus on the person also explains the common phenomenon that the more we know of a hero of ours, the less we admire them: we come to realize that even if they do approximate one ideal, they fall short along many other dimensions (for example, any number of successful men turn out to have been inveterate womanizers). The second, and related, reason is that admiration's effects on interaction with its target are pervasive, like the effects of love or shame. They're not limited to motivation to emulate the target in ways that are related to their perceived excellence. It's not unusual for us to start dressing like our heroes, for example, even if it's not sartorial elegance that grounds our admiration. But admiration also involves a disposition to pay attention to and find out more about its target, to recommend her as a model to others and to defend her against criticisms, to feel happy when the target is successful or gets recognized and sad when they suffer a loss or die, and so on.

There are several further reasons, too. Two of them have to do with relationships to other exhortative attitudes. Consider the possibility of self-admiration. If such a thing exists, it is virtually indistinguishable from hubristic pride. If what I say is right, they have basically the same intentional content—both portray me as living up to an ideal I endorse in virtue of my enduring features. Insofar as admiration motivates emulation, self-admiration motivates me to be like myself—or just glory in my magnificent self. And that's just hubristic pride. And since hubristic pride is uncontroversially person-focused, admiration must be the same, or the two wouldn't coincide in the case of self-admiration. The fourth argument is similar, except it begins with the observation that the contrary of admiration is contempt or disdain, which is also widely considered a person-focused attitude (Bell 2013). The difference between contempt and admiration is polarity, not difference in focus. Act-focused attitudes like resentment and anger do not have admiration as their contrary, but rather gratitude or contentment.

Finally, fitting admiration seems to have a higher bar than fitting pride. You might legitimately be proud of getting the kids to school in time when your spouse is away. Nevertheless, don't expect me to admire you for it. What explains this difference? Well, if admiration focuses on the person, it's harder to merit it, because you'll need to have a set of traits and lasting commitments that explains a pattern of praiseworthy performances. You could easily get the kids to school without such a psychology. (You'll also have to be superior to me, but that's probably true when it comes to this kind of case.) Since authentic pride, in contrast, is act-focused, in can be appropriate on the basis of a single act.

Some of these arguments point to admiration being focused on enduring features. I've already given reasons why such focus is holistic, but some might still insist that we can admire character traits. But I think this is misleading. I may admire your tenacity. But I'm not sure if it makes sense to admire tenacity as such—it's not really the character trait, even a virtuous one, that is the object of the admiration. (Nor do I envy wealth as such, but *your* wealth.) And in admiring *your* tenacity, it seems that I'm admiring *you*.

That's why I don't admire Margaret Thatcher's tenacity, though I grant that it was a virtue of hers. However, I confess I admire Lyndon Johnson's ruthlessness in twisting Southern senators' arms to ram through civil rights legislation, even though I don't think ruthlessness as such is a good thing. It's really Johnson I admire. Finally, it may be that a trait, such as acerbic wit, is both grounds for admiring and grounds for not admiring someone (assuming it hurts people, for example).

Given the difference between first- and third-person perspectives, person-directed admiration isn't ethically problematic for the same reasons as hubristic pride is, though they seem to be in many ways parallel attitudes. While hubristic pride is smug and in bad faith, admiration isn't. For me, your traits and abilities exist in a different way than they do for you—they're independent of the choices I make or am going to make. For me, they *are* facts about you, while for Sartrean reasons my own traits aren't simply facts about me for myself. I can predict you're going to keep doing good things, but I can't simply predict that of myself, since the truth of the prediction is in my own hands, or rather in the hands of my future self, who is free to decide otherwise. Unlike hubris, admiring you doesn't encourage complacency, but self-improvement or keeping it up. We may have good reason to do our best to resemble an exemplar.

But that is not to say person-focused admiration doesn't raise ethical questions. Indeed, it gives rise to what I'll call the Puzzle of Admiring the Imperfect: everybody falls short of some legitimate ideal of the person, so how can it be fitting to admire anyone? For example, I just said I admire Lyndon Johnson. At the same time, I know that he was a philandering bully and sycophant, who got his country into the Vietnam war in large part for reasons of domestic political expediency. How could he be admirable? But who is, then? Even saints have their flaws, as Susan Wolf (1982) famously pointed out. Will it turn out that admiration is after all never, or at best very rarely, a warranted attitude? I don't think so. I'll next consider two possible solutions to this puzzle.

The first way to try to avoid the puzzle is to distinguish between different kinds of admiration. It seems natural to say that someone like Picasso is aesthetically admirable, even if he's not morally admirable. One way to make sense of this is to say that it is fitting for us to adopt one kind of attitude, one of aesthetic admiration, towards him, but not moral admiration, which is a distinct kind of attitude. This would go at least some of the way towards solving the puzzle. I'm not happy with this proposal, however. It doesn't seem to me that there's a variety of attitudes of admiration. To be sure, there's some case for the notion that there are feelings of elevation that are distinctive of admiring those who are morally impressive. This is one reason why some psychologists, such as Algoe and Haidt (2009), distinguish moral elevation from other forms of admiration. We might nevertheless insist that as long as intentional and motivational content are the same, we don't really have a different attitude or emotion. Of course, the ideals and consequently grounds for admiration are different, but that doesn't make for a different attitude, any more than different normative expectations alone give rise to different forms of anger.

The second issue is that there seem to be too many different ways to be admirable for this strategy to be plausible. Even if we can distinguish between a couple of different species of admiration, it won't help explain why Lionel Messi is admirable as a footballer but not admirable as a taxpayer—even if there is an attitude of moral admiration, there isn't going to be an attitude of football admiration and taxpayer admiration.

So how, then, can we make sense of admiring the imperfect? I think we can make the case that admiration can be fitting in many different ways. Rather than a plurality of attitudes, there is a plurality of kinds of fit. Among other things, this solution has the benefit of generality: there are plenty of other attitudes that can be fitting in different ways (Kauppinen 2015). After all, it seems like someone can be, say, aesthetically as well as morally contemptible.

In the case of admiration and related attitudes, there is a straightforward way of explaining why there would be different kinds of fit: there are, after all, different kinds of ideal that a person might realize in their lives. Roughly, to be morally admirable, one must live up to a moral ideal, and to be aesthetically admirable, one must live up to an aesthetic ideal. But this is only the beginning, since our ideals can be quite fine-grained. This goes especially for ideals that derive from standards of excellence that are internal to our various practices. I mentioned the ideal of a scholar above. But there's also the ideal, or possibly many ideals, of a teacher, or a politician, or a doctor, or a father. All of these are possible ways of leading a life that can realize or promote something of genuine value, so that the standards they involve are authoritative. When somebody does approximate realizing such ideals in their lives in virtue of their enduring traits or commitments, they can be admirable in a specific way. Lyndon Johnson, for example, is politically admirable, or admirable from a political point of view, given his ability to find solutions that would persuade people with very different viewpoints.

This account has a number of interesting implications. First, according to it, there's no such thing as being admirable *tout court*, unless that means being admirable from every applicable perspective. It may be that no one is admirable in that way. But that's not a big deal, since it is still fitting to admire many people. Second, it is possible that it's fitting to admire someone from one point of view and disdain them from another point of view. Consider Erwin Rommel. He's generally recognized as one of the greatest German generals of World War II, an inspiring leader of men who achieved feats many had considered impossible. At the same time, though he wasn't personally a Nazi and even supported the conspiracy against Hitler, he fought for one of the worst causes in history. So while from a military perspective, he merits admiration, from a moral perspective we must condemn and even disdain him.

Now, it follows from what I've said that you can't, as a matter of fact, adopt both of these attitudes towards the same target at the same time. Both are person-focused and permeate interactions with the target in ways that are polar opposites. So how should we relate to Rommel, or Picasso, or Messi, then? Let me first emphasize that this is a distinct question from whether someone is admirable in some way (that is, whether admiration is fitting). To make this distinction clear, consider fear. Sometimes you shouldn't be afraid, because the target of your emotion isn't in fact dangerous (say, it's a spider). But if you're caught in the midst of a hurricane, say, fear might well be warranted. At the same time, it might paralyze you and result in great harm. This is a strong reason for you to want not to be afraid, and to do what you can to down-regulate your warranted response. I'm not sure if it makes sense to say you shouldn't feel afraid in such a situation, since it is an involuntary response, but you should try to get rid of it. Similarly, the question of whether it is fitting to admire Rommel from a military perspective is distinct from whether we *should* admire him. It seems natural to me to say that although he's militarily admirable, we have reason to want not to admire him, and perhaps, insofar as admiration is under direct voluntary control, that we shouldn't admire him, given that he fought for a terrible cause.

So, in short, it doesn't follow from that fact that it's in some way fitting to admire someone that we should admire her, just as it doesn't follow from something's being valuable that we should value it in the sense that implies emotional investment. Perhaps the simplest thing to say is that admiring can be appropriate, all things considered, when the target is admirable in some way and is not disadmirable or contemptible from the moral perspective. Morality, after all, has a unique function and authority in demanding or prohibiting certain attitudes, laying claim to a universal jurisdiction in a way that other perspectives don't.[4] No one thinks we shouldn't, all things considered, admire a scientific genius just because her personal hygiene leaves much to be desired. Alternatively, we might say that appropriateness of admiration is subject-relative—maybe it depends on which ideals are particularly important to you whether rating low enough by their standards disqualifies someone as an object of appropriate admiration for you, regardless of their achievements on other dimensions.

Whether we should admire someone who is in some way admirable may further depend on our own projects and life history. For example, it makes good sense for me to admire Nussbaum, since we're both engaged in the scholarly project, and she does it so much better than I do, while it is less sensible for me to invest in admiring someone who is good at woodworking, since such pursuits aren't a priority for me now.

CONCLUSION

To sum up, I've defended the following three theses regarding agential admiration in this chapter:

1. Admiration construes its target as (approximately) realizing a worthwhile ideal of the person to a greater degree than the admirer (or the norm).
2. Admiration is always person-focused rather than act- or trait-focused.
3. Admiration is *fitting* from a specific point of view as long as the agent (approximately) realizes the relevant worthwhile ideal of the person, even if they fall short of other ideals. Whether admiration is *all things considered appropriate* depends also on the relevance of the ideal they approximate to our own projects and on the target's not falling conspicuously short of moral (or subjectively important) ideals.

I suspect that what I've said is controversial, in particular when it comes to emphasizing the realization of excellent traits in action rather than merely possessing them, highlighting the holistic focus of the attitude, and noting the consequent restrictions on its appropriateness. But I believe we have good reasons to accept these theses, given the function of exhortative attitudes in general in guiding our personal development and the way agential admiration permeates our relationship to our idols.[5]

NOTES

1. For this sort of responsibility, see Watson 1996 on attributability.
2. Compare with Shoemaker 2015 on the grounds of attribution-responsibility.
3. Although, as Simon Robertson reminded me, there are other alleged forms of guilt, such as survivor guilt, which are controversial precisely because they don't relate to one's own acts.
4. It follows from this that my admiration of LBJ is all-things-considered inappropriate, insofar as he did morally terrible things (as well as morally admirable ones). Mea culpa.
5. I want to express my gratitude to André Grahle, Lilian O'Brien, and especially Simon Robertson for insightful written comments, which led me to make several important changes. I also owe a debt to the participants at the Munich Admiration workshop in September 2017.

REFERENCES

Algoe, Sara, and Jonathan Haidt. 2009. "Witnessing Excellence in Action: The 'Other-Praising' Emotions of Elevation, Gratitude, and Admiration." *Journal of Positive Psychology* 4 (2): 105–27.

Bell, Macalester. 2013. *Hard Feelings: The Moral Psychology of Contempt*. New York: Oxford University Press.

Fischer, Jeremy. 2012. "Being Proud and Feeling Proud: Character, Emotion, and the Moral Psychology of Personal Ideals." *Journal of Value Inquiry* 46 (2): 209–22.

Gottman, John, and Robert Levenson. 2000. "The Timing of Divorce: Predicting When a Couple Will Divorce over a 14-Year Period." *Journal of Marriage and Family* 62 (Part 3): 737–45.

Hume, David. 1739–1740 (1978). *A Treatise of Human Nature*. Edited by L. A. Selby-Bigge, revised by P. H. Nidditch. 2nd edition. Oxford: Oxford University Press.

Kauppinen, Antti. 2015. "Fittingness and Idealization." *Ethics* 124 (3): 572–88.

Kauppinen, Antti. 2017a. "Pride, Achievement, and Purpose." In *The Moral Psychology of Pride*, edited by J. Adam Carter and Emma Gordon, 169–90. London: Rowman & Littlefield International.

Kauppinen, Antti. 2017b. "Valuing Anger." In *The Moral Psychology of Anger*, edited by Myisha Cherry and Owen Flanagan, 31–48. London: Rowman & Littlefield International.

Mason, Michelle. 2003. "Contempt as a Moral Attitude." *Ethics* 113 (2): 234–72.

Shoemaker, David. 2015. *Responsibility from the Margins*. New York: Oxford University Press.

Tangney, June P., and Rhonda Dearing. 2002. *Shame and Guilt in Interpersonal Relationships*. New York: Guilford Press.

Tangney, June P., and Jessica L. Tracy. 2013. "Self-Conscious Emotions." In *Handbook of Self and Identity, 2nd Edition*, edited by Mark L. Leary and June P. Tangney, 446–78. New York: Guilford Press.

Tracy, Jessica, and Richard Robins. 2007. "The Psychological Structure of Pride: A Tale of Two Facets." *Journal of Personality and Social Psychology* 92 (3): 516–30.

Watson, Gary. 1996. "Two Faces of Responsibility." *Philosophical Topics* 24 (2): 227–48.

Williams, Lisa, and David DeSteno. 2008. "Pride and Perseverance: The Motivational Role of Pride." *Journal of Personality and Social Psychology* 94 (6): 1007–17.

Wolf, Susan. 1982. "Moral Saints." *Journal of Philosophy* 79 (8): 419–39.

Zagzebski, Linda. 2017. *Exemplarist Moral Theory*. New York: Oxford University Press.

Chapter Three

Happy Self-Surrender and Unhappy Self-Assertion

A Comparison between Admiration and Emulative Envy

Sara Protasi

> "Envy is concealed admiration. An admirer who feels that he cannot be happy by surrendering himself elects to become envious of that which he admires. So he speaks another language, and in that language of his the thing which he really admires is called a stupid, insipid, and queer sort of thing. Admiration is happy self-surrender; envy is unhappy self-assertion."
> (Kierkegaard, *The Sickness Unto Death*)

You did it! You won first prize. You just heard the speaker announce your name. You can't quite believe it. All the sleepless nights, all the work, all the fights with your partner and the yelling at the kids, followed by repentance, making amends, and explaining you are just so very tired, and you will do better next time. You tell yourself it was all worth it. You open your eyes, realizing only now that you closed them for a second, and you look around. Everyone is waiting for you to stand up and go to the podium. You can't help but look in the eyes of the people near you: they were all competing with you, and their hopes have just been dashed by your victory.

What would you expect to see in their gaze? And what would you rather see? Admiration or envy? Most people will say that they would rather be admired than envied, even though we often expect, and fear, to be envied. It's because you fear to be envied that when you give your little speech at the podium you start by collecting goodwill and thanking all of the people in front of you; it's because you fear to be envied and to avoid sounding boastful that you highlight your lack of desert and your good fortune, even though you actually believe you achieved success through your hard work. All socially apt adults know this much: even if you sincerely believe you are better than everyone else, you just don't say it out loud.[1]

Conversely, imagine that you are one of the people who has not won the prize. What would you rather feel? And what should you show that you are feeling on the outside? Envy or admiration? The answer here will be, I suspect, universal: admiration. No matter what you actually feel inwardly, consciously or unconsciously, you will clap your hands and put up a congratulatory smile on your face. Again, very few socially apt adults will stomp their feet and make a frowning face, and storm out of the ballroom, no matter how envious they are feeling.

None of the phenomena I described are surprising. Most people think of admiration as a positive emotion, both affectively and morally: it is pleasant to feel; it inspires the admirer; it is void of ill will and thus does not threaten the admired, who does not fear being deprived of their superior status or harmed in any way. Conversely, most people think of envy as a negative emotion, almost a perfect opposite of admiration: it is unpleasant to feel; it depresses the envier; it is malicious and thus scares the envied, who fears the envier's attempts to spoil the good they covet.

And yet, innumerable stores and products contain the word "envy" in their name, and any psychologist working in marketing or advertisement will tell you that many ads are aimed to elicit envy in the viewers. We do, secretly, want others to envy us. And we do, often, envy others. This gap between the story that emerges to the surface and the story buried in our hearts is not merely the chasm between ideal and reality, a chasm we so often confront when philosophizing about ethics. It is also an expression of the complexity of human moral psychology, a symptom of the variety and nuance of social-comparison emotions.

In this chapter, I argue that a certain kind of envy is not only morally permissible, but also, sometimes, more fitting and productive than admiration. Envy and admiration are part of our emotional palette, our toolbox of evolutionary adaptations, and they play complementary roles. I start by introducing my original taxonomy of envy, which allows me to introduce emulative envy, a species of envy sometimes confused with admiration. After reviewing how the two emotions differ from a psychological perspective, I focus in particular on the distinct and complementary roles they play in the ethical and political domains.

THE VARIETIES OF ENVY

Philosophers are used to lively ontological debates, but even psychologists seem far from a consensus on the thorny question of what emotions are. In both disciplines, emotions are argued to be feelings, judgements, perceptions, cultural constructs, innate responses, all of the above or even none of the above, given the recent popularity of psychological construction theories, according to which emotions are not discrete natural kinds.[2]

This ontological debate, however, has no direct bearing on the question I am tackling in this chapter, so I will use a relatively neutral definition of emotion as a syndrome of characteristic appraisals, feelings and physiological changes (including facial expressions), motivational tendencies, and behavioral outputs. Fear, for instance, can thus be individuated by its appraisal that a certain object is scary (because dangerous or harmful); by affective responses caused by specific bodily changes (e.g., increase in heart rate and blood pressure, accelerated breathing, release of stress hormones); and by the typical urge to flee or fight. Fear, like many emotions that have traditionally been called "basic," involves a two-place relation: the agent who experiences the emotion and the object that triggers it.

Envy is more complex, and so there is disagreement on whether it is better characterized as a two- or three-place relation. I assume here the view that I defend elsewhere (Protasi 2016, 2017b): that it is a three-place relation, composed of the *envier* (the subject who feels the emotion), the *envied* (the person toward whom the emotion is directed, or target), and the *good* (the object with regard to which the envier is in a disadvantageous position vis-à-vis the envied).[3]

But what is envy *about*? Envy's *appraisal*, or evaluative content, has to do with perceived superiority or advantage: the envied has something that the envier lacks and that they care about. As a consequence, envy's affect is negative: it is a painful or at least unpleasant emotion to feel. Such a pain is amplified by a further aspect of envy. In cognitivist terms, envy's appraisal involves a perception of similarity: that is, the envied is perceived as similar to the envier along some relevant dimension. (Note that envy's appraisal may not be conscious—in fact, envy itself often isn't [Smith and Kim 2007, 56].) In a noncognitivist account, perceived similarity may be considered a situational antecedent or part of the fittingness conditions.

Envy feels a lot worse than a simple wish for something or a general feeling of inferiority to another person: it compounds the two. The insult of feeling inadequate is added to the injury of lacking a valued good, so to speak. In addition, envy is never felt with regard to goods that are considered important, but not connected to the envier's identity. This aspect, too, may or may not be part of envy's appraisal depending on the account of emotions one chooses.

My working definition of envy will thus be: aversive response to a perceived disadvantage vis-à-vis a similar other with regard to a domain of self-relevance, which motivates the agent to overcome their disadvantage *either* by pushing themselves up to the envied person's position *or* by pulling the envied down to theirs.

Such a disjunctive motivational tendency (which we can informally call "leveling up" or "leveling down") gives rise to a variety of behavioral outputs, which in turn characterize four specific varieties of envy. In order to see how that works, though, we have to take a step back and look more carefully at envy's appraisal.

Recall my initial scene and adapt it to your professional context. The prize winner is a colleague of yours. They have achieved a significant professional milestone, while you haven't. This perceived inferiority of yours is painful. But it might be painful in two different ways: it might sting because you really care about that goal. Or it might sting because it is *that colleague* who has achieved it. That is, you might be primarily concerned with the lack of the good or you might be primarily concerned with the superiority of the envied.

If the former applies, you will be disposed to pursue the good further, because that is what you really want, what you value for its own sake, and the envied's success is only a reminder of your (perceived) failure. But if the latter applies, and what really bothers you is the envied's superior performance, then achieving the goal is a means to beating your rival and is thus valued only instrumentally. You will therefore be disposed to do everything it takes to bring the envied down.

Thus *focus of concern*, the first variable of envy, determines whether the envier is motivated to level up or level down: to overcome their disadvantage either by pushing oneself to the envied's level or by pulling the envied down to their level. What that means, in concrete action terms, varies depending on another variable: *obtainability of the good*. (For simplicity, I will speak as if the variables are dichotomous, even though they are continuous. Since they do not correlate, they give rise to four kinds of envy.)

The good might be perceived as obtainable or not, depending on many circumstantial factors. In the case of a professional achievement, this might be an exclusive or particular good, such as receiving an honorific title that cannot be shared. In that case, it is not possible for the envier to achieve the good: the envied already got it! Thus, leveling up is impossible, notwithstanding the envier's disposition. But sometimes goods are nonexclusive or shareable: imagine the professional achievement in question being promotion to a higher rank. In that case, it is possible for the envier to achieve their own goal (assuming they perceive themselves as being capable of it—if they don't, then the outcome is the same as before).

When enviers are concerned with the lack of the good and perceive themselves as capable of obtaining it, then they are disposed to *self-improve* and *strive* to level up with the envied. I call the emotion they feel *emulative envy*. When enviers are concerned with the good, but do not perceive themselves as capable of obtaining it, then their self-improvement disposition is frustrated and they end up being *sullen* and *sulky*. The resulting emotion is *inert envy*, which is self-defeating by definition.

When enviers are concerned with the superiority of the envied and perceive themselves as capable of bringing the envied down, then they are disposed to *steal* the good. Gaining the good thanks to one's own improvement does not matter to the envier; however, to obtain it for oneself is a nice bonus, the best possible way of bringing the envied's down. I call this emotion *aggressive envy*. But stealing the good is not always perceived as possible, in which case the envier is disposed to *spoil* the good, as the saying goes ("envy spoils the good it covets"). This last type of envy is *spiteful envy*. Note that spiteful envy is not self-defeating: even if the good is lost, the envied has been brought down, per the envier's goal.[4]

Figure 3.1, below, summarizes my taxonomy.

Emulative envy and admiration are close emotions, which are often confused with one another. In the remainder of this chapter, I am going to set aside the other subspecies of envy in order to show how sometimes emulative envy is a more appropriate and productive emotional response than admiration, *contra* what popular wisdom and traditional morality would argue.[5]

ADMIRATION AND EMULATIVE ENVY

Let me introduce you to Emma, our exemplary Emulative Envier. She is a hip-hop dancer, who wants to become a star; she trains in the same studio as a strong-willed and talented girl named Beyoncé.

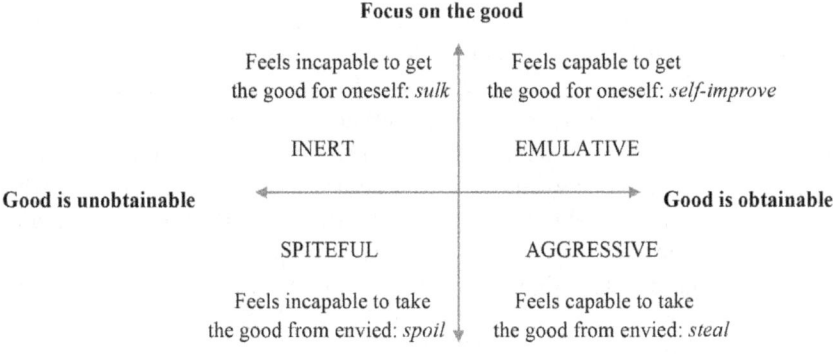

Figure 3.1.

Emma is a very good dancer, but Beyoncé is excellent, and regularly outperforms her in competitions. Emma feels a painful emotion toward Beyoncé when she sees her on stage: she is aware of her own inferiority and would like to become like Beyoncé. They have trained in the same studio since they were children, so Emma thinks that becoming as good as Beyoncé is within the realm of possibility. She keeps training hard and keeps hoping that one day she will achieve her goal.

Emma feels an aversive response to a perceived disadvantage vis-à-vis a similar other with regard to a domain of self-relevance, which motivates her to overcome her disadvantage by pushing herself up to the envied person's position. It is not an immoral response: it does not involve any ill will toward the envied. Emma never wishes that Beyoncé lose her talent. Watching her dance fills her with excitement and longing, the way a child looks at a lollipop behind a store window. She does not want to spoil the envied's talent, nor does she desire to steal it: she cares about becoming an excellent dancer through hard work, by her own means.

Emma's response is not a self-defeating or imprudent response either: it does not make her sulk in despair, nor berate her unlucky fate. Thus, her envy is neither morally nor prudentially bad: it is not harmful to the envier or the envied. While painful to experience, it is a productive kind of pain, which motivates to self-improvement.

But is Emma's emotional response really an envious one? How does it differ from admiration? The question arises naturally and legitimately. After all, emulative envy and admiration have much in common. Both emotions are complex, value-laden responses to upward social comparison: both the admired and the envied are perceived as superior to the self. The agent "looks up" to the target in both cases. However, the admiring gaze is only superficially similar to the envious one. The two emotions differ in affect, appraisal, antecedent, and affiliation tendency.

Starting with the most obvious difference: emulative envy is painful, admiration is pleasant (or "happy" versus "unhappy," in Kierkegaard's words). That is because emulative envy is focused both on the self *and* the other, while admiration is mostly (but perhaps not exclusively) focused on the other. Such a shift in appraisal correlates with a shift in the situational antecedent: emulative envy arises when comparison is toward someone who is similar in status or ability, and with regard to a self-important domain. Admiration typically arises toward people who are perceived as much superior to the agent and its "stimulus events . . . are not directly relevant to the individual's current goal pursuits" (Schindler et al. 2013, 90). Finally, and relatedly, admiration motivates to affiliate with the target, whereas emulative envy does not.

However, when it comes to action tendency and what these emotions motivate the agent to do, the evidence is mixed and still quantitatively limited. Earlier studies (van de Ven et al. 2011) showed that *benign envy*, as is generally called in psychology,[6] outperforms admiration in the effectiveness to motivate the agent to self-improve. Admiration was not shown to motivate agents to emulate the admired. But these results were contradicted by subsequent research by Ines Schindler and her collaborators (Schindler et al. 2013, 2015), which showed that admiration is in fact linked to the tendency to emulate the admired other. The emerging consensus is that admiration and benign envy serve two different functions and that they motivated different kinds of emulative behaviors (Schindler et al. 2015; van de Ven 2015).

Envy is a negative affective state that motivates to act immediately; it narrows the agent's cognitive processing and pushes one to pursue the coveted object right away (Harmon-Jones et al. 2012).[7] But there is another kind of emulation, the development of a commitment to abstract ideals, akin to being inspired. That is what "an emotion with lower motivational intensity that broadens cognitive processing" does (Schindler et al. 2015; Harmon-Jones et al. 2012).

To summarize, admiration is a pleasant emotional response to the perceived excellence of an object (often but not necessarily a person), whose primary function *may* be to "enhance one's own agency in upholding ideals" (Schindler et al. 2013, 86).

Emulative envy, *qua* envy, is an unpleasant emotional response to the perceived superiority or advantage of a similar other in a self-important domain, which *may* be the most adaptive and less harmful response to being outperformed in evolutionarily important domains of resource competition (Hill and Buss 2008).

Kierkegaard's pithy slogan of admiration as "happy self-surrender" and envy as "unhappy self-assertion" seems about right. Recall Emma and her envied target, Beyoncé. They both admire Misty Copeland, whom they perceive as a much more talented dancer than both of them. (This is all, of course, purely fictional.)

Setting aside their competitiveness, the two girls often get together to watch videos of the famous ballerina, and they lose themselves in the performance, emitting sighs of love and shrieks of pleasure as Misty pirouettes on stage. Watching Misty dance renovates, in both, the commitment to show up to the dance studio every day and to engage in outreach activities with younger girls of color in their local community, and it makes them dream of future success and fame. But when Emma looks at Beyoncé "pop and lock," she is focused on imitating her sharp arm movements, here and now.

That these emotions are so similar may suggest that they have evolved from some sort of common affective ancestor.[8] Nevertheless, as I define them here, they are cultural constructs that are typical of certain contemporary Western societies, like the current United States. We may not find them in ancient honor cultures, such as the Homeric one, where malicious forms of envy prevail, and we may not find them in contemporary collectivist cultures (such as China, Korea, and Japan), where an interconnected sense of self prevails over an individualistic one (Henrich et al. 2010).

THE MORAL VALUE OF ADMIRATION AND EMULATIVE ENVY

Emma has grown up and set aside her artistic ambitions. She is now a philosophy professor and admires both Beyoncé and Misty Copeland from afar. As it turns out, she is your departmental colleague, and she envies you for that prize you won. Does that make her a bad person? Is her envy morally impermissible or inappropriate? And, more pressingly for the topic of this chapter, shouldn't she admire you instead?[9]

If ought implies can, we cannot hold Emma to ethical standards that are psychologically too demanding. We have limited control over our emotions. As discussed above, admiration and emulative envy typically arise in different circumstances. Emma's professional status and her philosophical talents are similar to yours: she perceives you as similar to herself. Furthermore, she shares your goals and self-identity: like you, she cares a lot about being a good philosopher. Envy, not admiration, is the natural response in this case. Furthermore, it is also a *fitting* response: you did deserve your prize. Your work is, indeed, superior to Emma's at the moment. And Emma is right in thinking that she could improve and achieve what you have achieved.

That an emotion is a typical and fitting response to circumstances does not in itself make it morally appropriate. But emulative envy is not morally bad either, because it is fully void of ill will and malice. It does not involve either the desire or the effect of harming the envied.

It is possible that, upon discovering that Emma envies you, you might feel uneasy, especially if you are not sure what kind of envy Emma feels. However, many behaviors that are not morally impermissible have the potential of creating uneasy feelings in others (think of surgeons: they may induce fears in their patients, even if they benefit them). Thus, making someone feel uneasy is not in itself harmful and therefore is not morally impermissible.

One might argue that admirers are more disinterested and altruistic: they are focused on the admired, after, all, not on themselves. However, this rosy picture is not supported by empirical evidence, which shows that admirers do expect some advantage from the admired other (Schindler et al. 2013). In fact, emulative envy might be *more* disinterested than admiration, given its lack of desire to affiliate with the envied. Emma is focused on becoming like you, not on getting any favor from you.

What about Emma's character? Is her disposition to envy her colleagues morally bad? Shouldn't she habituate herself to feel admiration more frequently? Wouldn't that promote more harmonious relationships in your department?

Moving from single occurrences and actions to dispositions can help us see how admiration and emulative envy are complementary emotions that play different roles in our moral psychology. As we know, Emma is capable of feeling admiration. In fact, she did feel deep admiration for you when she was hired a few years ago. But, as time went by, she came to see you as a peer. She has grown intellectually, also thanks to your mentorship. That Emma now envies you is something you should respect and appreciate: she sees you as an equal. There does not seem any reason, then, to think that Emma is a bad person, provided she habituates herself to feel emulative envy, as opposed to the other varieties, and provided that she feels admiration when appropriate.

Might admiration, however, be more appropriate *prudentially*, that is, more conducive to the well-being of the agent? We have already seen that both emotions motivate to self-improvement, if in different ways and times, but admiration is more pleasant. This seems a strike in favor of admiration.

However, the importance of feeling pain can hardly be overstated. Negative affect is crucial to human survival. Without fear of predators, disgust for contamination and pollution, sadness for loss, and sheer physical pain for hunger, thirst, or wounds, we would not be here. Envy's pain can be a productive one, as is the case for emulative envy.

If Emma didn't feel envy for you, but only admiration, she would still go to work, teach her courses, and write her articles, but she would be less motivated on a day-to-day basis to try to achieve more and to fulfil her potential.

Furthermore, as highlighted above, that Emma feels envy for you is a sign that she perceives herself as a more talented philosopher and that she believes she can become as good as you are; provided that her self-assessment is correct, it seems good, other things equal, to be on terms of equality with others.

One might worry that such a claim, however convincing anecdotally, is not sufficiently supported by empirical evidence, given the consistent correlations between envy and poor mental and physical health (Smith and Kim 2007, 58–60). But *what kind of envy* is investigated in the studies that provide such evidence? Most of these studies do not distinguish between different kinds of envy. Those which do make this distinction provide evidence supporting the claim that emulative envy is not bad for the envier.

Furthermore, the study that is most often cited for the correlation between envy and poor health outcomes (Smith et al. 1999) only focuses on *dispositional envy*. But, as Kenneth Tai and collaborators observe, the Dispositional Envy Scale is construed so as to investigate the most negative aspects of envy, and thus it is unsurprising that it ends up tracking only negative outcomes associated with envy (Tai et al. 2012, 108).

In sum, I suggest that admiration and envy complement each other, prudentially speaking; one provides the big picture, the long-term goals, and the other sets up a schedule, the short-term steps to achieve those goals.

THE POLITICAL VALUE OF ADMIRATION AND EVALUATIVE ENVY

One way to think about the difference between ethics and politics is to think of the former as the realm of private interactions, between agents *qua* individuals, and of the latter as the realm of public interactions, between agents *qua* members of a polity.

What happens once we start thinking of multiple Emmas, and conceive of her not as a moral agent but as a citizen of a state? Indeed, envy has been widely discussed in political philosophy, but almost always with regard to its negative varieties, and almost always in the context of redistributive justice (e.g., Bankovsky 2018; Ben-Ze'ev 1992; Kristjánsson 2005; La Caze 2001; Morgan-Knapp 2014; Neu 1980; Nozick 1974; Rawls 1971). Here, I am rather interested in a comparative analysis of admiration and emulative envy in motivating citizen behavior. Particularly, I will focus on two kinds of relations: a "vertical" one between a political leader and their followers and a "horizontal" one between members of different racial groups.

Once again, admiration and envy seem to play complementary roles. Admiration, being affiliative but hierarchical, seems more apt in the context of vertical interactions, while emulative envy, being adversarial but equalizing, is more appropriate to the horizontal ones. Being capable of arousing admiration is an indispensable quality of political leaders, and successful politicians are indeed admired, or even adored, by their followers.[10]

Of course, admiration for a leader who is undeserving of it, because of lack of competence or immorality, for instance, can be detrimental and even very dangerous, as history has proven time and again; in this respect, admiration's power is also its weakness. Because it provides the ideals and long-term goals, it can set up not just an individual, but an entire society, to failure and even, in the most tragic cases, horrific events like genocide. Admiration is not unique in this respect: trust, respect, compassion, and love, which have all been defended as important political attitudes, have the same problem, that is, they can be directed at an undeserving target and inspire to commit moral atrocities. (Thus, I do not take this to be an effective objection against admiration specifically.)

But, when a leader is worthy, admiration for them can lead to momentous positive change: Malala Yousafzai inspired young women in Pakistan and all over the world to courageously pursue their education notwithstanding political oppression or other adverse conditions. Most political movements are thus associated with one or more admired leaders. If I say decolonization of India, you think Mahatma Gandhi; if I say American Civic Rights, you think Martin Luther King Jr., and so forth.

This association might be slightly less common in the internet era. Consider Occupy Wall Street and Black Lives Matter, two U.S. political movements of the early 2000s. Even though they were, in practice, organized and led by a handful of individuals, neither is obviously associated with a popular leader. However, admiration still plays a role in building these movements. For instance, the photo of a Black woman, Ieshia Evans, standing in front of the police in a protest in Baton Rouge, Louisiana, went viral in July 2016; many people felt deep admiration for her courage. Her graceful yet firm stance became iconic. Figures like this, and the admiration felt for them, are pivotal in creating political and social movements.

Envy, even of the emulative kind, cannot play this role. It does not bring people together; it does not arise in the presence of someone whom we perceive as much more capable than ourselves. Someone who feels emulative envy for a Barack Obama or a Benazir Bhutto ought to be part of their entourage. And such an envier will not be drawn to be their follower; quite the contrary, they will aim to surpass them in talent or status. They will aim to become like them.

However, relationships in a polity are not exhausted by the one between a leader and their followers. Contemporary democratic and pluralistic societies are made up of groups, which can be extremely different from one another, and among which hostility, mistrust, or resentment often surface.[11] It is hard to believe that in Aristotle's times *philia*, a form of love and friendship, was expected to be felt toward one's fellow citizens! But it becomes more plausible once we realize that only a relatively homogenous group of people composed the citizenry of fourth-century Athens: free male adult individuals. It is much harder to get along in more diverse societies.

Furthermore, diversity of values, goals, and background is made particularly problematic in a context of limited resources: citizens often strive to access goods, including essential ones, that are available to some but not others, and the competition is often unfair. Hence, the "war among the poor" kind of phenomenon: groups that would benefit from being allies tend to be hostile against one another.

In this kind of situation, envy is a double-edge sword; in its aggressive and spiteful varieties, it can be as dangerous as warned by its many detractors, tearing apart the delicate tissues of civic society. Emulative envy, however, is not malicious and is not counterproductive, and it may be an apt response to a situation of perceived disadvantage.

Consider the case of policies aimed to increase racial diversity at university level as a case study. The reaction of some social groups, such as lower-socioeconomic status (SES) Whites and highly educated Asian Americans, toward groups perceived as advantaged by these policies, such as African Americans, can be construed either as resentful *and* envious, or envious only. (I assume here the fairly common characterization of resentment as a moral emotion that necessarily involves perception of injustice, and of envy as an amoral emotion that requires no such perception. See Ben-Ze'ev 2002 and Miceli and Castelfranchi 2007, and *contra* La Caze 2001.)

Consider first a resentful and envious response.[12] Since resentment involves a perception of wrongdoing, it involves hostility toward a culprit or cause of the wrongdoing. This might be the response of a student who does not benefit from a diversity policy and who believes the policy to be unfair. Given that one does not have control over one's race, and that the perception of unfairness is likely to make the envied's success more bothersome than the lack of the good (e.g., access to a prestigious university), the student will likely feel spiteful envy.[13] In this scenario, *neither admiration nor emulative envy can arise*. When the parties involved are convinced that a certain situation is unjust, and thus resentment is called for, a resolution is very hard to achieve. We often witness a stalemate in which agreeing on the facts, in this case historical causes of present inequality and effective means to eliminate it, is prevented by entrenched hostility and lack of empathy. I do not believe that either envy or admiration can play a central role here. It is no coincidence that anger, resentment, and forgiveness are such popular topics in contemporary discussion of political emotions!

But there are contexts in which resentment is low or not salient. In those contexts, one could suggest to lower-SES Whites or highly educated Asian Americans that they emulate the political battles of their Black counterparts, while suspending judgement on whether those gains are deserved or undeserved. In fact, this could be a strategy meant to actively decrease resentment! Emulative envy only requires perceiving the envied as capable and successful; the envied's success is indicative of the possibility of one's own (because the envier is sufficiently similar to the envied) and thus the envier is set to emulate them. While changing race is not possible,[14] one can advocate for extending diversity policies to other underrepresented groups. Lower-SES Whites can argue that socioeconomic status is a source of discrimination comparable to race. Asian Americans can point out that, while not subject to the same kind of discrimination faced by African Americans, they suffer other kinds of disadvantage; for instance, Asian-American students are underrepresented in philosophy departments.

Here, admiration could actually play a supporting role, by fostering respect between groups. For instance, admiration for accomplished women may undermine sexism; admiration for great artists such as Toni Morrison or

Miles Davis may help undermine White supremacy; admiration for esteemed conservative figures such as John McCain might increase Democrats' respect for Republicans; and so forth.[15] Thus, admiration may make groups *like* each other more, decrease hostility, and allow emulative envy to motivate productive behavior.

It is important to highlight again that envy is susceptible to the agent's subjective assessment of the circumstances: we can shift our perspective and make salient factors that favor perception of autonomy and control in our lives. We do see such a shift in perspective in the calls, for instance, for African Americans to refuse victimization and to see themselves as powerful and agentic. Consider the #Blackgirlpower and the #Blackexcellence memes on social media.[16]

One may object, at this point, that emulative envy is too adversarial an emotion, a far cry from the ideal of political *philia*, the civic friendship invoked by philosophers such as Martha Nussbaum under the auspices of revered figures like Martin Luther King Jr. and Gandhi (Nussbaum 2015). I have argued elsewhere that Nussbaum's model does not take sufficiently into account empirical findings, and I have defended the view that love and envy are two sides of the same coin, rather than radical opposites (Protasi 2017a). At the same time, the increased acrimony and dividedness that we are witnessing in the U.S. and European political scenes, the hostility between different social groups that is seemingly ripping countries apart, does give me some pause. While neither civic friendship or admiration seem available in such cases, it seems that we might need to find ways of reestablishing basic sympathetic responses to each other. After all, even envy is not possible when we cease to see others as fundamentally akin to us. And dehumanization is a constant threat in our history, and, possibly, our present (Livingstone Smith 2011, and under contract).

In a short chapter such as this, I can only gesture toward how to start thinking of very complex issues. My aim here was only to suggest that admiration and emulative envy can both be political emotions and play a positive role in civic society: neither is uniquely productive, nor detrimental, quite like in the private domain.

CONCLUSION

In this chapter, I have presented my original taxonomy of envy, which helps differentiate emulative envy from admiration. I have argued that these emotions play complementary roles in both the moral and political domain: in our private interactions, admiration helps us elaborate and achieve our long-term goals, while emulative envy aids us in setting up intermediate steps; in our public interactions, admiration is often targeted at our leaders and helps build community of like-minded citizens, while emulative envy may motivate fair competition between social groups.

I have long advocated for the rehabilitation of envy, and there is a general trend of re-evaluating negative affect emotions in both psychology and philosophy: we should not fear the dark side of human nature, for there is no light without shadow. We should not recoil from pain, for it is as crucial to our flourishing as pleasure. As Michelle Mason aptly puts it, "an enlightened morality need not be a gentle morality" (Mason 2003, 271). But it need not be a harsh one, either. Practical wisdom sometimes requires happy self-surrender, sometimes unhappy self-assertion, and sometimes something else altogether.

NOTES

1. This is a social behavior that we are taught early on in life. For most of us, a certain kind of modesty, whether sincere or not, becomes automatic and intuitive, an internalized norm of etiquette. Some adult individuals flout the norm, either because of a disability or neural atipicality, or because they can afford to do so given their social position and power. However, there are significant cultural variations in what counts as "modesty." While these behaviors can be observed cross-culturally, here I focus on contemporary Western society.
2. See Scarantino and de Sousa (2018) for a review.
3. For a fuller explanation and defense of my account of envy, see Protasi (2016). Therein, I also provide extensive references to the empirical literature supporting my descriptive claims.
4. Anthropological research (Foster 1972 and Lindholm 2008) shows that the fear of enviers stealing or spoiling the good is a common element of the stigma attached to envy cross-culturally.
5. There are, however, fierce critics of admiration as well. See Jan-Willem van de Rijt's contribution to this volume: "Admiration and Self-Respect."
6. Most psychological taxonomies distinguish only between malicious and benign envy, as defined by the motivational tendency to level down or up. The main explanatory factor for this difference is taken to be perception of control over the situation. I think this taxonomy neglects significant nuances, and I defend my own account in comparison to the psychological one in Protasi (2016). However, emulative envy does coincide with benign envy in many of the aspects studied by psychology, and especially with regard to the comparison between envy and admiration, so I will use psychological findings about benign envy as applicable to emulative envy as well.
7. These empirical findings nicely dovetail with envy's iconography and cultural tropes of the envious gaze as one that comes through squinted eyes, which well-represents the envier's focus on the lacked good.
8. Heidi Maibom (2012) hypothesizes that human shame and animal expressions of submission evolved from "protoshame," an emotion felt by the ancestor primates and human beings share. Perhaps something similar could be argued for the varieties of emotions that stem from social comparison.
9. To reiterate, this essay is narrowly focused on a comparison between emulative envy and admiration, rather than a comprehensive analysis of the moral value of either emotion. For an argument that admiration plays a pivotal role in morality, see Zagzebski (2017). For some well-founded critiques of Zagzebski's views, see Irwin (2015) and van der Rijt (2017).
10. For the difference between admiration and adoration see Schindler et al. 2013.
11. When I talk about *groups* feeling emotions, that is a shorthand for individuals of a certain group who feel emotions for individuals of other groups *qua* members of those groups.
12. I'm thankful to Jan-Willem van der Rijt for helpful criticisms of this section.

13. Such an envy might be excusable (Rawls 1971). Miriam Bankovsky argues for the stronger thesis that in conditions of deep injustice, (what I call) spiteful envy might be rational and prudentially appropriate (Bankovsky 2018).
14. I am setting aside cases of "passing" or even permanent race change, assuming they are possible, since they are not available to most people anyway.
15. I thank André Grahle for this suggestion.
16. See https://www.instagram.com/explore/tags/blackgirlpower/; https://twitter.com/hashtag/blackexcellence?lang=en. Note the difference with so-called respectability politics: making one's power and excellence salient need not imply that systemic disadvantage is unreal, nor that individual agency is full and complete, nor that talking in terms of victims and perpetrators is never appropriate or effective.

REFERENCES

Bankovsky, Miriam. 2018. "Excusing Economic Envy: On Injustice and Impotence." *Journal of Applied Philosophy* 35 (2): 257–79.
Barrett, Lisa F., and James A. Russell, eds. 2014. *The Psychological Construction of Emotion.* New York: Guilford Publications.
Ben-Ze'ev, Aaron. 1992. "Envy and Inequality." *The Journal of Philosophy* 89 (11): 551–81.
Ben-Ze'ev, Aaron. 2002. "Are Envy, Anger and Resentment Moral Emotions?" *Philosophical Explorations* 5 (2): 148–54.
Bers, Susan, and Judith Rodin. 1984. "Social-Comparison Jealousy: A Developmental and Motivational Study." *Journal of Personality and Social Psychology* 47 (4): 766–79.
de Balzac, Honoré. 1901. *The Complete Works of Honoré de Balzac.* Boston: Dana Estes and Company.
Fiske, Susan T. 2011. *Envy Up, Scorn Down: How Status Divides Us.* New York: Russell Sage Foundation.
Foster, George M. 1972. "The Anatomy of Envy: A Study in Symbolic Behavior." *Current Anthropology* 13 (2): 165–202.
Harmon-Jones, Eddie, Tom F. Price, and Philip A. Gable. 2012. "The Influence of Affective States on Cognitive Broadening/Narrowing: Considering the Importance of Motivational Intensity." *Social and Personality Psychology Compass* 6 (4): 314–27.
Henrich, Joseph, Steven Heine, and Ara Norenzayan. 2010. "The Weirdest People in the World?" *Behavioral and Brain Sciences* 33 (2-3): 61–83.
Hill, Sarah, and David Buss. 2008. "The Evolutionary Psychology of Envy." In *Envy: Theory and Research,* edited by Richard Smith, 60–71. New York: Oxford University Press.
Irwin, Terence H. 2015. "Nil Admirari? Uses and Abuses of Admiration." *Proceedings of the Aristotelian Society Supplementary Volume* 89 (1): 223–48.
Kierkegaard, Søren. 1941. *The Sickness unto Death: A Christian Psychological Exposition for Upbuilding and Awakening* (1849). New York: Oxford University Press.
Konstan, David. 2007. *The Emotions of the Ancient Greeks.* Toronto: Toronto University Press.
Kristjánsson, Kristján. 2005. "Justice and Desert-Based Emotions." *Philosophical Explorations* 8 (1): 53–68.
La Caze, Marguerite. 2001. "Envy and Resentment" *Philosophical Explorations* 4 (1): 31–45.
Lindholm, Charles. 2008. "Culture and Envy." In *Envy: Theory and Research,* edited by Richard Smith, 227–44. New York: Oxford University Press.
Livingstone Smith, David. 2011. *Less Than Human: Why We Demean, Enslave and Exterminate Others.* New York: St. Martin's Press.
Livingstone Smith, David. *Making Monsters: The Uncanny Power of Dehumanization,* under contract at Harvard University Press.
Maibom, Heidi. 2012. "The Descent of Shame." *Philosophy and Phenomenological Research* 80 (3): 566–94.
Mason, Michelle. 2003. "Contempt as a Moral Attitude." *Ethics* 113 (2): 234–72.
Miceli, Maria, and Cristiano Castelfranchi. 2007. "The Envious Mind." *Cognition and Emotion* 21 (3): 449–79.

Morgan-Knapp, Christopher. 2014. "Economic Envy." *Journal of Applied Philosophy* 31 (2): 113–26.
Neu, Jerome. 1980. "Jealous Thoughts." In *Explaining Emotions,* edited by Amélie O. Rorty, 425–63. Oakland: University of California Press.
Nozick, Robert. 1974. *Anarchy, State and Utopia.* New York: Basic Books.
Nussbaum, Martha C. 2015. *Political Emotions: Why Love Matters for Justice.* Cambridge, MA: Belknap Press.
Rawls, John. 1971. *Theory of Justice.* Cambridge, MA: Harvard University Press.
Protasi, Sara. 2016. "Varieties of Envy." *Philosophical Psychology* 29 (4): 535–49.
Protasi, Sara. 2017a. "Invideo et Amo: On Envying the Beloved." *Philosophia* 45 (4): 1765–84.
Protasi, Sara. 2017b. "'I'm Not Envious, I'm Just Jealous!': On the Difference between Envy and Jealousy." *Journal of the American Philosophical Association* 3 (3): 316–33.
Scarantino, Andrea, and Ronald de Sousa. 2018. "Emotion." *The Stanford Encyclopedia of Philosophy* (Winter 2018 Edition), edited by Edward N. Zalta. https://plato.stanford.edu/archives/win2018/entries/emotion/.
Schindler, Ines, Veronika Zink, Johanne Windrich, and Winfried Menninghaus. 2013. "Admiration and Adoration: Their Different Ways of Showing and Shaping Who We Are." *Cognition and Emotion* 27 (1): 85–118.
Schindler, Ines, Juliane Paech, and Fabian Löwenbrück. 2015. "Linking Admiration and Adoration to Self-Expansion: Different Ways to Enhance One's Potential." *Cognition and Emotion* 29 (2): 292–310.
Smith, Richard H., and Sung Hee Kim. 2007. "Comprehending Envy." *Psychological Bulletin* 133 (1): 46–64.
Smith, Richard H., W. Gerrod Parrott, Edward F. Diener, Rick H. Hoyle, and Sung Hee Kim. 1999. "Dispositional Envy." *Personality and Social Psychology Bulletin* 25 (8): 1007–20. https://doi.org/10.1177/01461672992511008
Tai, Kenneth, Jayanth Narayanan, and Daniel J. McAllister. 2012. "Envy as Pain: Rethinking Envy and Its Implications for Employees and Organization." *Academy of Management Review* 37 (1): 107–29.
van der Rijt, Jan-Willem. 2017. "The Vice of Admiration." *Philosophy* 93 (1): 1–22.
van der Rijt, Jan-Willem. 2019. "Admiration and Self-Respect." In *The Moral Psychology of Admiration,* edited by Alfred Archer and André Grahle, 61–76. London: Rowman & Littlefield International.
van de Ven, Niels. 2015. "Envy and Admiration: Emotion and Motivation Following Upward Social Comparison." *Cognition and Emotion* 31 (1): 193–200.
van de Ven, Niels, Marcel Zeelenberg, and Rik Pieters. 2011. "Why Envy Outperforms Admiration." *Personality and Social Psychology Bulletin* 37 (6): 784–95. https://doi.org/10.1177/0146167211400421.
van de Ven, Niels, Charles E. Hoogland, Richard H. Smith, Wilco W. van Dijk, Seger M. Breugelmans, and Marcel Zeelenberg. 2014. "When Envy Leads to Schadenfreude." *Cognition and Emotion* 29 (6): 1007–25.
Zagsebski, Linda. 2017. *Exemplarist Moral Theory.* New York: Oxford University Press.

Chapter Four

Admiration and Self-Respect

Jan-Willem van der Rijt

Viewed from a moral perspective, admiration is a peculiar attitude in at least three ways. First of all, admiration is not an exclusively moral attitude. Indeed, a case can be made that it does not primarily belong to ethics at all, and that in as far as it is a moral attitude, it is a spillover or import from aesthetics. The most natural objects of admiration are just that: objects. We admire, for instance, works of art that represent extraordinary beauty, or a vast and overpowering landscape. At first glance, therefore, it seems that admiration is typically a relation between a subject and an object. Certainly, persons can be the object of aesthetic admiration, too; for example when one admires a dancer's gracefulness or someone's striking physique, but when this is the case, we relate to these persons in an objectifying way: we evaluate them from a particular perspective and not in their capacity as persons as such. In a certain sense, aesthetic admiration by its nature objectifies persons. This need not be problematic, but it is worth noting that what one could call "moral admiration" is importantly different in this regard. In moral admiration the object of admiration is a person in her capacity as a moral being, the very capacity that makes her a person in the first place.[1] Moral admiration is an attitude that is adopted towards so-called moral exemplars: persons who embody the very essence of morality, who seem to excel at always doing the right thing, in the right way, at the right time. Since our capacity for morality is what grounds our personhood, moral admiration expresses a relation not between a subject and an object but between two subjects. It is directed at a person *as* a person, to put it in a slightly cryptic way.

This leads to the second issue with moral admiration. Surely it is possible to feel moral admiration towards another person, but is it appropriate to do so? Obviously we can admire, but *should* we do so (and if so, when and why)? Are subjects proper targets of admiration, or are there reasons to think that it is more properly directed exclusively at objects? When viewed from the perspective of the admirer, most appear to assume that moral admiration is not in itself objectionable. Surely, admiration *can* be problematic in certain cases, but this is mostly thought to be a matter of misdirection, for instance when people who are not moral exemplars are taken as such. If, however, admiration is directed at a genuine moral exemplar, then it seems to many that admiration is the right attitude to adopt. Zagzebski, for example, believes that moral exemplars are fitting objects of admiration and famously touts admiration's virtues (2017). It is through admiration, so she contends, that we become aware of examples of moral excellence and at the same time become motivated to improve our own moral conduct.[2]

Admirers themselves often appear to believe that their admiration constitutes a (great) compliment to the object of their admiration—at least, that is how it is intended when admiration is expressed in public. "How nice it must be to be openly admired by all present," so the thought appears to go, and if the admired were to openly rebuff the admirer's admiration, this tends to be quite painful for the admirer.

And yet, when we focus on the perspective of the admired, things become more ambiguous. For one, a desire for admiration is widely regarded as problematic—a thought that goes back at least as far as Hume, who described it as one of the basest of human desires. And this seems to be correct. If one were to answer the question "What do you want to achieve in your life?" with "To be admired!," one sounds, at best, rather juvenile, or, at worst, slightly megalomaniacal. One might think that this wariness towards a desire for admiration is based on the suspicion that such a desire means the actions wherefore the persons are admired would not be done for the right reasons. Doing something for the purpose of being admired immediately disqualifies it as a virtuous act. There appears to be more to it than that, however; even somebody who has done the right thing for the right reasons is not expected to respond to public expressions of admiration with an "And rightly so! You all indeed ought to admire me!" attitude. Instead, moral exemplars are standardly portrayed as spurning admiration—compare the irony and/or humility that moral exemplars are described as showing in Zagzebski (2017, 67, 163).[3]

In my view, this indicates that moral admiration may not be quite as unobjectionable as it is often taken to be. For if admiration were the appropriate response to moral excellence, why then would moral exemplars typically seek to evade it, rather than accepting it as the normal and fitting attitude for their behaviour to elicit? In this chapter, I argue that we can explain these reactions on the part of moral exemplars from the fact that there is something inherently objectionable about moral admiration.[4]

Before turning to my argument to that affect, a third matter needs to be addressed. This issue concerns the various (and shifting) ways in which the term "admiration" is used.[5] Here I will assume that admiration is best described as "approbation mixed with wonder,"[6] but there are and have been many other ways in which the term is applied. Historically, admiration was strongly related to awe, and at times it even seems to have been a full synonym of wonder simpliciter (i.e., without approbation). Nowadays the link with awe is much weaker, and in a time where hyperbole appears to have become the norm, admiration can also be used to express no more than high appraisal or approval (i.e., without wonder).[7] Nonetheless, to me it seems that the statements "I (highly) appreciate you for what you have done" and "I admire you for what you have done" are not fully equivalent, even to contemporary ears. Moreover, whereas the latter may be expected to lead to the reticence on the part of the admired described above, the former has no such connotations and can be unproblematically embraced as a welcome compliment. In order to find out what makes the moral difference between admiration and (high) appreciation, the aforementioned definition is particularly useful, as it clearly identifies what distinguished the two, a difference that also has clear etymological roots: admiration involves an ineliminable element of wonder, which mere (high) appreciation lacks.[8]

Since moral admiration, as opposed to aesthetic admiration, is an attitude adopted towards another subject as a subject, the moral evaluation of the attitude of admiration needs to be aimed at the nature of the relationship admiration creates between an admirer and the admired. I contend that moral admiration distorts this relationship in a problematic way.

My argument to this effect is based on the incompatibility between admiration and self-respect. In the following section, I first introduce the notion of self-respect, and its close cousin self-esteem. Subsequently (section 3), I determine how self-respect and self-esteem are impacted by admiration. In doing so, I also suggest that so-called "benign envy" is a more appropriate response to moral exemplars than admiration. Sections 4 and 5 address two complications that could occur as a result of distinguishing two different aspects of moral excellence that admiration could target: steadfast moral commitment and superior moral judgement. In the concluding section, I return briefly to the distaste that moral exemplars are expected to display towards admiration.

SELF-RESPECT AND SELF-ESTEEM

What does it mean to have self-respect? In current philosophical literature, it is standard to distinguish between a moralised notion of self-respect and a descriptive notion of self-esteem. The latter notion is many ways the easier to summarise. Self-esteem refers to a person's own evaluation of herself. Broadly speaking, a person is said to have high self-esteem when she has a favourable opinion of herself. That is, a person judges her actions, accomplishments, or character according to whatever subjective standards she deems to be relevant to this adjudication. If she then concludes she measures up favourably to them, her self-esteem increases, and if she judges herself to have performed poorly, her self-esteem suffers. There are many things that can contribute to a person's self-image, but her success and failure in endeavours she deems worthwhile count among the more significant ones.

Self-esteem is of considerable importance to a person. First of all, it can give a person information on how well she is doing in her capacity as an agent. If our self-evaluations are accurate, it tells us a lot about our personal strength and weaknesses. High self-esteem indicates we are—broadly speaking—on the right track, doing things that we are good at and care about, whereas low self-esteem tells us we need to either improve our skills or activities, or consider the possibility of dedicating ourselves to other pursuits to which we are better suited. Self-esteem also influences our psychological health. Those who have high self-esteem tend to be confident and active, whereas chronically low self-esteem can lead to depression and self-loathing. What is the point of doing anything, when you are not able to bring anything worthwhile to a successful conclusion? Thus, Rawls famously regards it as the most important primary good, arguing that a lack of self-esteem can undermine a person's ability to enjoy anything he does (1971/1999, §67).

As important as high self-esteem is from a psychological viewpoint, it must also be stressed that from a moral perspective high self-esteem is not unconditionally good. Because of the subjectivity of self-esteem, it is in principle possible that a person has high self-esteem when she should not. This can occur, for instance, through erroneous judgements or self-deception, when a person believes she has performed much better than she has. It can also occur when a person adopts inappropriate standards, regarding things as worthwhile that are not—evocative examples include various gruesome, but successful, despots from history, stereotypical hedge-fund managers, ruthless real-estate tycoons, and, since 2007, bankers. When you have behaved abominably and/or dedicated your life to base projects, then, morally speaking, you ought to feel bad about yourself, even if—or especially when—you are successful in your pursuits. Hence, in certain cases low self-esteem is, as unpleasant as it is, actually a good thing.

Let us now turn to self-respect. Unlike self-esteem, self-respect is an unabashedly moralised notion. It does not refer to how a person evaluates herself, to having a high opinion of oneself, but to the way someone behaves and what this behaviour says about the attitude she has towards herself. Having self-respect is a matter of appropriately valuing oneself as a moral agent, and to act accordingly. Another way of putting this is that self-respect is a matter of respecting one's own dignity. Exactly what this means in practice is something about which there is considerable disagreement, but a number of its core aspects are fairly uncontested. The requirements of self-respect are probably most vividly illustrated in the negative: there are certain things that show a person clearly fails to respect herself. Various forms of servility are classic examples. These include the deferential housewife, who subordinates her whole life to pleasing her husband; the Uncle Tom, a black man who believes blacks are worth less than whites (Hill 1995); and the spineless sycophant, who is willing to perform any act of self-humiliation in order to achieve a benefit or make his life easier.[9]

It is important to stress that the problem with these cases is not one of low self-esteem. For instance, the deferential wife may, notoriously, take great pride in performing her adopted role well. Similarly, many a successful career has been built on sycophancy (Schaber 2010, 76), so a successful brown-noser who thinks that all that matters is achieving one's goals, may actually think very favourably of himself. Failures of self-respect do not, unfortunately, necessarily lead to low self-esteem.

So what makes all these cases paradigmatic illustrations of lack of self-respect? Though the errors of the deferential wife, the Uncle Tom, and the sycophant are not fully identical, they all share one distinctive feature. Each in their own way, they fail to *see and/or express themselves as the full equals to others*. The deferential wife's total subordination to her husband shows she does not regard herself equal in importance to her husband, the Uncle Tom explicitly endorses his own inferior status, and the sycophant's obsequious willingness to kowtow shows he has no understanding of his own dignity.

When we exhort the sycophant, deferential wife, or Uncle Tom to *"have some self-respect!"* we are not trying to make them feel better about themselves, which we would do if we were simply trying to increase their self-esteem. In a way, we are actually trying to make them feel bad about themselves, at least in the short term, by making them aware of the undignified way they are behaving. What we want them to realise, is that there are certain standards of conduct that every person has to live up to simply because they are human beings—standards of which their current behaviour falls well short.

If we look a bit closer at self-respect, one of its most striking features is that though it is primarily concerned with how we relate *to ourselves*, it is typically expressed through the way we relate *to others*. This is a result of the fact that we are at the core of our nature social and political beings; there can be no moral individuality without a broader society that we are part of, a fact that is sometimes expressed through the notion of "the moral community." Having self-respect, then, is a matter of fully embracing one's own status as a full and equal member of this community, taking on all the rights and duties that come with it. A staunch belief in one's fundamental equality to all others, then, is a vital part of self-respect, and it is this fundamental equality that servile persons renounce or betray through their unworthy behaviour.

With the notions of self-respect and self-esteem in mind, let us return to admiration. Though I leave open the question of whether admiration amounts to a subtle form of servility, I argue that admiration is similar to servility in at least one respect: that it, too, is at odds with a full respect for the basic equality that underlies all proper relations between moral agents.

THE EFFECT OF ADMIRATION ON SELF-RESPECT AND SELF-ESTEEM

Let us imagine that you are a fairly ordinary moral agent. That is, your moral track record is not too horrendous, but it does contain a few blemishes. Not that you have committed any major crimes or massive betrayals, but there are several actions you aren't too proud of, and a few things you've done that you recall with shame. Perhaps you are aware that many others have a much worse track record than you do, but if you are honest with yourself, you recognise you, too, could have done better. If you look to the future, you like to believe you will indeed do better, but if you are truly honest with yourself, you expect your future performance to be rather similar to your past record: you do not expect to perform any grossly immoral actions, but you are not very confident you will really manage to improve your shortcomings and minor vices either. In moral terms you are "okay-ish."

Now imagine that you meet a person whose moral track record is much better than yours. A true paragon of virtue, someone who has the uncanny ability to seemingly always know what is to be done, and who has the type of character that also allows her to follow through on that judgement. Moreover, where you often have to struggle against temptation to do what you believe to be morally required, she seems to carry out her moral beliefs with relative ease. It is not that she is wholly immune to temptation, but her commitment to morality is so strong that even when she faces temptation it is never really in doubt that she will do the right thing in the end. In short, she is a veritable moral exemplar. The question now is, How should you relate to this person? What is the attitude you ought to adopt towards this embodiment of moral excellence?

Let us first query whether your encounter with the moral exemplar is a pleasant experience. Well, that depends on what perspective you adopt. Perhaps you never thought that the level of moral excellence the exemplar has reached was really achievable for human beings and are now both pleasantly surprised by this undeniable proof regarding the unexpected heights that humanity apparently is capable of reaching, and slightly awestruck by this particular specimen that embodies it. Isn't the world a wonderful place that it contains such excellences, and aren't you blessed to find yourself in the presence of such greatness? In short, you could adopt an admiring attitude towards the exemplar.

There are, however, also other possibilities. Since, presumably, you care about your own moral track record, your encounter with the moral exemplar may also emphasise your own shortcomings. When you compare yourself with others you regularly encounter, you tended to come out looking quite okay, but the comparison with this individual is far less flattering to your ego. Psychologically speaking, being confronted with our betters is far from pleasant and tends to evoke envy.

Envy is often assumed to be a vice, but it is important to stress that envy comes in (at least) two forms.[10] One possibility is that you begrudge the moral exemplar's excellence, and, somewhat pathetically, decide to try and take her down a peg or two. How dare she make you look bad! Thus, for instance, you might deliberately start to look for small flaws in her character, and overemphasise their severity; or, if you cannot find any, you try to tempt her into performing some contemptible act. Anything to bring it about so that you do not have to feel her lesser. Moreover, if you succeed in your attempt to corrupt the moral exemplar, you take a significant amount of satisfaction in her downfall. This attitude is called malicious envy and should indeed be considered vicious.

Another option, however, is to adopt an attitude known as benign envy, which does not constitute a vice. Rather than begrudging the moral exemplar her excellence, the benignly envious person focuses on her own lack of it. To be confronted with another's excellence is anything but pleasant as it highlights your own imperfections, but rather than holding this against her, you hold it against yourself. If she represents proof positive of the fact that higher levels of moral excellence are achievable than you have currently reached, then you take this as what it is: proof that you ought to do better too. And if you are not that confident that you will indeed do better in the future, then that is something you will refuse to accept lying down, but regard as something you have to work on with some tenacity.

Which of these attitudes is the proper attitude to adopt? For obvious reasons, we can dismiss the hostile attitude of malicious envy. This leaves us benign envy and admiration. In order to decide which of these two is, morally speaking, the most appropriate one, let us see how they affect a person's self-esteem and self-respect. Before we do so, however, it is worth noting that benign envy is fully compatible with showing high appreciation to the moral exemplar—indeed, the attitude of benign envy is premised on a full recognition of her excellence. This means that in terms of the self-esteem of the moral exemplar,[11] admiration and benign envy both appear to be beneficial: both attitudes provide positive feedback on her moral performance and thus reflect a positive self-image.

If we are to look at the effects of admiration and benign envy on self-respect and self-esteem, we need to return to what distinguishes the two. Since benign envy involves positive appreciation, the major distinction between the two is the element of wonder that is part and parcel of admiration but is absent in benign envy. Wonder comes in many degrees, but one thing that is essential to it, is that it involves a *partial* apprehension of its object (cf. Sherry 2013, 351). Obviously, there must be some level of grasp of the object, or an admirer would not be able to approve of the object of her admiration, but wonder also implies that there is something that eludes the understanding. It is in the nature of wonder that there is something you do not fully comprehend. This, I will argue in a moment, has important implications for moral admiration.

But let us first return to benign envy. What are its effects on self-esteem? As described above, an envious person takes her encounter with the moral exemplar to highlight her own shortcomings. This tends to be a blow to one's self-esteem: it emphasises that one does not measure up to the standards one believes to be applicable to one's behaviour. The benignly envious person takes the exemplar's excellence as a reminder of what is possible and required, and commits to improving her own performance. What is interesting about benign envy is that though it thus involves a lowering of one's self-esteem, it also reaffirms the universal validity of the standards of morality. The benignly envious person asserts in her envy that the same standards that apply to the moral exemplar also apply to her. Though she may have failed to live up to them to the same degree, by reasserting the fact that morality's standards bind both of them equally, the benignly envious person also reaffirms her fundamental equal standing with the exemplar. Thus, the benignly envious person incurs a blow to her self-esteem, but by accepting this blow maintains her self-respect.

For the admiring person, however, things are different. In fact, they are exactly opposite. The admiring person responds to the moral exemplar with approval, but also with wonder: how could someone be so excellent! Since wonder implies that there is something that eludes one's full grasp, we must query what it is that the admirer holds to be so difficult to grasp. It cannot be the standards that the moral exemplar has lived up to as such. If she would fail to grasp the standards by which moral actions are to be judged, she could not approve of the exemplar's accomplishments: she would not be able to recognise them as excellent. Hence, it seems that what the admirer holds to be so incredible must be the moral exemplar's living up to these standards.

But herein lies a problem. Morality binds unconditionally.[12] Hence, to recognise the standards that make the behaviour of the exemplar so excellent as moral standards is to believe that one *must* live up to them, too. At the same time, however, morality is a rational enterprise: to regard the standards of morality as *binding to oneself* implies seeing their demands as doable (ought-implies-can). Since admiration implies wonder, this cannot fully be the case for the admirer, however (cf. above).[13] But that also means that the admirer cannot regard herself as *unconditionally bound* to display the same level of excellence as the moral exemplar.

In order to admire, therefore, one must assume there are moral standards that bind the exemplar, but that do not bind the admirer, to whom another set of (less-exacting) demands are applicable. This, however, would mean that there are two different sets of moral standards, one binding ordinary people like the admirer, and one binding for extraordinary people like the moral exemplar. That, in turn, would mean that the admirer is committed to assenting to two classes of moral agents, which implies denying the basic equality between moral agents and thereby constitutes a violation of self-respect.

If this argument is on the right track, then an obvious question is why persons would adopt the attitude of admiration, rather than that of benign envy? Why would you be willing to recognise two classes of moral agents and put yourself in the lower one? The psychological reason, I believe, is that benign envy is, as stated, painful. It damages our self-esteem. Admiration, however, does not have this effect. Because the admirer implicitly allows for two sets of moral standards, she does not have to believe her own performance is subpar. Since she believes it cannot be *demanded* of her that she meets the exemplar's excellence, as she cannot see how she could do so, she does not have to believe she falls short of the standards that apply to *her*. Hence, according to her own standards, she may still perform well enough, and thus her self-esteem stays intact. Admiration is comfortable and easy; benign envy, however, is hard.

Moral admiration, then, can be viewed as a psychological mechanism that shields one from the painful experience of recognising that one is not doing well enough when confronted with the uncomfortable fact that others have actually done so. That something is psychologically explainable, however, does not make it morally appropriate.

ADMIRATION AND EQUALITY

The crux of my argument against admiration is the basic equality between moral agents, an equality that implies that we are all bound by morality in the same way, which is incompatible with the element of wonder that is part of admiration. Though this basic equality is not very controversial in contemporary moral theory, it is worthwhile to explicate a bit more what this equality does and does not entail. The basic equality between moral agents is an equality of status. Status equality is expressed in an equality of rights and duties. If one moral agent has a right or a duty to something in a certain situation, then another moral agent who finds herself in the same situation, also has that right or duty. It is crucial to emphasise that the equality of rights and duties only applies to identical cases: if there are relevant differences between two moral agents, then their rights and duties can differ, too. A common example of this are role-dependent duties: you have certain duties towards your family members that I do not have towards them simply because I do not stand to them in the same relation.

The equality of status between moral agents is independent of our abilities and physical characteristics. Whether we are physically strong or weak, tall or short, have brown or blue eyes, and so on, we all have the same basic standing as moral agents, and the same general rights and duties attached to that standing.

It is important to note, though, that such differences in abilities can have an impact on our *specific* duties in particular situations. Let me illustrate this with a variation on a standard case in ethics education, that of a drowning child in a lake. The scenario here is as follows. A child is on a sinking dinghy in the middle of a large body of water. You and I are on the shore and see the tragedy that is about to occur. Standard morality has it that we are under a duty to help the child if we can do so without serious threat to our own life and limb. At first glance, it would seem that we both have the same duty to rescue the child. Assume, however, that you are a world-renowned long-distance swimmer, whereas I am a very lousy one. In fact, I am so bad at swimming that if I were to try to reach the child, I would in all likelihood be swept away by the current and drown. For you, however, it would be a cinch. Even if it perhaps would still be highly inconvenient for you to go and rescue the child—you would get your suit wet and miss your flight, for instance—you have a duty to do so and I do not. None of this affects the basic equality between us, for basic equality is only at issue when there are no relevant differences between us, and your ability and my inability clearly do constitute a relevant difference here. Had I also been able to rescue the child, I would have the same duty as you do, but since I am not, I do not.

Let us assume you swim out to the child and bring it back safely ashore. The question now is if I have reason to admire you for rescuing the child or not? At least at first glance, it would seem that the argument I have described so far would not quite work: clearly, I can see no way *I* could have done what you did. Hence, perhaps admiration is still possible in this case. But what would I be admiring in you if I were to admire you? One thing I could admire you for is your outstanding swimming skills. That, however, would be a kind of admiration akin to aesthetic admiration: I admire you not as a person but as a swimmer, of which you are undoubtedly an excellent specimen. Such admiration has no effect at all on our relation as moral agents. Indeed, it is not moral admiration at all, and hence falls outside of the scope of this analysis. Your swimming skills as such have no relevance to whether you are a moral exemplar or not.

For me to have moral admiration for you, I would have to admire you for the commitment to morality you showed by rescuing the child. Do I have reason to do that? Undoubtedly I should acknowledge that you underwent some notable discomfort in order to rescue him or her, and I should probably show my recognition and appreciation for the fact that you did your duty. But that amounts to (perhaps significant) appreciation, not yet to admiration; in order to admire you, I would also have to feel an element of wonder towards your decision to rescue the child. But do I have reason to regard you with wonder for that? True, perhaps other excellent swimmers would have shirked, hid their skill, and walked on to catch their flights. That, however, only shows their lack of virtue and has no impact on how I ought to regard you. Given your swimming skills, I fully recognise that you were under a duty to save the child (as I would have been had I your skills), and there does not seem to be anything that challenges the understanding in your deciding to swim out and save him or her. In fact, had you refused to save the child, my attitude towards you would probably be quite negative.[14]

This example shows, I believe, something important about moral admiration: its target is normally not one of special skill. Possessing special skills or abilities that others lack may mean that you are, in certain circumstances, subject to duties that these others are not, but given these special abilities, your living up to these duties do not give cause to wonder at your carrying them out, for you may be fully expected to do so. An unwavering commitment to morality, then, is certainly worthy of high appreciation, but it falls short of warranting or legitimating admiration.

ADMIRATION AND MORAL JUDGEMENT

There is, however, another aspect to the outstandingly strong commitment to morality that may set moral exemplars apart from most of us. This is the fact that they are not only uncommonly strongly committed to doing what they believe is required but also that they are exceptionally often correct in their assessment of what is morally required. Moral exemplars do not just possess a stronger-than-average strength of will, they also possess potentially superior moral judgement. In some cases what we find so excellent about moral exemplars is less a matter of their overcoming the temptation to shirk from doing what they recognise as their duty, as it is the fact that they noticed what their duty was in a situation where we would have likely missed it. Since moral judgement does not come ready-made but needs to be acquired and honed over time, perhaps a moral exemplar's judgement is something we may rightly admire her for?

To illustrate the importance of a keen sense of moral judgement, let us stay with the example of someone in acute distress. Empirical research has shown that when it comes to failures to help often the problem is not one of weakness of will but of simply not noticing the morally relevant features of a situation. A famous example is the case where seminary students who were tasked to go give a lecture on the parable of the Good Samaritan passed by an injured person without helping on their way to the venue where they were to give their talk (Darley and Batson 1973). There is little reason to doubt that these seminary students would consider it their duty to help an injured person or to believe that they are not committed to carrying that duty out. The problem was simply that they failed to fully notice the injured person's distress in the first place.

There are many things that may affect our judgement, and many cases of faulty judgement are much more complicated than this example,[15] but it should suffice to illustrate the type of issue at hand: one of the things that moral exemplars are assumed to lack is a proclivity towards these and other kinds of shortcomings of judgement. A moral exemplar, presumably, would have noticed the injured person.

Could we, then, legitimately admire a person for their superior moral judgement? A number of issues seem relevant to answering this question. First of all, moral judgement cannot elicit moral admiration all by itself. Someone who possesses superior moral judgement, but fails to act on it, would not be an appropriate object of moral admiration. Unlike the above example of the swimmer, for whom we can maintain admiration as a swimmer even when she chooses not to display these skills at particular instances in which it would have been appropriate for her to display them (e.g., she elects not to compete in a specific competition), a moral exemplar cannot choose not to act in accordance with her belief of what is demanded.

Another relevant issue is the way we normally respond to failures in judgement. Someone who did the wrong thing believing it to be right, can, in many cases, offer this inaccurate belief as viable grounds for excuse, but never as a plausible justification of her action. Someone who "did not know any better" can often be rightly excused, but it does not make what they did right. The standard by which to judge a person's actions remains whatever it is that morality demands. This brings us back to the crux of the question: do we have reason to regard a moral exemplar who has shown exemplary judgement with wonder?

An analogy with exemplars in other fields may prove helpful, in this case mathematics. What makes someone an exemplary mathematician is (amongst other things) that she is exceptionally good at solving mathematic problems. Clearly, this is an ability that we do not all possess, and which requires significant training to develop even if you are born with a talent for it. Yet, how do we recognise who is an exemplary mathematician? If you are sufficiently bad at mathematics, and cannot judge the validity of mathematical proofs yourself, you perhaps have no other way of identifying exemplary mathematicians than by the testimonial evidence of others whom you believe capable of such assessments. If you are sufficiently baffled by mathematics, you can certainly wonder at those who apparently excel at it. I doubt, however, this would provide a useful analogy to admiration for moral exemplars. Indeed, one can even question if it would really constitute genuine admiration for the exemplary mathematician. Admiration combines wonder with approbation; in this case there may be wonder, but it seems that the person who understands nothing of higher mathematics lacks even the minimal skills necessary to genuinely approve of the exemplary mathematician's skills. Genuine admiration, or at least the type of admiration that seems to be advocated as an appropriate response to moral exemplars, should not be based solely on blind trust in others' say-so.

There is, of course, another way to identify exemplary mathematicians: if you possess sufficient skills, you can adjudicate the validity of their proofs yourself. To ascertain the validity of a mathematical proof does not imply you have the ability to come up with original proofs yourself, but it does suffice for you to appreciate and approve the quality of the mathematician's work and thereby determine her exemplary status. Oddly enough, however, it seems this is very difficult to square with continued wonder. If you base your appreciation of an exemplar on your own assessment of the validity of the proofs they delivered, you do so on the basis of a *full* understanding of the validity of their work. A full understanding of excellence, however, is compatible with the highest form of appreciation, but it excludes genuine wonder, which requires only a partial understanding.

Perhaps this does not exclude feeling admiration in mathematics altogether: when you first encounter a mathematician presenting her proof to a well-known hitherto unsolved problem, seeing the proof developing before your eyes whilst you do not yet fully grasp it may elicit astonished marvel. Yet this seems to be a fleeting condition: once you grasp the validity of the proof, wonder ceases and a deeper appreciation sets in.[16]

Though not all readers may be equally enamoured by the idea of drawing an analogy between ethics and mathematics, I believe something similar applies to moral admiration.[17] What makes a highly developed moral judgement so impressive is that it allows persons who possess it to recognise moral issues and their solutions, if you wish, *ex ante*: in advance of the decision to act. Moral judgement is particularly impressive from a forward-looking perspective. Hence, perhaps a short flicker of moral admiration may indeed be felt when, for instance, you witness superior moral judgement "in action," but that seems a momentary matter. Moreover, one cannot legitimately assign the status of moral exemplar to someone based on a single action. To confidently assign someone the status of moral exemplar we need to know that her actions have consistently been in accordance with what morality demanded. This not only requires that we have a thorough understanding of the moral worth of her actions over time, but also means that assigning the status of moral exemplar to someone can only be done on the basis of our *ex post* judgements of her actions. From that backward-looking perspective wonder is no longer applicable, as argued in the previous sections, but must be replaced by a deeper form of understanding of the correctness of their actions. As a result, the settled attitude that governs our relationship to moral exemplars, should be one of deep appreciation for their person, but not one of admiration.

CONCLUSION

I have argued that admiration is an inappropriate attitude to adopt towards moral exemplars. The reason for this is that admiration, implying wonder, is incompatible with regarding oneself as equally bound by morality as the exemplar. Thus, admiration is implicitly premised on the acknowledgement of two classes of moral agents, so that admiration constitutes a violation of self-respect on the side of the admirer.

This, I believe, also puts us in a position to explain the evasive behaviour exemplars are typically described as displaying when dealing with public expressions of admiration, such as the mentioned humility and irony. Not only does public admiration, being based on an only partial understanding, constitute faint praise compared to a genuine appreciation based on a full understanding of their excellence, but, more importantly, moral exemplars will not want others to engage in public displays of self-disrespect. Moreover, in order to avoid becoming complicit in such acts of self-depreciation, moral exemplars will have no choice but to distance themselves from the expression of admiration in some way. As mentioned, however, publicly rebuffing admiration tends to be quite embarrassing to the admirer, if not outrightly humiliating. When repudiating admiration, tact is required. Luckily, tact is something that moral exemplars presumably possess in abundance. Hence, so I would proffer, the humility or irony that moral exemplars display in the face of expressed admiration is not to be interpreted as a self-effacing denial of their own merit, but as the gentlest, most face-saving way of signalling to the admirer that they should not behave in such a self-disrespecting fashion.

NOTES

1. Throughout this chapter I assume a broadly Kantian perspective on the nature of morality. For a more detailed discussion of this outlook, see Van der Rijt (2018).

2. As plausible as this emulation argument may sound, there is reason for wariness. The empirical literature on admiration is still very small (and that on moral admiration even smaller), and though studies suggest that admiration leads to people reporting feeling inspired or

motivated (e.g., Algoe and Haidt 2009; Van de Ven 2017), most of such works do not ascertain whether this inspiration also leads to emulative action. Indeed, some research suggests that admiration, being a feel-good emotion, is not all that effective in incentivizing self-improvement (Van de Ven et al. 2011)—this combination of increased enthusiasm with lack of emulative action is fully in line with the argument I put forth here.

3. As this would be false humility on the side of the exemplars if it were based on a denial of the merit of their actions (which would be incompatible with their being moral exemplars), it seems more plausible that this response is based on the belief that meritorious actions do not constitute appropriate grounds for admiration.

4. My argument in this chapter draws on ideas first presented in Van der Rijt (2018).

5. This variety of usages also complicates the direct incorporation of research findings from psychology, as it is often unclear how participants in experiments use the term admiration.

6. Compare *The New International Webster's Comprehensive Dictionary of the English Language, Deluxe Encyclopedic Edition* (1996).

7. This appears to be especially the case for the adverb "admirable."

8. Both in Latin (*ad- mirare*) and in Germanic languages (*be wunder n*), the link to wonder is very explicit.

9. For a useful overview of the various ways in which self-respect can be violated, see Dillon (1992).

10. For other works that present a more positive view on the appropriateness of (certain forms of) envy, see, for example, Protasi (2016; this volume) or Thomason (2015).

11. We do not need to consider the self-respect of the moral exemplar, as her moral-exemplariness guarantees that she meets the demands of self-respect by assumption.

12. It is perhaps worth mentioning that certain (especially non-Kantian) views on the supererogatory can be difficult to square with the unconditional bindingness of morality. As both the precise nature of supererogation and its coherence are highly contested, however, and the debate on supererogation is not easily summarised, I will not dwell on any possible complications caused by particular views on supererogation (cf. also Van der Rijt 2018, 75–76).

13. This also offers an explanation of Van de Ven et al.'s (2011) finding that admiration does not lead to emulation, whereas benign envy does. If you find something wondrous, this may make you feel enthused, or "elevated" as some psychological studies call it (e.g., Algoe and Haidt 2009), but since it also implies you cannot see how you could do the same, there is little point in trying.

14. Note that this also applies in cases where one is aware of one's own lack of commitment to duty, for example, in cases of cowardice or weakness of will; even if I were aware that I would likely have shirked my duty, that amounts to a reason to reproach myself, not a reason to regard you with wonder.

15. In the case at hand, the researchers note that the students being hurried played a significant role in their oversight.

16. Note also that the exemplary mathematician is likely to put more value in the appreciation expressed by those who fully understand the quality of her work than any admiration shown by those who only have a partial understanding of it.

17. It is probably not a coincidence that those who are more favourably disposed toward moral admiration tend to adopt a less rationalistic perspective on the nature of morality than the Kantian framework I have been using. An example is Zagzebski (2017), who believes we can reliably identify moral exemplars on the basis of emotions rather than on understanding.

REFERENCES

Algoe, S., and J. Haidt. 2009. "Witnessing Excellence in Action: The 'Other-Praising' Emotions of Elevation, Gratitude, and Admiration." *The Journal of Positive Psychology* 4 (2): 105–27.

Darley, J. M., and C. D. Batson. 1973. "'From Jerusalem to Jericho': A Study of Situational and Dispositional Variables in Helping Behavior." *Journal of Personality and Social Psychology* 27 (1): 100–8.

Dillon, R. 1992. "How to Lose Your Self-Respect." *American Philosophical Quarterly* 29 (2): 125–39.
Hill, T. 1995. "Servility and Self-Respect." In *Dignity, Character, and Self-Respect*, edited by R. Dillon., 76–92. New York: Routledge.
Keltner, D., and J. Haidt. 2003. "Approaching Awe, a Moral, Spiritual and Aesthetic Emotion." *Cognition and Emotion* 17 (2): 297–314.
Protasi, S. 2016. "Varieties of Envy." *Philosophical Psychology* 29 (4): 535–49.
Rawls, J. 1971/1999. *A Theory of Justice*. Oxford: Oxford University Press.
Schaber, P. 2010. *Instrumentalisierung und Würde*. Paderborn: Mentis.
Sherry, P. 2013. "The Varieties of Wonder." *Philosophical Investigations* 36 (4): 340–54.
Thomason, K. 2015. "The Moral Value of Envy." *The Southern Journal of Philosophy* 53 (1): 36–53.
Van der Rijt, J. 2018. "The Vice of Admiration." *Philosophy* 93 (1): 69–90.
Van de Ven, N. 2017. "Envy and Admiration: Emotion and Motivation Following Upward Social Comparison." *Cognition and Emotion* 31 (1): 193–200.
Van de Ven, N., M. Zeelenberg, and R. Pieters. 2011. "Why Envy Outperforms Admiration." *Personality and Social Psychology Bulletin* 37 (6): 784–95.
Zagzebski, L. 2017. *Exemplarist Moral Theory*. Oxford: Oxford University Press.

Part II

History

Chapter Five

Gazing Upwards to the Stage

*Mendelssohn's Notion of Admiration
and Its Consequences*

Anne Pollok

The German Enlightenment is a source of fascinating ideas, even though at times the arguments for these ideas seem outdated or even outlandish to the contemporary reader. A discussion of the notion of admiration, however, is never complete without recourse to the German Late Enlightenment in particular, in which a higher sensibility towards the emotional and sensory aspect of human ratiocination becomes visible. Overall, we can diagnose a clear trend towards an anthropological perspective in this time. The main indicators of this are the growing importance of empirical over rational psychology, the extensive reception of medical theories to explain human behavior and emotions, the development of aesthetics, and, therewith, a turn towards an inclusion of the non-discursive, sensory part of humanity as a relevant branch of philosophy, and, finally, an immense interest in the "vocation of humankind" on both the individual and historical level, thus covering the areas of metaphysics, psychology, moral theory, and philosophy of history.

In light of these trends, this chapter reflects on the concept of admiration in eighteenth-century Germany as an anthropological category. As far as I can see, philosophers like Mendelssohn, Lessing, Schiller, and Kant[1] understand the function of admiration to be an emotional reinforcement of our vocation to realize our full capacity, and that it is hence not a moment of awe (as the recognition of a force that is decidedly *beyond* me), but a moment of *recognition*: of an enlarged, grander notion of myself, of my humanity, in the "other." The better self that we admire—a decisively humanized version of divine perfection[2]—becomes the goal of my own aspirations towards personhood and a better society. This idea clearly indicates that a seemingly overcome era such as the Enlightenment can still influence contemporary philosophical thought.

However, admiration thus understood involves two seemingly contradictory aspects. It requires at the same time intimacy with the object of admiration (in order for it to be a realistic object of aspiration) and distance from it (in that the moral quality of mine and the object's behavior are indeed decisively different, as I look up to the object of admiration), thus reflecting an internal tension within aesthetic appreciation.[3]

I will first discuss the role of admiration in the debate on tragedy between Friedrich Nicolai, Gotthold Ephraim Lessing, and Moses Mendelssohn,[4] in which this inner tension becomes apparent in the distinction between sympathy[5] (favored by Lessing) and admiration (championed by Mendelssohn and Nicolai). Whereas it seems as if Mendelssohn just argues for a straightforward emulation of a perfect model, the hero, I intend to show that his position in the *Briefwechsel* was more sophisticated. For him, admiration is not mere adoration, or a mere recognition of the moral superiority of the hero, but a sympathetic immersion in a struggle of which the observer is only virtually a part. This makes his account compatible with Lessing's more progressive approach on the effect of tragedy, and critically widens its scope: the new citizen (which tragedy was supposed to educate) is not just capable of *more* feeling but can also critically evaluate her emotions. As such, Mendelssohn's defense of admiration gains a critical dimension as well.

This complex structure of aesthetic appreciation as a mixture of admiration and repulsion will figure prominently in the emerging theory of the sublime, an aesthetic category with a decisively anthropocentric undertone. For this, I reflect on the influence of Shaftesbury and Burke on the respective development of Mendelssohn's theory, which envisages the sublime in relation to humanity, rather than a Kantian notion of the moral good.

A closing outlook will explicate how such a take on admiration opens the way for a genuinely modern, essentially open understanding of human nature. This, however, is not Mendelssohn's view, but can be established through a combination of Kantian criticism with Enlightenment philosophy, as exemplified by Friedrich Schiller's aesthetic writings after his readings of Kant's *Critique of the Power of Judgment* in the 1790s.[6] Key here is the alleged impossibility of closing the gap between the human and the divine, between our potential for and the realization of perfection. As we will see, admiration can claim to offer the enraptured audience a sense of direction, but it can never fully realize this goal, thus marking a transition from a medieval "closed world" to an "infinite universe" of modernity[7] that transfers the weight of the aesthetic onto the recipient.

THE DEBATE ON TRAGEDY

Right after the publication of his psychological-aesthetic essay *On Sentiments* (1755), Mendelssohn becomes involved in Lessing and Nicolai's debate on the function and merits of tragedy. It is puzzling that Mendelssohn seems unwilling to put the theory of sympathy as developed in his previous publication to the test. Whereas the 1755 essay defends the worth of sympathy, and insists on the distinctive independence of the stage in particular in all things moral, in the *Briefwechsel* he seems to make the straightforward moralistic claim against Lessing that it is not sympathy but admiration that grounds our enjoyment of tragedy.[8] Does he revert back to the moralistic sense of theatre which claims to educate its audience by parading moral models on the stage?

Lessing, in contrast, sees the function of tragedy in the heightening of our overall sensibility: our capacity to feel should be heightened—no moral questions asked. We reach such a refinement of our sentiments through the experience of sympathy, to which Lessing reduces all other possible candidates such as horror and admiration. After distinguishing *Bewunderung* from *Verwunderung*,[9] Lessing argues that admiration is not an emotion in its own right but only a form of "sympathy that became expendable" (*entbehrlich gewordenes Mitleiden*, November 1756, Mendelssohn 1929, *Jubiläumsausgabe* [hereafter JA] 11, 66). It is a bit confusing, though, why it cannot be the other way around: that sympathy is only of interest for the dramatist if it is paired with admiration—since only then can we explain why we care about the protagonist in the first place.

But this seems to have been Mendelssohn's very starting point; before we develop any interest in the well-being of the protagonist, we first have to connect to her. A general feeling of sympathy for another *qua* human being is insufficient; we need to positively *care* about the other as this particular, well, admirable kind of person. Such a connection is forged through admiration, which Mendelssohn understands as a deep awareness of the superior moral quality of the protagonist. But, now arguing pro Lessing's position, why should this be our entryway into the emotional mess of tragedy? Isn't admiration a feeling that—*qua* moral distance between the ordinary me and the protagonist—negates the possibility of a genuine emotional connection? Isn't the person we admire so far from us that we rather strain to even see her humanity, a humanity that is always all too obvious in ourselves? In other words, doesn't admiration presuppose a distance between mine and the protagonist's moral qualities that should hinder the process of identification, and hence make it less effective in an aesthetic experience?

I shall put my explanation *ex negativo*: what was it that Mendelssohn wanted to *avoid* when rejecting Lessing's insistence on sympathy? To him, Lessing's theory of improvement claims that the arousal of our general capacity to feel rests on too many questionable assumptions concerning human benevolence.[10] Instead of speculating about an inborn tendency to feel positively about any other human being, Mendelssohn seeks to utilize the then widely accepted rationalist position, which claims that all human beings—may it be through their emotions or their thought—seek overall perfection. In Baumgarten's parlance (which Mendelssohn mostly follows), this is also put as a tendency towards more "reality," or, in other words, towards more and sufficiently founded concepts[11] rather than a speculative human conception of "goodness" (as would be required for Lessing's conception of sympathy).

Consequently, Mendelssohn first assumes that our drive for perfection draws us towards any exhibition of it. Hence, we become interested in a character that shows said perfection. Then, a misfortune that befalls this character arouses our sympathy—and this sympathy is well founded, in that it is based on a conception of perfection rather than mere human closeness. Where we find no opportunity to admire the protagonist, no amount of pity will actually bring us to seek for more perfection ourselves.

Hence, the tragic hero should be not exactly of my kind—morally speaking—but higher, so that I look up to her. At first glance, this seems like an outdated insistence on the old, aristocratic form of theatre (in which our aesthetic experience strengthens society as it is), whereas Lessing defends its new version, enabling and improving the citizen: *das bürgerliche Trauerspiel*. Up close, however, Mendelssohn's call for self-improvement is as novel as Lessing's idea: with (critical) self-perfection we do not conserve the old but establish the new era of the citizen. Our witnessing such an example as the tragic hero enables us to aspire to greatness in ourselves. The hero may seem unreachable at first and takes our breath away in her ability to deal with her bad fortune (that, since this is a tragedy, is bound to catch up with her). But this feeling of admiration, says Mendelssohn, also enables us to see *ourselves*—albeit in an already improved version—in the hero. The hero's actions surprise us in terms of their quality when we see them played out on the stage. But, after the moment of mere surprise, we identify with her, and see with our own eyes that we should—and *can*—aim higher. In a way, it is through the hero's example that the possibility to an improved way of acting is put right in front of our eyes, in a situation where we are already emotionally invested.

On the one hand, Mendelssohn here exploits our emotional involvement, which makes us take the hero as an example on the emotional level. Following his theory of sentiments, such emotions are not completely reflected, but, as being merely clear and confused, pass our mental apparatus more quickly and are hence more efficient. On the other hand, Mendelssohn argues that the admired hero does not just "refine" our sentiments (as Lessing has it), but also serves as a compelling call to action—but an action that we can also relate to critically. Mendelssohn recognizes the aspect of distance in our admiration as a means to enable *judgement*. As he later quips, "Who just increases a person's sensitivity didn't make her more virtuous—if he has not simultaneously improved her power of judgment."[12] Instead, we seek the exemplar, to which we are drawn *qua* superiority (which is a judgement concerning moral perfection), but to which we can still connect emotionally qua sympathy. The resultant, more elaborate emotional construct is what Nolte (1931, 325) calls "exultant sympathy." And this is exactly the realm in which Mendelssohn situates tragedy.[13]

However, in the *Briefwechsel*, it is not very clear how a *feeling* of admiration could be accompanied by such a judgement, since feeling presupposes clear and confused, but judgement clear and distinct notions. Under "aspects still under dispute" (*streitige Punkte*) of their "capitulation" on May 14, 1757, Mendelssohn and Nicolai still do not offer a clear solution. There, they contrast sympathy and admiration accordingly: "Sympathy moves our heart, admiration uplifts our soul."[14] We could assume that the "heart" is the target of the emotions, but the soul has either the capacity of judgement—or the faculty—that brings rational judgement and sentiment together. Strikingly, Lessing seems to move into this direction when he requires the "best" character (presupposing our moral judgement) in a tragedy to be the most unfortunate (to arouse the most sympathy).[15] He tries to realign this with his preference for sympathy by characterizing the thus required admiration as only "the half-part of sympathy,"[16] which only has value if it accompanies sympathy. But this, as Nolte rightfully notes, is an "improper deduction."[17] Even if admiration is felt in tandem with sympathy at times, it does not follow that it is hence not a feeling on its own—or the same would count for its counterpart. And hence, it seems that Lessing has to concede to Mendelssohn's point regarding their dynamic interdependency in tragedy.

Mendelssohn's conception, if completed, turns out to be more comprehensive,[18] in that it perceives of the ultimate aim of tragedy as a dynamic relation[19] between sensibility and reason: the dynamic interplay of various emotions, pleasant and unpleasant, is either accompanied by, or finds its firm grounding in a particular form of reasoning: in our immediate, but already intelligible[20] grasp on the good and perfect.

In the end we could say that both sides win: as Mendelssohn holds, our emotional involvement in a tragedy must be founded of the feeling for a perfection (which engenders admiration). But, as Lessing points out, the impression of a perfection is only poignant in a tragedy if it is paired with the feeling of sympathy. And this feeling is only invoked if the perceived perfection is in danger. Sympathy needs a grounding in admiration—but without a tragic event that endangers the perfection, we do not feel enough. In other words, without the lure of sympathy, we do not become involved with the action on the stage.

Mendelssohn does not want *Schadenfreude* to be the main reason for our enjoyment of tragedy. Since *Schadenfreude* merely rejoices in our luck as compared to any other person's misfortune, it is not founded on a notion of overall perfection, but sheer contrast (in which I just happen to stand on the positive side). Hence, he does not accept the mere involvement into unfortunate events as the main drive of the dramatic force, but this involvement must be sparked by an idea of perfection.[21] This Mendelssohn finds founded in the notion of admiration, which makes us aware of an idea of perfection that we find in another, but that we learn to see as if it were within our reach (through sympathy). This helps to explain why he argues in the 13th Letter in *On Sentiments* that tragedy functions under a completely different set of moral rules (which seems like an embrace of a-moral, that is, non-perfect agents and acts on the stage)[22]: the contrast to our understanding must be "well hidden" (JA 1, 94) and thus the illusion of the stage be perfect, so that we first identify and then feel a rush of sympathy as an expression of our common humanity.

For both Mendelssohn and Lessing—with implicit reliance on Adam Smith—"the spectators' sympathy with the affections and intentions of the agent is made possible by imaginative projection or identification: sympathetic feelings arise when the spectator conceives himself in the observed situation, if he can share and approve the agent's motives."[23] However, Mendelssohn is more reluctant than Lessing to let go of the rationalistic theory of perfection. Rather, he ties our interest in the agent's fall back to our interest in her perfection—and this is why he underscores the prevalence of the rational emotion of admiration over mere sympathetic passion.

MENDELSSOHN ON THE SUBLIME

What Mendelssohn and Lessing discuss, in a rather nit-picking fashion, in the debate on tragedy is an early version of the theory of mixed sentiments, which Mendelssohn develops in the late 1760s.[24] What we enjoy in the theatre (or at the movies, for that matter) is less of a feeling of contentment, but more of the exciting emotions—we grieve, weep, or admire the good in its loss. As we have seen, Mendelssohn does not trust emotion alone to do the trick. His aim is to refine both our emotions and our reasoning. The enjoyment of tragedy does not just rest in our being swept away by the action, but also by our appreciation of the grandness of the deed. The effect of tragedy should not be just a refined capacity to feel, but a higher level of critical, and at the same time emotionally invested self-knowledge. Mendelssohn's theatre connoisseur is a tad more sober than Lessing's,[25] even though she is still smitten.

My interpretation of Mendelssohn's notion of admiration is grounded in Shaftesbury's reflections of the artist as the "second maker under Jove."[26] This divine maker is not the creator of awe-inspiring sublimity, but foremost exemplifies the Socratic quality of self-knowledge. Such an artist, Shaftesbury holds, in line with the earlier *Moralists* (1709), has not only grasped the world's deeper structures, but also aligned her own stance to them. This "fundamental knowledge" (p. 92) of science and of mind is mostly a knowledge of proportion and, ultimately, of perfection. The "moral artist" sees the whole and its parts, understands their respective functions, and can represent them in an artwork. As such, what we admire in the artist's work is order, unity, and wholeness, but also something striking, something extraordinary, which, incidentally, can be understood as the ultimate reality, the all-embracing ordinariness of the whole of creation—which only becomes extraordinary through its rephrasing in the artwork, striking because we can finally perceive it easily and as a whole. She knows of all "inward form and structure of every creature" (93), including herself. The idea of self-knowledge as a precondition for genuine artistry seems akin to Mendelssohn's philosophie—where the artist can achieve full perfection and sublimity in her presentation only if she understands the essential structure of world and self. What Mendelssohn needed was simply an adequate "enemy" who could help him to sharpen his own view on the aesthetic effect. He found this counterpart first in Lessing, and then in Edmund Burke.

Overall, I side with Beiser[27] and Koller's interpretation that Mendelssohn initially resisted Burke's theory of the sublime, since he, Mendelssohn, wanted the effect of the sublime to rest in the object's (or the artist's) perfection, and not, as Burke, "in the realm of fundamentally unanalyzable passions, outside the jurisdiction of reason" (Koller, 2011, 332). Not by accident are the two philosophers' examples quite different: Mendelssohn concentrates on sublimity-inspired awe, whereas Burke focuses more on the fearful jolt, verging on terror (Koller, 2011, 331). Both agree, however, that the experience of the sublime is immensely moving and *transformative*.[28]

And this is how Mendelssohn's theory of the sublime connects with the theory of admiration that I have focused on so far: the aspect of admiration is, for Mendelssohn, a necessary ingredient in the experience of the sublime, which must contain some reference to a higher perfection: either in the grandness of the object that overwhelms our sensible apparatus, or in the genius of the artistic presentation of a subject.

This comes fully to the fore in the version of *On the Sublime and Naïve in the Beautiful Sciences* from 1771.[29] Now he is finally able to take over most of Burke's examples and include them in his own theory of perfection, utilizing the theory of mixed sentiments.[30]

The first kind, which I call the "objective" sublime, is due either to the utter perfection of the object, but also to its mere vastness in its breathtaking dimensions, or its capacity to stun us in its intensive quality (as power, genius, or virtue). His distinction between extension (*Größe*) and intensity (*Stärke*) focuses on the latter two subcategories—but whereas intensity is still capable of delivering the impression of perfection, mere extension leaves the limits of perfection behind, and feels monotonous (JA 1, 457). Mendelssohn mentions the effort we have to put into grasping this first kind of sublime, but judges this as a negative sensation (JA 1, 455). Instead, the extensively great must at least contain some possibility of order, or structure, so that we can engage with the presentation of it fully. It must, as Koller points out (Koller, 2011, 340), be the great multitude in a vast unity that we struggle to actually comprehend but which hints at a harmonious bigger picture. The effect is a combination of attention (*Aufmerksamkeit*) and a pleasure in the assumed perfection of an extensive magnitude, where the imagination is deeply engaged in the sheer number of impressions. This evokes a sweet shudder (*süßer Schauer*) that engages the whole human being. In conclusion, Mendelssohn defines the sublime as the "sensuous-perfect in art that is capable of arousing admiration" (JA 1, 458).

Even more engaging is the second kind of sublime, which has its roots in the perfection of the presentation, and that lets us sense the "footprint of genius."[31] Hence, "a great genius, great virtuous people whom we admire but cannot attain: who can behold these without shuddering, who can proceed to consider them without a pleasant dizziness?" (JA 1, 398).

It is interesting that Mendelssohn refrains from the rather obvious consequence that we also reflect on our own perfection (which should console us in light of the immensity of the sublime). We only get this result if we combine the 1771 introductory paragraphs from the *Rhapsody*[32] with the 1771 version of *On the Sublime*. Within the first couple of pages of the former, Mendelssohn not only recasts the theory of mixed sentiments (taken over from Wolff, but now far more intricate), but also connects it closely to the sublime—since the *prima facie* non-pleasurable feeling of horror, abhorrence (*Abscheu*), or dread can also evoke some positive effect. How else would we come to enjoy them "in the sublime or the majestic" (JA 1, 387), Mendelssohn asks.

Overall, our pleasure in the sublime is due to the activity of our rational and sensible capacities (JA 1, 389, the first "general reason"). This gain in "reality" is neutral concerning the quality and direction of the perception, and hence captures both positive and negative emotions and cases. Sensitive people are more likely to react adversely toward negative presentations, since they tend to place themselves in the role of the other (whose tragedy they have just witnessed). Hence, in their experience the negative outweighs the positive—they flee the presentation and abhor it (JA 1, 389–90). In order to make such presentations digestible for sensitive people, they need to be framed *as* an artwork to prevent complete identification (JA 1, 388).

In the artwork, the experience of our rejection of a displeasing or bad situation is a "very attractive engagement of our faculties [*Seelenkräfte*], which in itself cannot be without pleasure" (JA 1, 390). As such, our very rejection is a *positive* reaction on the part of our soul: the negative development on the stage enables a mixed emotion: we reject the development, but at the same time take pleasure in our capacity to disapprove of it (JA 1, 400).[33] Mendelssohn also stresses this self-reflective tendency of negative emotions in a footnote on Lessing's interpretation of Aristotle in the *Laocoon* (see *Rhapsody*, JA 1, 396). Mendelssohn doubts that we need to have first-hand experience of a certain situation in order to feel sympathy for anyone enduring it on the stage. Though it does help to be acquainted with at least a similar experience, we are not in fact reflecting on ourselves, but aim at a better "Selbstgefühl"[34]: we can connect to such a feeling because of the structural similarity it has to our experience. We reflect on the shudder these impressions evoke in us, not because we are glad not to be the victims, but because we engage in a form of positive refusal; we reaffirm our perfection through the proper rejection of the bad. This is a reality—and hence a genuine perfection—in its own right.

This allows Mendelssohn to link a metaphysical notion of perfection with our aesthetic activities. Thus admiration becomes an important category in an anthropological theory of aesthetic effectiveness: through admiration, we are lured into the tragic conflict, and become capable of grasping its full, devastating, but at the same time uplifting potential. As Mendelssohn holds in 1758, in a tragedy the jolt of admiration is even more effective if accompanied by a soft sentiment "that kindles its flame" (1758, JA 1, 196). In this regard, it is the sympathy we feel with the hero, whose perfection flashes up in some of her actions and evokes a more deeply felt admiration (out of surprise at the sudden perfection of the act). Through this feeling (as spelled out in the theory of mixed sentiments), we also become conscious of the underlying message in tragedy: that the faulty, but ultimately virtuous human being is capable of fulfilling her vocation to develop her full capacity. This is the ultimate mixed sentiment: we have an impression of the terrifying and consuming force of tragedy, but this points us toward our own capacity to withstand these tragedies in our good deeds. Sympathy and abhorrence make us feel that we might indeed (if we follow in the hero's footsteps) develop our own perfection.

In his discussion with Thomas Abbt regarding the vocation of man, the *Phädon*,[35] and in the *Morning Hours*, Mendelssohn utilizes admiration as a way of detecting our vocation. We can sense our vocation by taking in the world around us; and this ability is, as a "positive ability of the soul," on a level with rational understanding.[36] From the overall perfection of creation, we proceed to grasp the perfection of the human race that is reflected in our capacity of doing the good for its own sake. For Mendelssohn, moral perfection lies in the nobility of the soul,[37] another indirect espousal of admiration. Such nobility, as he argues, allows us not only to hope for, but also to be certain of the soul's personal immortality.

Historically, however, Kant's critical philosophy destroyed this optimistic belief in immortality—at least in its theoretical dimension. But it seems that the practical–aesthetic notion of admiration is still a viable candidate for the unifying force of the beautiful and the sublime towards a general improvement of humanity, both on the individual and social level. In the third part of this chapter, I shall briefly discuss Schiller's peculiar contribution to this question, which reads like a combination of Kantian and Mendelssohnian ideas.

THE POST-CRITICAL FUNCTION OF ADMIRATION IN SCHILLER'S *AESTHETIC EDUCATION*

With Kant's practical–aesthetic philosophy, admiration is given a rather straightforward framework—which, in Schiller's famous misunderstanding, comes at the cost of finally abolishing the rights of the sensible.[38] Admiration, in Kant's view, breaks through the world of sensibility, and lets us feel that there is indeed a higher order beneath everything, showcasing the ultimate purposiveness of the world. In his *Critique of the Power of Judgment*, Kant takes care to distinguish between mere emotion (*Rührung*) and admiration. Some people, he remarks drily, feel that tragedy transforms and improves them, whereas they are actually just glad to have a little diversion (see Kant 2006, *Kritik der Urteilskraft* [hereafter KU B], 124). Genuine admiration, in contrast, has an effect on our "*Denkungsart*" (ibid.), in that ideas of reason (*Vernunftideen*) gain dominance over our sensibility (*Sinnlichkeit*). In the end, such dominance cannot be adequately represented (since it negates the reign of the sensible)—but, as Kant holds, our imagination fills in the gaps in the "negative" presentation of these ideas, and keeps us fruitfully (albeit mainly intellectually) entertained.

Ultimately, tragedy shows that this demand comes from within us, not from an external source (see KU B 477–78). Admiration of the hero thus does not mean emulating somebody else, but following the calling of the moral law that we recognize to be within us. The hero just makes it visible. This seems like an endorsement of the *Briefwechsel*, but—of course—in critical terms, focusing on the overarching requirements for freedom.

Schiller grappled both with Kant's notion of morality as an overcoming of sensibility and with the intellectualized streak of Kantian tragedy. If Mendelssohn's certainty that the human being can indeed fulfil her vocation crumbles with the transcendental turn, with Schiller we find it being recuperated in (and limited to) aesthetics.[39] His reception of Mendelssohn's main ideas, brought into the realm of critical philosophy, brings about a new theory of the emulative and critical force of admiration: it becomes the force of human education, in that it enables us to recognize the good (externally as well as inside us), and live according to it. However, Schiller is also clear that, tied as we are to the sensible realm, we have to limit our expectations of our ability to realize the ideal—but at least we can be brought into the position to realize the best *possible* course of action through our involvement with such artworks.

In his aesthetic essays of the 1790s,[40] Schiller replaces (similar to Mendelssohn[41]) sympathy with the sublime as the main function in tragedy. We admire both the "female" grace and the "male" dignity,[42] one showing the harmony of sensibility and reason in (willful) motion, the other stating the superiority of intelligibility over sensibility in morality. In relation to Schiller's evocation of the "whole human being" as the goal, this means that we need to learn to appreciate—and learn how to balance—sensibility and intelligibility, in order to enable appropriate, civilized action and the formation of a just society even while an appropriate political framework is missing (to avoid the mistakes of the French Revolution, as Schiller argues in letters 3–5 of the *Aesthetic Education*), and to compensate for modern working conditions (letter 6). The goal is *Idealschönheit*[43] as the perfect marriage of the good, the beautiful, and the necessary. How we can reach this ideal depends on our character, in that we are either in need of *melting* or *energizing beauty*.[44]

Unfortunately, Schiller remains the faithful idealist and wants to have it all. Both beauties, grace and dignity, should still be unified in one entity, the aforementioned *Idealschönheit*. But how is this supposed to happen? Since the two concepts stand in contradistinction to one another,[45] they ultimately cannot—neither in experience, nor conceptually—perfectly harmonize, nor become unified. In the *Aesthetic Education*, Schiller attempts to avoid this conundrum by dynamizing the ideal: in an "anthropological estimation" [*antropologische Schätzung*] with undeniable idealistic undertones (letters 11–16), the lawful, regular, and necessary are represented by the concept of "person," whereas change, manifold, and development/experience are situated within the concept of "condition" (*Zustand*, see in particular letter 11). Both are *Wechselbegriffe*,[46] and are thus in continual flux. They are in perfect harmony in the aesthetic play—that we cannot pinpoint to one particular position nor condition, but which has to be in perpetual motion. In his essays on tragedy, Schiller goes a step further. On the stage, the artist should seek neither to just arouse emotions (vs. Lessing), nor admiration (vs. the earlier Mendelssohn), "but the final aim of art is the presentation of the supersensible" (*On the Pathetic*, Schiller 1962, *Nationalausgabe* [hereafter NA], 20, 196). However, this "supersensible" does not outright deny the validity of our emotional investment, but *plays* with it; in contrast to moral appraisal, on the stage we are more concerned with the idea of freedom *in general*,[47] and if the artist is to evoke our aesthetic appraisal, then it is in her best interest to depict characters that stir this idea up in us—which, most of the time, the morally problematic characters do better than the good ones. Schiller, more resolutely than Mendelssohn, here reaches out through the fourth wall and directly engages the audience. The peculiar mixture of repulsion and attraction within a sublimated concept of admiration is finally set free but requires an educated and reflective audience that is capable to admire what is only present structurally, not personally. This audience Schiller wanted to educate through aesthetic education. However, what he did not say was how we are to enter this peculiar hermeneutic circle without losing our way.

NOTES

1. This chapter woefully underrepresents another aspect of the change within German philosophy, and that is the reception of "European Philosophies," in particular from Great Britain. Following Manfred Kuehn's groundbreaking work in this respect (see in particular *Scottish Common Sense in Germany*. McGill: Queen's Press, 1987), there is still a lot of work to be done to highlight the influence of David Hume, Alexander Gerard, Shaftesbury, Adam Smith, and others on these German thinkers—but also, the influence of the latter on the former. For instance, it is not entirely clear where Smith got his ideas about sympathy from, may it be Rousseau, Shaftesbury, or even Mendelssohn himself. Smith's *Theory of Moral Sentiments* appeared in 1759, four years after Mendelssohn's *Letters* (I thank André Grahle to remind me of that fact). Smith famously espouses the principle of sympathy to replace the rather fickle and speculative assumption of a sixth moral sense, as put forward by his teacher Hutcheson (for which thinkers like Mendelssohn and Lessing prominently criticized Hutcheson, too). Smith also argues that it is only the imagination that can carry us towards an understanding of the feelings of another person, and that it is admiration that engenders imitation—the step to a theory of the beneficial influence of tragedy then is a small one indeed.

2. Adoration would be the adequate emotion towards the divine (see Ines Schindler's contribution to this volume, 181–99).

3. In this regard, this chapter is structured following Rueger's diagnosis that the late eighteenth century entertained a "stimulating" and a "regulating" principle in aesthetics; here, the stimulating aspect is the sympathy, the regulating aspect the distance to the object of admiration (see Rueger, "Enjoying the Unbeautiful," 182).

4. Henceforth referred to as the *Briefwechsel*, all cited from JA 11 (letters between 1756/57).

5. *Mitleid* is a rather ambiguous term. Whereas Martinec ("The Boundaries," 744) mentions "pity and compassion," which we feel when we see another person suffer, and "empathy," which relates to me putting myself virtually in the place of the sufferer, I have translated *Mitleid* as sympathy, since it allows for more "personal space" on the part of the audience: we feel a common bond, but the passion does not make us virtually identical.

6. How Kant and Mendelssohn influenced each other, in particular via Kant's *Beobachtungen über das Gefühl des Schönen und Erhabenen*, 1764, is a fascinating topic, but one that goes far beyond the limits of this paper.

7. As Alexandre Koyre titled his study of the development of science (*From the Closed World to the Infinite Universe*. Baltimore: Johns Hopkins University Press, 1968).

8. Historically speaking, his insistence is less surprising, given that Nicolai ended his *Abhandlung vom Trauerspiele* with four groups of tragedy, of which Lessing accepted only the first: the *bürgerliches Trauerspiel* that arouses horror (*Schrecken*) and sympathy. The second and third kinds, however, the heroic and mixed tragedies, respectively, aim at admiration (the

fourth category is rather superfluous, since the arousal of admiration, as Nicolai admits, is actually impossible without arousing sympathy, too).

9. Following Gottsched, who argues that Corneille's notion of admiration boils down to a mere surprise (*Verwunderung*, see Michelsen, "Erregung des Mitleids," 561). In his review of Burke, Mendelssohn makes it clear that admiration/*Bewunderung* is indeed fundamentally different from surprise/*Verwunderung*, in particular because the former is independent of the element of novelty that the latter depends on; see JA 3, 237–53, here 241.

10. As an *ad hominem* aside, it is surely understandable that Mendelssohn is wary of believing in such benevolence, with his ample experience of all the insidious kinds of oppression that the Jews had to suffer in enlightened Prussia. Lessing's stance is closely related to Francis Hutcheson's theory of moral sentiments (Lessing translated his *System of Moral Philosophy* from 1755 in the subsequent year to *Sittenlehre der Vernunft*), according to which the more powerful passions regard more important issues. We feel sympathy easier than we feel joy for another person, because helping her in distress, for which sympathy calls, is more important and necessary than sharing in her joy (see Heidsieck, "Disput," 15–16). Ultimately, our sentiments aim at avoiding pain first, and only then at elevating pleasure. For Hutcheson, our moral sentiment is the ultimate cause of good works, since no reasoning can figure out what is morally good. Reason is nothing but a "helping hand" of understanding and volition (see Heidsieck, "Disput," 18, citing Lessing's translation).

11. In the Leibnizian tradition, this means as clear and distinct concepts as possible.

12. Mendelssohn, *Jubiläumsausgabe* [JA] 2, 147–155, here 154. Nolte offers a rather convincing account of why sympathy as such is also a dubious moral category: all too often, we sympathize not with the hero, but with a morally untrustworthy candidate such as Othello (see Nolte, "Lessing's Correspondence," 319).

13. Note that Mendelssohn is here standing in a long-ranging tradition, starting with Aristotle and culminating in France with Racine, whom Mendelssohn explicitly references (see Heidsieck "Disput," 9). Heidsieck's interpretation of Mendelssohn should be treated with caution, though, since he offers a rather ahistorical reading of Mendelssohn's philosophy: most of the aspects he mentions rely on his theory of mixed sentiments, which he does not fully develop until 1771.

14. JA 11, 129.

15. Lessing in his letter from November 1756, JA 11, 64–69, esp. 68.

16. Both Mendelssohn and Lessing have no patience for fear; which Mendelssohn subsumes under sympathy that surprises us (see his *Letters on Sentiments*, JA 1, 110)—a reading that Lessing takes up in his letter from November 1756 (JA 11, 66).

17. Nolte, "Lessing's Correspondence," 323.

18. Schillemeit, "Differenz," 85 *passim* offers a very convincing alternate reading: Mendelssohn focuses on pleasure (*Lust, Vergnügen, angenehme Empfindung*) because it is a perfection in itself and offers the possibility of a heightened sense of self (a "reality"). I find this particularly interesting since it fits well with Mendelssohn's theory of the sublime—see here section 2.

19. See also the various attempts to marry sentiment and reason in the early German Enlightenment, for example by Gottsched, Johann Ulrich König (in his *Untersuchung von dem Guten Geschmack in der Dicht- und Rede-Kunst*, 1727), and Nicolai (*Abhandlung vom Trauerspiele* [first in *Bibliothek der schönen Wissenschaften und der freyen Künste*, I.1, Leipzig 1757], in *Über das Trauerspiel: Briefwechsel mit Mendelssohn und Nicolai*, edited by Robert Petsch (Leipzig: Reclam, 1910), 1–42, here 23: "Das Trauerspiel ist die Nachahmung einer einzigen, ernsthaften, wichtigen und ganzen Handlung durch die dramatische Vorstellungen derselben; um dadurch heftige Leidenschaften in uns zu erregen"). Nicolai (without offering too much reasoning to bolster the description—but at least said description is pretty blunt and straightforward) even reflects on the distinction between theatrical and "real" emotions. Certain displeasing emotions feel "good" when experienced through art. However, he limits those emotions to fear (*Schrecken*), admiration, and sympathy.

20. In *On Sentiments*, Mendelssohn argues how in aesthetic appreciation our rational understanding is already operative (see Pollok, *Facetten*, 170–78).

21. Even the pleasure of the masses in beheadings or gladiator fights is interpreted as "actually" a pleasure in the finesse, power, or dexterity of the "actors" (see the "Beschluss" in *On Sentiments* etc.). On Mendelssohn's aversion to *Schadenfreude*, see Zelle, *Angenehmes Grauen*, 340; Schillemeit, "Differenz," 87; and Pollok, *Facetten*, 150.

22. "Die Schaubühne hat ihre eigene Sittlichkeit," JA 1, 94; see Pollok, *Facetten*, 318–22.

23. Heidsieck, "Adam Smith's Influence," 127.

24. On this, see Anne Pollok, "Beautiful Perception and Its Object: Mendelssohn's Theory of Mixed Sentiments Reconsidered," *Kant-Studien* 109 (2018), 270–285.

25. As we can also see in his discussion of the sublime with Thomas Abbt: "Daß die Empfindung des Erhabenen mit der Empfindung der Bewunderung übereinkommt, lehrt die Erfahrung" (to Abbt, March 9, 1761; JA 11, 201).

26. See his 1710 *Soliloquy, or, Advice to an Author*, 93. Both Mendelssohn and Abbt were deeply impressed by Shaftesbury's philosophy and even planned to translate parts of his works. However, they only ever got to a partial translation, see JA 5.2, lv.

27. Beiser, *Schiller as Philosopher*, 196: "Against these challenges Mendelssohn continued to uphold the aesthetics of perfection of Leibniz, Wolff, and Baumgarten, according to which all aesthetic experience is a sensible perception of rational structure." However, I do not agree that Mendelssohn's position did not develop a more intricate theory of subjective involvement in tragedy (see also Koller, "Mendelssohn's Response," 330–31).

28. Koller, "Mendelssohn's Response," 332, discusses this with reference to Boileau.

29. The first version from 1758 differentiates between two kinds of sublimity, which both rest on the presentation of perfection: either it is an expression of such perfection that evokes admiration (1758 JA 1, 194–95)—this pleasurable sentiment overcomes us suddenly and nearly overwhelms us. Or this overwhelming impact stems from our understanding of the immense skills of the artist. Admiration thus either stems from the perfect object itself, or from its perfect presentation. However, only after his discussion of Burke is Mendelssohn ready to include the psychologically positive effect of negative impressions through artistic representations. On this, see Pollok, *Facetten*, 228–40.

30. First in 1761 (with only minor revisions), and finally in 1771, Mendelssohn published his essays *On Sentiments, Dialogues (vol. 1), Rhapsody, On the Main Principles, On the Sublime*, and *On Probability* under the general title *Philosophical Writings*. It is noteworthy that in order to get the full impression of Mendelssohn's theory of mixed sentiments in their final version, one needs to read *Rhapsody*, *Main Principles*, and *On the Sublime* together.

31. "Fußtapfen des Genies," JA 1, 479.

32. The 1761 version already contains the seeds for this, see JA 1, 570–72 (Lesarten). We may seek what is objectively bad to indulge our desire for knowledge—hence marking these events as evoking mixed sentiments (disgust on the one hand, pleasure at the training of our faculties on the other). However, only the 1771 version offers the theory it is full scale (contra Beiser, *Schiller as Philosopher*, 255).

33. This aspect is new in 1771.

34. Literally: self-feeling—not a feeling of oneself, but one that one has felt, is familiar with *qua* having felt it formerly (JA 1, 396).

35. See Anne Pollok, "How to Dry Our Tears? Abbt, Mendelssohn, and Herder on the Immortality of the Soul," *Interdisziplinäres Jahrbuch Aufklärung*, edited by Gideon Stiening, Udo Thiel (Hamburg: Meiner, 2018), 67–81.

36. See *Morning Hours*, JA 3.2, 138. The sublimity of creation and its overarching harmony is the point of departure from which he attempts to prove the immortality of the soul as the final stone in the perfect edifice of creation. It is the starting point both in the *Oracle* and in the third dialogue of the *Phädon* (see JA 3.1, 106).

37. What Mendelssohn develops here is a practical philosophy that can do without the notion of "reward" (which is what Abbt diagnosed as the main mistake in Spalding's work; see Pollok, "Dry Our Tears").

38. See Kant's discussion of Schiller's *On Grace and Dignity* in a footnote in the second edition of his *Religion within the Boundaries of Reason Alone* (in *Kants Gesammelte Schriften* [Berlin: De Gruyter, 1902 ff.]), VI, 23n, and, for further background, Beiser's discussion of it in chapter 5 of his *Schiller as Philosopher* (169–90). Beiser does a great job of clarifying the

actual point of their discussion and pointing out that Kant subsequently embraced the aesthetic character in his *Metaphysics of Morals* (181–82).

39. Note that Schiller starts his essay "On the Reason of Our Pleasure in Tragic Objects" (NA 20, 133–35) with a version of Mendelssohn's theory of mixed sentiments (Beiser, *Schiller as Philosopher*, 255), but under a Kantian lens. It is not an awareness of perfection or love for humanity, but our "awareness of freedom itself" (256) that is the source of subjective pleasure.

40. Most notably in *On the Sublime: Toward the Further Development of Some Kantian Themes* (1793).

41. Beiser, *Schiller as Philosopher*, 256, seems to overlook this.

42. Compare this treatment to Kant's *Observations*, third part, which discusses beauty and the sublime in its distribution among the sexes.

43. The ideal of beauty (letter 16, NA 20, 361) that functions as the "symbol of man's essence carried to completion" (letter 14, NA 20, 353).

44. See NA 20, 360. In *On the Sublime* he discusses the latter type (see Zelle, "Notstandsgesetzgebung," 464)—however, this comes with a much more negative estimation of the role and telos of history (see ibid., 466).

45. As Zelle holds, Schiller's theory of grace aims to harmonize this dualistic image of humanity. But in turn, his theory of dignity widens the chasm even more (Zelle, "Notstandsgesetzgebung," 455).

46. Reciprocal concepts, which establish their essence only in dynamic relation to each other.

47. I follow Beiser's analysis here, see Beiser, *Schiller as Philosopher*, 2005, 250.

REFERENCES

Beiser, Frederick. 2005. *Schiller as Philosopher. A Re-Examination.* Oxford: Clarendon Press.

Heidsiek, Arnold. 1979. "Der Disput zwischen Lessing und Mendelssohn über das Trauerspiel." *Lessing Yearbook* 11 (1979): 7–34.

Heidsieck, Arnold. 1983. "Adam Smith's Influence on Lessing's View of Man and Society." *Lessing Yearbook* 15 (1983): 125–43.

Kant, Immanuel. 2006. *Kritik der Urteilskraft.* Edited by Heiner Klemme. Hamburg: Meiner.

Koller, Aaron. 2011. "Mendelssohn's Response to Burke on the 'Sublime.'" In *Moses Mendelssohn's Metaphysics and Aesthetics*, edited by Reinier Munk, 329–50. New York: Springer.

Martinec, Thomas. 2006. "The Boundaries of 'Mitleidsdramaturgie': Some Clarifications concerning Lessing's Concept of 'Mitleid.'" *The Modern Language Review* 101 (3): 743–58.

Mendelssohn, Moses. 1929. *Gesammelte Schriften: Jubiläumsausgabe.* Edited by Alexander Altmann et al. Stuttgart-Bad Cannstatt: Frommann-Holzboog.

Michelsen, Peter. 1966. "Die Erregung des Mitleids durch die Tragödie: Zu Lessings Ansichten über das Trauerspiel im Briefwechsel mit Mendelssohn und Nicolai." in *Deutsche Vierteljahrsschrift für Literaturwissenschaft und Geistesgeschichte* 40 (4): 548–66.

Nolte, Fred. 1931. "Lessing's Correspondence with Mendelssohn and Nicolai, August 31, 1756 to May 14, 1757." *Harvard Studies and Notes in Philology and Literature* 13 (1931): 309–32.

Pollok, Anne. 2010. *Facetten des Menschen: Zur Anthropologie Moses Mendelssohns.* Hamburg: Meiner.

Pollok, Anne. 2018. "How to Dry Our Tears? Abbt, Mendelssohn, and Herder on the Immortality of the Soul." In *Interdisziplinäres Jahrbuch Aufklärung*, edited by Gideon Stiening and Udo Thiel, 67–81. Hamburg: Meiner.

Rueger, Alexander. 2009. "Enjoying the Unbeautiful: From Mendelssohn's Theory of 'Mixed Sentiments' to Kant's Aesthetic Judgments of Reflection." *The Journal of Aesthetics and Art Criticism* 67.2 (Spring): 181–89.

Schiller, Friedrich. 1962. *Schillers Werke: Nationalausgabe.* Edited by Norbert Oellers et. al. Vol. 20 *Philosophische Schriften: Erster Teil.* Edited by Benno von Wiese. Weimar: Böhlau.

Schillemeit, Jost. 1984. "Lessings und Mendelssohns Differenz: Zum Briefwechsel über das Trauerspiel (1756/57)." In *Digressionen: Wege zur Aufklärung*, edited by Gotthardt Frühsorge et al., 79–92. Heidelberg: Winter.

Shaftesbury [Anthony Ashley Cooper, Third Earl of Shaftesbury]. 1999. *Characteristics of Men, Manners, Opinions, Times*. Edited by Lawrence Klein. Cambridge: Cambridge University Press.

Zelle, Carsten. 1987. *"Angenehmes Grauen." Literarhistorische Beiträge zur Ästhetik des Schrecklichen im achtzehnten Jahrhundert*. Hamburg: Meiner.

Zelle, Carsten. 1994. "Die Notstandsgesetzgebung im ästhetischen Staat: Anthropologische Aporien in Schillers philosophischen Schrifen." In *Der ganze Mensch: Anthropologie und Literatur im 18: Jahrhundert*, edited by Hans-Jürgen Schings, 440–68. Stuttgart, Weimar: Metzler.

Chapter Six

Nietzsche on Admiration and Admirableness

Simon Robertson

Nietzsche advances a perfectionist ethics, valorising above all else the highest human excellences. We might expect his category of *excellence* to align neatly with a conception of *admirableness*. For both concepts identify something surpassing what is *merely good*. As ever with Nietzsche, however, matters quickly become more complex, both conceptually and substantively. I'll be using him to motivate two specific, perhaps surprising, claims: first, the normative concept *admirable* works in an *agent-relative* way; second, admiring something, even something excellent, is often bad, even *dis-admirable*. The wider goal is to illuminate various features of the concept *admirable*, plus the potential value and snares of admiring. The first three sections introduce Nietzsche's perfectionism, raise an interpretative puzzle about how admiration fits in, and outline some target theses I'll be using to engage with him. The next three sections build the case for our two specific claims. The final section pulls the interpretative and philosophical threads together and notes their wider import.

NIETZSCHE'S PERFECTIONISM

Nietzsche valorises over all else the highest human non-moral excellences. More than that is interpretively contentious, but it will be useful to map some further contours to his perfectionism.[1] Much of this can be gleaned from what he writes about "higher types"—those rare individuals who realize the highest excellences. Such figures embody two distinct kinds of excellence.

One is *flourishing*: an ongoing process (without a fixed end-state) that concerns how well a person is configured psychologically and how well she fares in relation to her environment. This is inextricably bound up with Nietzsche's enigmatic dictum to *become who you are* (or could be): a process of self-improvement that involves actively realizing *your* highest potential. How fully you flourish depends on (*inter alia*) how fully you realize that potential. What a particular person must do to flourish depends on the particularities of that person: who she already is, as circumscribed by her character and abilities, and what she could make of herself or become. Nietzsche nonetheless emphasises two general sets of conditions constitutive of human flourishing, which we could call *psychological efficacy* and *effective agency*. Psychological efficacy involves *self-understanding* (understanding who you are, what you could make of yourself) and *self-mastery* (governing your conflicting drives and forging an integrated self). Effective agency involves setting and realizing your own goals (an ideal of *autonomous self-determination*)—but goals that are *appropriate* for you, by being goals the pursuit and realization of which expresses who you are and realizes your potential (yielding a form of *authentic self-expression*). In short, a flourishing human is a self-governing agent who, by achieving goals that are truly her own, expresses who she is in ways that fulfil her and her potential.

People besides higher types can flourish. A higher type, though, excels in some further *external* sense, by achieving something great or excellent in its own right beyond flourishing. Indeed, a higher type flourishes *by* so excelling, thereby realizing her potential. It will be useful hereon to reserve "excellence" to denote only those externalised excellences distinct from flourishing. (Nietzsche centres upon great artistic, intellectual, and cultural achievements, though one could extend that.) An achievement may be recognised as excellent once achieved. But we cannot specify in advance a set of precise, informative, manual-like conditions the meeting of which is necessary or sufficient for excelling: excellence does not admit a single unifying formula across all domains; it also marks something *exception*al, going beyond, bending, violating, rules; moreover, it is the result of immense *creativity*, which, by its nature, is innovative, novel, transformative. For such reasons, excellence on Nietzsche's view is uncodifiable.

Nietzschean flourishing and excellence have different *evaluative qualities*. The value of flourishing is primarily *personal* and *relational*: flourishing is good for the person whose flourishing it is. "Excellent" is a thin evaluative notion, denoting not what is *merely* good but *highly* so. As used here, it is an evaluative predicate identifying something exceptionally good in some respect not picked out by merely attributive uses: Beethoven's *Emperor Concerto* is not just excellent *qua artwork* but, simply, an instance of excellence. The evaluative core of excellence is *non-personal* and *non-relational*. Even if his composing the *Emperor Concerto* was good for him or us, that doesn't get to the nub of its value. Its value, rather, has something to do with simply being excellent as an expression of humankind's highest potential.

AN INTERPRETATIVE PUZZLE

Now for a peculiarity. In his published works Nietzsche rarely uses the words "admire" and "admiration" (or their cognates), and never, as far as I've found, uses "admirable."[2] This seems odd because there appears a close (conceptual and extensional) alignment between *excellence* and *admirable*, both implying something that exceeds what is *merely good*. Indeed, we might expect a perfectionist to hold:

> (E → A) x is excellent → x is admirable.

So this raises an interpretative puzzle: Given that Nietzsche is a perfectionist, why does he never use words like "admirable" (and only rarely use "admiration")? And what, if anything, might he think about *admirableness*? Here are two possible answers:

> Answer 1: There's no deep philosophical rationale for such omissions—it just happens that these are not amongst his preferred words. Nonetheless, we could recast his views on *excellence* into talk of "admirableness" and accept E → A.

> Answer 2: There are important differences between how he thinks of *excellence* and *admirableness*—differences that require rejecting E → A.

I'll (tentatively) advance a version of Answer 2. To make headway, we'll need to further clarify the E → A thesis. That will raise some wider theoretical issues about admiration and admirableness. Given these two dimensions—interpretative and philosophical—I'll briefly say something about my approach.

Various methodological difficulties attend any attempt to resolve the interpretative puzzle.[3] But I'll proceed as follows. The next section sketches some core ideas underlying some relatively ordinary conceptions of *admiration* and *admirableness*, to ensure that the views attributed to Nietzsche map onto these. The rest of the paper draws upon what he actually writes on admiration and the kind of attitude he displays towards figures he appears to admire. I doubt there is a knockdown, non-question-begging case for either answer to the interpretative puzzle. Even so, the case for Answer 2 yields some interesting ideas of wider philosophical import. The strategy, then, is to "use" Nietzsche to explore this philosophical terrain; and I'm more interested in that than in "getting Nietzsche right."

ADMIRATION AND ADMIRABLENESS

Our ordinary concepts *admiration* and *admirableness* are connected: the foci of admiration and what we think admirable typically come together; and admiration is a characteristically appropriate response to what is admirable. An explication of these concepts should be sensitive to our actual views and practices. But these are multifarious and fluid. So we should resist rigidifying the concepts too much. We do nonetheless need enough traction on some basic features to ensure we are talking about the right thing. Let's start with *admiration*.

First, "admiration" can be used to pick out a certain sort or range of *attitude(s)*, possessed by someone who admires and expressed in acts of admiring. Admiration can be an occurrent attitude (consciously experienced *as* admiration or not) or a standing attitude/disposition (you can be said to admire someone you are not presently thinking about). The occurrent attitude may have a certain phenomenology—hard to pin down, perhaps varying across contexts, but often involving a sense of being impressed or inspired, esteem, reverence, wonder, or awe. It need not be a brute feeling devoid of reflective input, though: we usually admire things for qualities they exhibit, regarding them as admirable because of those qualities. Already, then, "admiration" picks out an assortment of ideas.[4]

Second, an admiration-involving attitude has an *object*. Ordinary thought suggests a range of possible objects: *agents* (individuals, groups, cultures, etc., typically human, though perhaps extendable); various *qualities* exhibited by those agents (e.g., qualities of character, especially those whose exercise a person has some control over); and what those agents *do* or *achieve*. I'll focus on what is involved in admiring persons. Usually, though, we do not admire someone in complete abstraction from what she does or achieves, or from the qualities of character enabling her to do/achieve those things or be like she is. This can make it unclear whether "the" object of admiration is really the person, her achievement, the qualities she displays, or some combination. I won't try to resolve that here. But I will assume that the person and what she does (what she achieves, the qualities she exercises) typically come together within the focus of admiration. Thus, when we admire someone, we admire her in virtue of something she did or achieved, or the qualities she thereby exhibited. That, at any rate, marks a paradigmatic case.[5]

Third, admiration involves a *pro-evaluative* stance: it casts its object in a positive evaluative light. The pro-evaluative stance for admiration goes beyond thinking the object (merely or quite) good: the object is regarded *especially good*—impressive, say, perhaps excellent.[6]

Fourth, *admiration* is sometimes explicated via the *response*-types it characteristically elicits, disposes to, or merits. Adam Smith (1790/1976, III.2.3) thought the characteristic or fitting response to admiration is *emula-*

tion. This seems too strong. I can admire a musical achievement yet have no wish to (be able to) emulate such achievements—because I know I can't, or because there are other things I care about achieving in life instead (wanting or attempting to emulate it might then be inappropriate). John Skorupski (2010, 288) suggests that the admiration-prompted response is *support*.[7] However, I doubt there is a single characteristic or fitting response-type. Some cases suggest emulation, others support, others just an emotional response (awe, reverence, etc.—though, we'll see, admiration can elicit something less genial).

These remarks suggest that admiration is fluid and takes many forms. They should nevertheless give enough clarity to fix on some basic ideas: admiration is a pro-evaluative attitude that casts its objects (paradigmatically agents, in virtue of their achievements or qualities) as especially good and disposes its bearer to some (contextually sensitive) practical or emotional response.

Let's now turn to *admirable*. This is an *evaluative* concept. Thus "x is admirable $\to x$ is thereby good in some (typically non-attributive) respect." If x is admirable, it is so in virtue of some set of facts that explain this or make it so. A person's being admirable might be explained by facts about what she achieved; there might be further facts that explain why those achievements make her admirable. These would be the same facts in virtue of which, by achieving something admirable, what she achieved is good. Letting "that p" stand for a relevant set of facts: "that p makes it the case that x is admirable $\to$ that p makes it the case that x is good."

Admirable is also a *normative* concept. This can be unpacked in different ways: something admirable *merits* or *is worthy of* admiration; admiration is a *fitting* or *appropriate* response to it; there is (sufficient) *reason* to admire it; and so on. I'll mostly frame matters in terms of admiration being *merited*. Thus,

(MERITS): (that p makes it the case that) x is admirable $\leftrightarrow$ (that p makes it the case that) x merits admiration.[8]

MERITS captures something right about the basic concept *admirable*—that it is normative and that its normativity is connected to what makes admiration a relevant response. However, it is open to two quite different, substantively more loaded, readings: an agent-*neutral* and an agent-*relative* interpretation. On an agent-neutral reading, whether x is admirable does not depend on whether x merits the admiration of any particular agent A. Thus,

(NEUTRAL): ($\forall x$, $\forall A$) (that p makes it the case that) x is admirable $\leftrightarrow$ (that p makes it the case that) x merits A's admiration.[9]

I suspect NEUTRAL represents a common folk and philosophical view. Here are two possible rationales for it. First, it tallies with common intuitions about some cases. Suppose Beethoven's (composing the) *Emperor Concerto* marks an admirable achievement. Whether that is so does not depend on whether it merits my, or any particular person's, admiration; it is, simply, admirable. Second, *admirableness* seems closely aligned with *excellence*. Suppose, as I'm assuming Nietzsche holds, that whether something is excellent does not depend on my, or any particular person's, relation to it. If we accept that plus E → A, NEUTRAL follows. However, I'll be drawing upon Nietzsche to advance the following claim:

(RELATIONAL): whether *x* merits A's admiration (qua *p*) depends on A's relation to *x* and/or *p*.

I'll use this to argue against NEUTRAL and for the claim that *admirableness* is agent-relative (thereby casting doubt on E → A). The next section begins the case against NEUTRAL.

A KEY NIETZSCHEAN THOUGHT

So Nietzsche never uses the evaluative-normative word "admirable." Why not assume he thinks of *admirable* as he thinks of *excellent* (and accept E → A)? That would keep things simpler. Two features of his thought push against it, though. First, what he writes about admiration, which could reveal something about his views on what is admirable, is typically ambivalent in a way his views regarding excellence are not. Second, his admiration towards various people appears to change over time, even when his view that they achieved something excellent does not. Assuming that his admiring someone (or not) implies he thinks the person admirable (or not), what he regards as excellent and admirable then come apart in a way directly opposing E → A. I'll hereon pursue this second thought, focusing on his attitudes towards Schopenhauer as evinced in his 1874 essay *Schopenhauer as Educator* [hereafter SE].[10] Two themes pervading SE are important for immediate purposes: self-improvement/becoming; and the role exemplars can and should play in this process. These give a clue to his views on admiration and admirableness.

Schopenhauer played a transformative role for Nietzsche. Nietzsche first encountered his work in 1865, immediately admiring the man in virtue of his philosophy.[11] By 1868, though, he opposed Schopenhauer's central doctrines, vehemently criticising them thereafter (see Breazeale 1997, xvi–xvii). *Schopenhauer as Educator* nonetheless pays homage to "the *great* Arthur Schopenhauer," giving "expression to my reverence for my one and only educator" (HA vol. 2, preface). Despite the philosophical break, Schopenhauer remains Nietzsche's "educator" due to the role he plays as an "exemplar" (SE 6.i).

An exemplar is someone you initially recognise as better (more excellent) than you, but who makes vivid to you that you could be better than you now are in ways you care about (SE 6.i–ii, 1.i). Suppose you initially admire *x*—there's something about *x* you esteem, perhaps aspire to, seek to emulate. However, you are unlikely to improve *yourself* in the ways needed to flourish or excel by *emulating another*, trying to be like *that* person or mimicking *her* achievements (ibid.; *Thus Spoke Zarathustra* [hereafter Z] I 22; *The Gay Science* [hereafter GS] 270). *Your* potential, or what you could become and make of yourself, is circumscribed by antecedent facts about *you*; and becoming who you could be, by fulfilling your potential in ways most appropriate to *you*, requires doing things (setting, pursuing, and realizing goals, say) that express important parts of who *you* are and create a better *you* (SE 6.ii, 1.iii–iv). Nor will you *excel* by merely mimicking someone or something else excellent (mere copies of excellence do not inherit its excellence; this connects to its creativity and uncodifiability). So an exemplar can make you aware that you could be better, inspire you, and perhaps indicate general directions to take (SE 2.ix, 1.iv, 5.v); but to flourish and excel you've got to work out how to do it, and do it, in a way appropriate to you, by creating something (and someone—yourself) novel (SE 1.iii, 5.viii).

Grasping this should already alter your attitude to the exemplar in a far less emulative direction (SE 1.i; 2.ix, 3.i). Moreover, if and when you surpass your exemplar by excelling, your attitude towards the exemplar might no longer be one of admiration. This seems to be what happened with Nietzsche; he continues to regard Schopenhauer and his philosophical achievements as excellent (hence worth engaging critically with), but no longer admires Schopenhauer.[12] The crucial point is that this seems perfectly reasonable. That an exemplar embodies something excellent could initially merit your admiration; but once you excel, attaining a level of excellence rivalling or surpassing that of the exemplar, the exemplar's achievements may now seem to you far less worthy, indeed not worthy, of your admiration. (Admiration may then be superseded by a different pro-evaluative attitude now more fitting or merited, just as Nietzsche continued to *respect* Schopenhauer.) You could still reasonably regard the exemplar or her achievements as excellent. But she no longer *merits your admiration* (she may still merit the admiration of someone less excellent, of course). And that attitudinal shift is reasonable, precisely because you are now able to achieve similar or higher levels of excellence.[13] Thus, what explains why admiration, though initially merited, is no longer merited is the fact that your *relation* to the object has changed.

This gives a case for RELATIONAL: whether *x* merits a person's admiration depends on *that person's* relation to *x*. The relation in question concerns the comparative excellence of the candidate admirer and object of admiration: whether *x* merits *my* admiration depends on how excellent *I* am (in relevant respects) in relation to *x*. That is the key Nietzschean thought I'll be using in the next section to argue that the normative concept *admirableness* is agent-relative.[14]

ADMIRABLENESS AS AGENT-RELATIVE

Let's suppose that *x* is excellent and add two assumptions:

> 1. At time t_1, A believes (truly, with justification, etc.) that *x* is excellent and A admires *x* (in part because A recognises that *x* is sufficiently better than A).
>
> 2. At t_2, A no longer admires *x* (because A recognises that now *x* isn't that much better than A).

The last section suggested the following could be true:

> 3. A's attitudes in 1 and 2 are merited.

The key Nietzschean thought then claims that

> 4. Premise 3 is explained by RELATIONAL: whether A's admiring *x* is merited depends on A's relation to *x*, by depending on how excellent A is in relation to *x*.

The thesis MERITS, recall, captures something right about the concept *admirable*—that it is normative and that its normativity concerns what makes admiration a relevant response. If MERITS and NEUTRAL were both true, admiration would be the merited response for *every* agent. That's what RELATIONAL denies. Then, however,

> 5. If MERITS and RELATIONAL are true, it's possible that *x* is admirable but, for some agents, *x* does not merit their admiration.

Thus, if the consequent of 5 is true, *admirableness* does not work in the agent-neutral way. Therefore,

> 6. NEUTRAL is false—*admirableness* is agent-relative.[15]

That's the basic argument. It is worth warding off some possible doubts about it.

First, one might challenge premise 3. I've motivated 3 by using the Nietzsche-Schopenhauer case to illustrate how diachronically changing attitudinal stances towards a single object can be merited. So if the objection is that the status of an attitude as merited cannot change over time, it begs the question. Moreover, it looks plain false: there are numerous cases in which a response (action, belief, feeling, attitude) that is merited or reason-supported today would not be merited another time (last week, ten years hence), precisely because, as RELATIONAL claims, our relation to its object has changed.

Second, then, one might object to RELATIONAL and hence 4. One source of objection might be that whether an attitude directed towards an object is merited must depend solely on that object, not our relation to it. Again, though, that begs the question and is precisely the assumption I've used the Nietzsche-Schopenhauer case to argue against. Moreover, there are good independent grounds for rejecting that assumption. Consider fear. There is a generic sense in which typically dangerous objects in one's vicinity merit fear—that "tigers nearby merit fear" is a useful, norm-stating generalisation. Even so, whether the presence of this tiger merits *your* fear depends on various facts about you in relation to the tiger: how strong you are in comparison to it, say, or whether you have a close bond with it (facts that likewise can change over time). In some cases, fear is not merited. This is just one of many examples in which an attitude's being merited (or not) depends not just on the (independently characterisable) object the attitude could be about, but also one's relation to it (other plausible examples include love, joy, amusement, anger, envy, etc.). In general, then, a response that is merited at one time (or for one person) might not be merited at (or for) another. If that's not true of admiration, we are owed an explanation.

Third, one might instead reject MERITS. I've already suggested that MERITS looks plausible as a way to capture the normativity of the concept *admirable*—it is meant to mark a shared and innocuous assumption. Nonetheless, one might object next, combining MERITS with RELATIONAL, by treating the "merited" relation in MERITS as agent-relative, seems to imply the following: if my admiring x is merited but your admiring x is not merited, then x is admirable "for me" but "not for you." Yet that sounds strained: ordinary use of "admirable" doesn't sit comfortably with this sort relativisation. Something must therefore have gone awry—namely, reading MERITS in the agent-relative way given by RELATIONAL. I agree it sounds strained. There are nevertheless several options here.

First, one could just jettison talk of "admirable," using only the idiom of "merited admiration," which more naturally allows relativisation to particular agents (and the greater precision that comes with that). One could thereby abandon MERITS (the argument for agent-relativity can indeed run without it, by moving straight from premise 4 to the conclusion 6). This might seem unduly revisionary to some, so it is worth seeing if we can retain MERITS. A second response, Nietzschean in spirit, is to claim that if relativising "admirable" to agents sounds odd, that's because ordinary normative talk is infused by concepts the surface grammar of which invites non-relativised syntactic constructions and reifying thought (bearing more "objectivist" connotations); but surface grammar is an unreliable, often misleading, guide to how things are. If we want to retain "admirable" talk, we'll just need to put up with some peculiar sounding linguistic constructions. We can nonetheless supplement this thought, or indeed replace it, with a third option, viewing "admirable" as a generic that we can still use to make informative norm-stating generalisations. Applying "is admirable" to an object (or type) implies that the object (type) characteristically or normally merits admiration (just as this tiger, or tigers generally, would merit fear amongst most people). That can be true even if it does not merit *everyone's* admiration. We can then treat both "admirable" and "merits admiration" in MERITS as generalisations and accept the biconditional. This is so far acceptable whether we read MERITS in an agent-neutral or agent-relative way. The agent-relative reading then just delivers an additional constraint on the scope of the normativity: even when "*x* is admirable" and "*x* merits admiration" are true in the generic sense, it remains an open question whether it merits *this particular person's* admiration—and that's what the agent-relative reading allows us to precisify. The biconditional connection thus holds at the generic level; but the connection between something's being *admirable in the generic sense* and its *meriting some specific person's admiration* is *defeasible*. We can thereby combine MERITS and RELATIONAL.

I won't decide here between these three responses. For whichever way one goes on that issue, the crucial point is that, if the case for RELATIONAL is sound, the normativity implicated by the concept of *admirableness* is agent-relative. That's our first, "perhaps surprising," conclusion.

THE DISVALUE OF ADMIRING

Whether something is overall valuable typically depends, in Nietzsche's view, on the role it plays in relation to flourishing and excellence. The same goes for the value of admiring. Even when the act/attitude is directed towards what is excellent, the value of admiring depends on the responses it provokes—in particular, whether it prompts self-improvement. Admiring can be good for you by inspiring you to better yourself (SE, e.g., 1.i–iv, 6.i–ii). But it can also be bad in various ways. We can group these into two camps.

One concerns how the attitude itself can go wrong. It can be *misdirected*: towards inappropriate exemplars whose example prompts you along paths not conducive to your flourishing or to people and achievements not worthy of (your) admiration (Nietzsche, *Daybreak* [hereafter D] 70, 113; *Twilight of the Idols* [hereafter TI], "Ancients" 2). It can be *superficial*, reflecting a shallow understanding of its object (*Human, All Too Human* [hereafter HA]

35, 79; GS 213; see Nietzsche's remarks on "educated philistinism": *Untimely Meditations* [hereafter UM] I; *Ecce Homo* [hereafter EH] "Untimelies" 2). Admiration can also dispose you to, or shade into, a range of *disadmirable responses*. These include mimicry, discipleship, hero-worship (UM I; SE). They also include various feelings and attitudes associated with harmful *inferiority* and *superiority* complexes. Fixating on how much better than you someone else is can produce a sense of inferiority; or, failing to emulate what you admire or unable to achieve what you hope, you may become increasingly prone to a brewing sense of frustration and impotence that generates the poisoning, vengeful disposition Nietzsche labels "*ressentiment*" (*On the Genealogy of Morals* [hereafter GM] I 10–11). Alternatively, admiration can foster a stultifying sense of *superiority*: basking in the success of emulating those you admire can lead to arrogance and complacency, symptomatic of what Nietzsche calls "*décadence*," a dwindling aspiration to push or improve further (TI "Expeditions" 37).

These are possible pitfalls, which is not to say that admiration always misfires. Nietzsche nonetheless has more systemic worries. That a person admires another is typically a sign that she, the admirer, has not properly begun to be (or develop) herself. She is likely to be too focused on (captivated, enthralled, fixated by) the person she admires. Although an exemplar can inspire you, admiring another for too long or too much distracts or misdirects you from doing what *you* need to flourish or excel. You instead need to focus more on yourself—setting and realizing goals that enable you to develop your potential and appropriately express who you are.

Both worries suggest that the admirer is, in virtue of admiring, unworthy of others' admiration, even disadmirable: admiring shades too easily into disadmirable attitudes and, moreover, admirers neglect their self-improvement in ways inimical to fulfilling their potential and excelling. Admiring is (often, perhaps typically) a symptom of something disadmirable in the admirer.[16] The remedy is to admire only fleetingly and carefully, to provoke self-improvement.

CONCLUSIONS

By way of conclusion, I'll draw together various threads. The first concerns our interpretative puzzle: why, given Nietzsche's perfectionism, does he never use words like "admirable" and only rarely uses "admiration" (often in a less than positive way)?—and what does or would he think about *admirableness* and its relation to excellence? I've been pushing a version of Answer 2. Perhaps Nietzsche doesn't use such terms, not even when discussing people who excel, because there are important differences between *excellence* and *admirableness*: x's being excellent (the evaluative core of which is non-relational) does not entail that it merits your admiration (admirableness is agent-relative).

This raises some important *theoretical* points. First, assuming that excellence is non-relational, if admirableness is relative we should reject the E®A thesis. (Even if excellence were relational, we still get the provocative thesis that *admirableness* is agent-relative.) A second point concerns the normativity of attitudes. On "object-based" views, whether an attitude is merited or reason-supported depends only on the object the attitude is a response to. But suppose that whether A's admiring *x* is merited depends in part on how excellent A is in relation to *x*. Then the normative notion of *merit*, as applied to admiration, or of what there is *reason* to admire, is not wholly object-based. Furthermore, we might now begin to question the extent to which there is a completely sharp distinction between *admiration being merited* and its being *good (practically speaking) to admire*. For whether *x* merits A's admiration depends on how excellent A is in relation to *x*; and A's admiring *x* is merited only if, and in part because, *x* is sufficiently more excellent than A in a way that admiring *x* would be good for A by prompting A's self-improvement or excellence. This kind of value, concerning what is good for A, is *practical*. We then get the beginnings of a case for thinking that the normativity attending attitudes like admiration could be subject to "pragmatic encroachment"—that whether the attitude or feeling of admiration A has for *x* is overall merited, or whether there is good enough reason for A to admire *x*, depends not just on *x* but on the value of A's admiring *x*. This is not a detailed argument for such a view. Nonetheless, it might motivate that view and could be of significance for debates about irreducibly or wholly affective normativity.[17]

Finally, given that Nietzsche is rarely motivated by theoretical issues for theoretical sake, it seems appropriate to close by emphasising the substantive import of the views attributed to him: we should be wary of admiring too readily—because admiring, even what is excellent, is generally disadmirable and, moreover, can be inimical to your living a life that's good for you.[18]

NOTES

1. The later arguments *rely* on very few of these specific interpretative claims; so the following serves mainly to introduce some background assumptions. For more on the interpretation itself, see Robertson, forthcoming, chapter 9–11.

2. "Bewundern," "Bewunderung," and "bewundernswert" are the most obvious German terms for "admire," "admiration," and "admirable." Of the smattering of passages where he uses "admire" and "admiration," many convey something *negative*, highlighting certain dangers of admiring (HA 141, 142; *The Wanderer and His Shadow* [hereafter WS] 308, 355, 370; D 70, 113) or mocking those whose admiration is misdirected or superficial (UM I 6; HA 35, 79; WS 123, 282; TI "Ancients" 2, 3). Some passages indicate how admiration *can* be more positive; even here, though, one often detects ambivalence (SE 2; HA 107; D 85, 135, 138, 306; GS 79, 213; *Beyond Good and Evil* [hereafter BGE] 118, 224; GM I 11; EH "Untimelies" 2).

He uses these words in more passing ways at UM I 5, 9; HA 92, 127; WS 127, 144, 210, 219; D 4, 113, 398; GS 364; Z IV 6; GM III 17; TI "Morality" 1; EH "HA" 4. I've found nothing in secondary literature devoted to Nietzsche on admiration, so this is a welcome opportunity to explore uncharted territory.

3. Given that Nietzsche doesn't say much about admiration, where should we even start from? Should we begin with "our" (or some "ordinary," "everyday") conceptions and then see how he might fit in? (But is there even a stable, everyday conception we could call "ours"? And might Nietzsche not be challenging folk conceptions?) Or should we look only at what he explicitly writes about admiration and the ways he seems to admire others? (How can we tell, though, that his attitudes are of admiration specifically?) We have to start somewhere, though.

4. I here leave aside wide-ranging questions about the structure and content of these attitudes/acts of admiration/admiring: whether they are wholly or partly cognitive/non-cognitive; whether admiring something necessarily involves thinking it admirable; whether that requires prior evaluative commitment to things of that genus; and so on.

5. An "achievement" need not mark an unmitigated success: nearly making the summit could be a notable achievement you admire the climber for. There *might* be instances of admiring an achievement without admiring the person who achieves it. (You might admire [*de dicto*] "whoever" painted the Sistine Chapel ceiling, yet have false (uncertain, no) beliefs about who that was. We can also grasp what someone means by saying "I don't admire *her*, but I admire what she achieved," though whether this could be literally true raises further issues. But we needn't take a stand on that here.

6. On ordinary views, one needn't regard the object as (uber-)excellent, though one presumably thinks it pretty good relative to certain (contextually and person-sensitive) expectations. I could admire her for the determination she showed in finishing the marathon (given how tough *she* found it), even though I don't think there is anything incredible about running that distance or mustering that level of resolve. One *might* even admire someone partly in light of her achieving goals one thinks have no deep (final, intrinsic) value: you admire her for completing the world's biggest jigsaw, say, given the patience it required.

7. He purposively leaves this open-ended and context-dependent: it "may take the form of attention and applause, or can extend to more extensive support in the form of private or public patronage, relief from duties, defence against criticism, and so on" (Skorupski 2010, 288).

8. This is a conceptual thesis, elucidating part of the conceptual content of *admirable*. The later discussion could be framed via other normative notions (I'm not imposing a view about which is most apt or basic). One reason for using "merits," though, is that it may have less strong *practical* connotations than other idioms, suggesting that admiration is a suitable response aside from whatever practical benefits there could be to admiring (or to forming the attitude, etc.). This is an issue we'll return to.

9. I follow the neutral/relative distinction drawn by Skorupski 2010, 60–67, though the later arguments reapply with relevant modifications to other accounts. Skorupski frames it in terms of "reasons" and, for the case of "evaluative" reasons, including to admire, labels them *patient*-neutral/relative (to distinguish these from practical reasons); that won't matter here. The central idea is this: whether a reason is neutral or relative depends on whether the reason-giving (admirableness-conferring) facts essential to its normative force include an essentially indexical reference back to the agent for whom it is a reason. If they do, the reason is agent-relative; if not, it's agent-neutral. Thus, a reason-predicate with a free occurrence of an essentially indexical agent-denoting term (one not governed by a universal quantifier) denotes an agent-relative reason; otherwise it is agent-neutral. Skorupski assumes that reasons to admire are agent/patient-neutral (2010, 287–89). We then get: ($\forall x$, $\forall A$) that p makes it the case that x is admirable $\leftrightarrow$ that p gives A (sufficient) reason to admire x.

10. This might seem a peripherally esoteric work to draw upon. However, it introduces numerous ideas central to his mature perfectionism and gives an unusually extended account of his shifting attitudes towards a thinker he initially admires. He continues to regard SE highly positively, regarding its theme of self-becoming as integral to his later achievements (EH "Untimelies" 3). For illuminating discussion of SE, see Conant 2001. References to SE specify section number and paragraph.

11. In a letter to Wagner: "[T]he best and most elevated moments of my life are linked with your name, and I know only one other man . . . Arthur Schopenhauer, who I regard with such admiration" (May 22, 1869; quoted in Janaway 1998, 17–18). At this stage, Nietzsche has a pro-evaluative attitude towards Schopenhauer and supports his philosophy (he is "keen to 'make propaganda' for it" and wishes "for a journal . . . to further [its] cause"; Janaway 1998, 16, n.16). Nietzsche's attitudes towards Wagner—shifting away from admiration, despite continuing to extol his music—might give a further example of the phenomenon outlined in the main text next (though the Nietzsche-Wagner relationship is rather complex).

12. This seems a common phenomenon (e.g., in sport, music, etc.): often, the better a person becomes at an activity, the less she admires the exemplars she initially looked up to. See BGE 118: "There is an innocence in admiration: he has it to whom it has not yet occurred that he too could one day be admired."

13. This is indicated by the thought that admiring someone for qualities you likewise possess, or for achievements you have equalled or exceeded, can be ethically immature or plain ignoble, narcissistic, self-conceited, and so on. (Also, even if I have reason to *emulate* A, someone exceeding A's excellence typically wouldn't; nor is it obvious that she would have reason to *support* A, in any non-vacuous sense; so those who think there are reasons to emulate/support what is admirable should agree that admiration need not be merited here.) This should help ward off the following worry (thanks to Antti Kauppinen and André Grahle for raising it). Imagine that, as a beginning swimmer, you admire Michael Phelps and want to be like him, but you eventually beat his times and achieve more golds; however, it might seem, continuing to admire him could be perfectly merited. Or suppose that one of your students overcomes considerable adversity to achieve a commendable standard given where she started from, even though your academic achievements far surpass hers; again, couldn't admiring her be merited? Two points in response. First, whether your admiration is merited depends on what exactly you admire (and why), and the relation between that and your achievements. What merits your admiring the student, presumably, is her overcoming such adversity to get to where she did. Yet if you achieved what you did under similarly adverse circumstances, it would be odd for you to *admire* her on such grounds—indeed worryingly *narcissistic* to admire someone else for possessing qualities very much like your own. Admiration may nonetheless be merited if and because your student surpasses you in relevant ways. Likewise, you might admire Phelps for what he achieved given the standards (equipment, training, etc.) of his day; but admiring him for qualities you possess or achievements less impressive than your own again seems troublingly narcissistic. Second, it may nevertheless be reasonable to *respect* and commend people for achievements it would be narcissistic to admire. Admiration and respect (even "appraisal" respect) are overlapping but distinct, as are the conditions under which each is merited. One difference is that admiration is properly directed only at people who are better than you in relevant respects, whereas respect need not be.

14. Although I've presented things in terms of intrapersonal diachronic attitudinal changes, an analogous argument for agent-relativity could be made via interpersonal considerations. It seems reasonable for *me* to admire Andy Murray for his tennis achievements but odd for *Roger Federer* to do so (for Federer to *admire*, not just *respect* him, that is, given how good Federer is), even though we agree that Murray's achievements are pretty excellent. RELATIONAL also explains this.

15. It is agent-relative because whether the facts, which make *x* admirable in a generic sense, merit *A*'s admiration depends essentially on (makes essential reference back to) A; given RELATIONAL, those facts not universally quantified over.

16. The "need *for* the noble [admirable?] is fundamentally different from the needs of the noble soul itself . . . [a] dangerous sign of its lack" (BGE 287); "a human being should *attain* satisfaction with himself . . . only then is [he] at all tolerable to behold" (GS 290).

17. Pragmatic encroachment is usually discussed in relation to (putatively normative) *epistemic* notions. In the current context, some authors differentiate irreducibly and wholly *affective* reasons for attitudes from *practical* reasons to form them (e.g., Skorupski 2010, 53–55, 480–84; Kauppinen, this volume; perhaps Parfit 2011, 50–51). Pragmatic encroachment would not by itself entail the denial of irreducibly or wholly affective normativity, though it does raise questions about the extent to which affective and practical normativity are so cleanly separable.

There are good theoretical reasons for keeping them separate and various ways to resist pragmatic encroachment. But I've thrown it out there as a different way to think about these issues, on the assumption that Nietzsche is not so concerned with theoretically driven cleanliness or the categorial rigidity it tends to produce.

18. This chapter was originally presented as a paper at "The Moral Psychology of Admiration" Workshop, hosted by the Ludwig-Maximilians-Universität München, organised by André Grahle and Alfred Archer. Many thanks to the audience there and to everyone with whom I've discussed the topic—Alfred and André, Sophie-Grace Chappell, Antti Kauppinen, Charis Marwick, Ben Matheson, Gudrun von Tevenar, and Alan Wilson. Additional thanks to Antti for really useful written comments on the penultimate version.

REFERENCES

Works by Nietzsche

UM [1873–1876]. *Untimely Meditations*, translated by R. J. Hollingdale, edited by Daniel Breazeale. Cambridge: Cambridge University Press, 1997.
SE [1874]. *Schopenhauer as Educator*, in *Untimely Meditations*, translated by R. J. Hollingdale, edited by Daniel Breazeale. Cambridge: Cambridge University Press, 1997.
HA [1878]. *Human, All Too Human*, translated by R. J. Hollingdale, edited by Richard Schacht. Cambridge: Cambridge University Press, 1996.
WS [1880]. *The Wanderer and His Shadow*, in *Human, All Too Human*, translated by R. J. Hollingdale, edited by Richard Schacht, 301–95. Cambridge: Cambridge University Press, 1996.
D [1881]. *Daybreak*, translated R. J. Hollingdale, edited by Maudemarie Clark and Brian Leiter. Cambridge: Cambridge University Press, 1987.
GS [1882/1887]. *The Gay Science*, translated by Walter Kaufmann. New York: Vintage Books, 1974.
Z [1883–1885]. *Thus Spoke Zarathustra*, translated by R. J. Hollingdale, London: Penguin Books,1969.
BGE [1886]. *Beyond Good and Evil*, translated by R. J. Hollingdale. London: Penguin Books,1990.
GM [1887]. *On the Genealogy of Morals*, translated by Douglas Smith. Oxford: Oxford University Press, 1996.
TI [1888]. *Twilight of the Idols*, translated by R. J. Hollingdale. London: Penguin Books, 1990.
EH [1888]. *Ecce Homo*, translated by Duncan Large. Oxford: Oxford University Press, 2007.

Other

Breazeale, Daniel. 1997. "Introduction." In *Untimely Meditations*, edited by Daniel Breazeale, vii–xxxiii. Cambridge: Cambridge University Press.
Conant, James. 2001. "Nietzsche's Perfectionism: A Reading of *Schopenhauer as Educator*." In *Nietzsche's Postmoralism*, edited by Richard Schacht, 181–257. Cambridge: Cambridge University Press.
Janaway, Christopher. 1998. "Schopenhauer as Nietzsche's Educator." In *Willing and Nothingness: Schopenhauer as Nietzsche's Educator*, edited by Christopher Janaway, 13–36. Oxford: Oxford University Press.
Parfit, Derek. 2011. *On What Matters* (Volume One). Oxford: Oxford University Press.
Robertson, Simon. Forthcoming. *Nietzsche and Contemporary Ethics*. Oxford: Oxford University Press.
Skorupski, John. 2010. *The Domain of Reasons*. Oxford: Oxford University Press.
Smith, Adam. 1790/1976. *The Theory of Moral Sentiments*. Oxford: Oxford University Press.

Part III

Social and Political Dimensions of Admiration

Chapter Seven

Towards a Concept of Revolutionary Admiration

Marx and the Commune

Vanessa Wills

Working men's Paris, with its Commune,
will be forever celebrated as the glorious harbinger of a new society.
Its martyrs are enshrined in the great heart of the working class.
(Marx 1871, *Marx Engels Collected Works* 22: 355)

Here, I offer an account of "revolutionary admiration," drawing heavily upon Marx's admiring remarks on the Paris Commune, the popular revolutionary republic that governed Paris from March 1871 until May of that same year.

It may seem surprising to ground in Marxist theory as affective, subjective, and inherently psychological a phenomenon as admiration. Marx, after all, the "mature" Marx, the "serious" Marx, is oft perceived as a theorist wholly unconcerned with the aspects of human life having to do with spirit and ideas. It is too typical to split Marx into two theorists opposed to one another: an "early" humanist poet, and a "later" economist who eschewed his youthful interest in abolishing alienation and concerned himself rather with ascertaining only the inexorable, iron laws of history that drag human beings along in their wake to the end of history.

In fact, there is no such sharp "break" to be found in Marx's theoretical development but rather an ongoing deepening of his understanding of how it is that human beings make their own history, albeit not under circumstances of their own choosing.[1] As Marx's comments on the role of love in revolutionary practice make clear, not only "objective" factors such as strictly economic concerns play a role, but also "subjective" factors such as the part played by human emotion in motivating and rewarding action. In his 1844 "Comments on James Mill," Marx appeals to the emotion of love as a frame for understanding how unalienated labor would be manifested in a fully developed communist society. There, in a beautifully evocative account of labor, freedom, and recognition, he writes that if

> we had carried out production as human beings ... [i]n your enjoyment or use of my product I would have the direct enjoyment both of being conscious of having satisfied a human need by my work, that is, of having objectified man's essential nature, and of having thus created an object corresponding to the need of another man's essential nature. I would have been for you the mediator between you and the species, and therefore would become recognised and felt by you yourself as a completion of your own essential nature and as a necessary part of yourself, and consequently would know myself to be confirmed both in your thought and your love. (Marx, 1844, *Marx Engels Collected Works* (hereafter *MECW*) 3: 227–28)

In his first draft of *The Civil War in France*, Marx echoes these sentiments about the significance of affirming, unalienated labor carried out *humanly*, in his admiring remarks on the Commune. Marx's concern with the themes of alienation and human emancipation has not disappeared; far from it, the example of the Commune allows Marx to combine these revolutionary aspirations with a practical revolutionary model. The Commune, for Marx, is "*the political form of the social emancipation*, of the liberation of labour from the usurpation of the (slaveholding) monopolists of the means of labour, created by the labourers themselves or forming the gift of nature. . . . The Commune does not [do] away with the class struggles, through which the working classes strive to the abolition of all classes and, therefore, of all class rule (because it does not represent a peculiar interest. It represents the liberation of 'labour,' that is the fundamental and natural condition of individual and social life" (Marx 1871, *MECW* 22: 491).

Proceeding from the informed presumption that Marx the poet and Marx the scientist remain always one and the same, an account of revolutionary admiration is salutary in its highlighting of the interplay between objective description and subjective affective response in Marx's treatment of revolutionary moments. More, it allows us to identify the specifically political significance of admiration, as such, and to account for this political significance as we investigate the moral psychology of this mental state. In this respect, an account of revolutionary admiration builds on an insight articulated by Frederick G. Whelan in his "Marx and Revolutionary Virtue," where he notes that attending to the traits Marx found admirable can shed some light on the question of what Marx's thought offers us in the way of normative moral theory. There, Whelan builds the case for interpreting Marx as a virtue ethicist, and reminds us that virtue "is a moral concept, and a doctrine that delineates traits or qualities that should be construed as excellences of character, or grounds for admiration and praise of an individual's character (and the actions that flow from it), is a kind of moral theory" (Whelan 1983, 55). My focus here is distinct from Whelan's—not on the objects of admiration but rather on the moral psychological nature of the admiration itself—yet this attention to Marx's invocations and expressions of admiration is similarly poised to inform our understanding of Marx's larger philosophical system, including his moral thought.

The nature of admiration as a generic concept is highly contested, and thus the philosophical literature is not univocal on the question of what, exactly, ought to be picked out by the English word, "admiration." There is, however, agreement that admiration constitutes a complex psychological state, incorporating elements of some combination of attention, judgement, and affect. In English, "admiration" is typically associated with an approving regard of the unusually fine, beautiful, excellent, or virtuous. Perhaps more controversially, as an attitude which one takes up toward what one regards as exemplary, admiration is an attitude that incorporates an incentive to mirror or mimic the admirable oneself, or to prefer that it be mimicked, even if only at a very general level of description (for example, admiring another's excellence at sport, an excellence instantiated in their dedication, drive, and maintenance of high personal standards, might inspire my own similarly instantiated pursuit of excellence at, say, music or philosophy).

The concept of revolutionary admiration that I put forward here draws on an understanding of admiration as a complex psychological state that brings together judgement and feeling. In this way of thinking about admiration, one judges that the object of one's admiration is excellent in some way or ways that the admirer finds to be significant and valuable, and this judgement is accompanied by a positive affective state, a feeling of joy or pleasure taken in one's perception of the admirable object.

One does not *generally* admire what one judges to be defective. We might say, perhaps, that one typically admires "under the guise of the good." Even in cases of so-called "grudging admiration," what we typically begrudge is that we have been compelled somehow to acknowledge the presence of some excellent characteristic possessed by an otherwise perhaps thoroughly unadmirable individual, or to marvel at the level of skill and dedication evinced in the defectiveness itself. (In her book, *Romantic Outlaws, Beloved Prisons*, Martha Grace Duncan refers to this phenomenon as "reluctant admiration," an experience of inner conflict over one's admiration of another. Writing specifically of our affective response to those who commit odious crimes, Duncan employs this phrase to refer to observers who "exhibit both admiration for criminals and resistance to their admiration" [Duncan 1996, 65].) This peculiar fact about how admiration can manifest is important to theorize; however, my aim here is not to offer a complete account of admiration as such, but rather, of just one specific form of it. Revolutionary admiration is neither grudging nor reluctant, but rather *wholehearted*. It does not spur the kind of inner conflict that emerges where judgement and affect come apart, as it were, and, quite in spite of oneself, one is positively disposed toward that which one judges to be unworthy of admiration. In revolutionary admiration, judgement and affect are in agreement.

Admiration is intimately linked with wonder; indeed, the English word "admire" derives etymologically from the Latin "*admirari*," often translated as "to wonder at," as one might a miracle. This raises the question of admiration's relationship to knowledge, given that the miraculous is typically also construed as that which is necessarily inexplicable and impervious to understanding. This association with a wondering attitude toward the mysterious and seemingly miraculous has given rise to skepticism about the place of admiration in a scientific approach to the world (I will discuss one influential example of such skepticism, in my comparison, which appears later in this chapter, of Cartesian *admiration* with revolutionary admiration).

In the *Marx Engels Collected Works*, Marx's "*bewundern*" is translated as "to admire."[2] My aim here, however, is not to offer any specific account of Marx's use of "*bewundern*" in his writings on the Paris Commune. Rather, it is to base an account of revolutionary admiration in an examination of Marx's reasons for holding the Paris Commune up for celebration and emulation, as he does. In that vein, I offer an account of admiration that is partially grounded in Aristotle's observation that "[i]t is owing to their wonder that men both now begin and at first began to philosophize; they wondered originally at the obvious difficulties, then advanced little by little and stated difficulties about the greater matters" (Ross 1924, I.2). This is an account of admiration not as still, passive, or contemplative wondering, but rather as an instigation, a spark, a prod eventually to that unity of inquiry and action that merits the name, "praxis."

I invoke the phrase "revolutionary admiration" here to signal the inherently political nature of the account of admiration to be offered in what follows. Revolutionary admiration links together feeling, judgement, and action in such a manner as to make a better world more possible. How admiration can serve this role is one of the tasks of this chapter to describe.

MARX'S ADMIRATION OF THE COMMUNE

Working, thinking, fighting, bleeding Paris—almost forgetful, in its incubation of a new society, of the cannibals at its gates—radiant in the enthusiasm of its historic initiative!

The circumstances of the Paris Commune are well known but nonetheless bear a brief retelling. The Commune was a short-lived revolutionary popular republic that existed for a brief moment in Paris, inaugurated on March 18 and finally extinguished by the bullets of the French Army on May 28, 1871. It emerged from the fallout of the Franco-Prussian war and the refusal of Parisian workers to follow Napoleon III in capitulating to Prussian Chancellor Otto von Bismarck's onward march through Europe, opting instead to seize control of the French capital and defend it themselves. In this manner, the Parisian workers' refusal united anti-imperialist struggle with workers' emancipation, or as Marx puts it, "[t]he direct antithesis to the empire was the Commune" (Marx 1871, *MECW* 22: 330). As Roger Thomas demonstrates in his treatment of Marx's *Civil War in France,* this political significance of the Commune is notable in great part because it cuts against the notion that Marx's enthusiasm for the Commune was feigned in his final draft of *The Civil War in France*. Thomas notes that for Marx, "the Paris Commune had come to represent several inter-related themes. Firstly, it was the conquest of political power by the working class. Secondly, the existence of this workers' state signified that the road to socialism was to be through a new and unprecedented democratic state" (Thomas 1997, 491). As such, Marx regarded the Commune as a practical confirmation of his theoretical commitment to the state as an instrument of social transition, in the hands of the masses, "the political form at last discovered under which to work out the economical emancipation of Labour" (Marx 1871, *MECW* 22: 334).

For Marx, then, the example of the Paris Commune served as a cornerstone of his radical theorizing and of his vision for what a future communist world might look like and how that world would be brought about. That the Paris Commune existed, even for only a brief time, makes immeasurably more credible the supposition that such a world is possible. In the Commune, Marx found living, concrete, practical expression of "that movement which abolishes the present state of things" (Marx and Engels 1846, *MECW* 5: 49). It is for this reason that in 1971, Monty Johnstone observed that "even after a hundred years, Marx's deeply democratic, anti-élitist, anti-bureaucratic *Civil War in France* retains its relevance as the starting point" for Marxist theorizing of revolutionary moments (Johnstone 1971, 458). Here, I approach it also as the starting point for a Marxist account of revolutionary admiration, for as C. L. R. James noted in 1946, "In 1871, when the workers of Paris established the Commune, Marx hailed it as one of the greatest events in human history," and one of the most worthy to be admired (James 1946).

Marx is frequently alleged to have offered frustratingly little in the way of a clear and concrete description of how a fully developed communist society would be structured, how people there would negotiate points of conflict and get their everyday needs met and desires fulfilled, and what the phenomenological character of such a society would be for human beings living their lives in it. In *The Civil War in France*, Marx simultaneously critiques this demand for a revolutionary blueprint, and identifies specific, concrete, praiseworthy aspects of the Paris Commune as exemplifying the proper tasks and aims of a revolutionary social liberation movement. While it is true that he did not focus his energies on predicting and detailing the minutiae of everyday communist life, Marx's reticence to offer an indication of how humans might organize their lives in a fully developed communist society is in general overstated.

By the time of the Paris Commune, Marx and Engels had already written in their 1846 *Critique of the German Ideology* that "Communism is for us not a state of affairs which is to be established, an ideal to which reality [will] have to adjust itself. We call communism the *real* movement which abolishes the present state of things. The conditions of this movement result from the now existing premise" (Marx and Engels 1846, *MECW* 5: 49). While Marx is frequently dismissed as a "utopian" theorist, he was himself highly critical of utopianism, insisting always that the work of a communist was not to dream idly of abstract possibilities but to identify the actual, already existing sociohistorical movement that would abolish the existing state of things and give birth to another. Twenty-five years after the *Critique of the German Ideology*, Marx would echo those earlier sentiments in his remarks on the Commune:

> The working class did not expect miracles from the Commune. They have no ready-made utopias to introduce *par décret du people*. Thy know that in order to work out their own emancipation, and along with it that higher form to which present society is irresistibly tending, by its own economic agencies, they will have to pass through long struggles, through a series of historic processes, transforming circumstances and men. They have no ideals to realize, but to set free the elements of the new society with which old collapsing bourgeois society itself is pregnant. (Marx 1871, *MECW* 22: 335)

The preparatory materials for Marx's *Civil War in France* offer additional insight into Marx's interpretation of the Commune as "the organized means of action" of a movement for not just French proletarian liberation, but of human liberation, ushered in by proletarian rule mediated by a state apparatus (Marx 1871, *MECW* 22: 490). In his first draft of the *Civil War in France*, published posthumously in the *Collected Works* of Marx and Engels, Marx speaks directly to the Commune's significance as a phase in abolishing the political state, and with it, one instrument and manifestation of human beings' alienation from their own powers. He writes that the Commune "was a Revolution against the *State* itself, this supernaturalist abortion of society, a resumption by the people for the people, of its own social life" (Marx 1871, *MECW* 22: 486). Marx goes on to describe the Commune in the following terms:

the reabsorption of the State power by society, as its own living forces instead of as forces controlling and subduing it, by the popular masses themselves, forming their own force instead of the organized force of their suppression— the political form of their social emancipation, instead of the artificial force (appropriated by their oppressors) (their own force opposed to and organized against them) of society wielded for their oppression by their enemies. (Marx 1871, *MECW* 22: 487)

This emphasis on the concretely democratizing tendency of the Paris Commune can be seen in Marx's discussion of the Commune's most notable achievements as a governing body. A list of what, in 1871, Marx identified as salutary policies of the Paris Commune includes the following:

1. "The first decree of the Commune was the suppression of the standing army, and the substitution for it of the armed people."
2. "The Commune was formed of the municipal councillors, chosen by universal suffrage in the various wards of the town, responsible and revocable at short terms. The majority of its members were naturally working men, of acknowledged representatives of the working class."
3. "From the members of the Commune downwards, the public service had to be done at *workmen's wages*."
4. The Commune achieved the "disestablishment and disendowment of all churches as proprietary bodies."
5. "The whole of the educational institutions were opened to the people gratuitously, and at the same time cleared of all interference of Church and State. Thus, not only was education made accessible to all, but science itself freed from the fetters which class prejudice and governmental force had imposed upon it."
6. "[M]agistrates and judges were to be elective, responsible, and revocable."
7. "The unity of the nation was not to be broken, but, on the contrary, to be organized by the Communal constitution, and to become a reality by the destruction of the State power which claimed to be the embodiment of that unity independent of, and superior to, the nation itself, from which it was but a parasitic excrescence."
8. "Instead of deciding once in three or six years which member of the ruling class was to misrepresent the people in Parliament, universal suffrage was to serve the people, constituted in Communes, as individual suffrage serves every other employer in the search for the workmen and managers in his business." (Marx 1871, *MECW* 22: 331–33)

Eight years after Marx's death, and on the twentieth anniversary of the Commune, his collaborator Friedrich Engels would point to the example of the Commune to illustrate how he and Marx conceived the initial aftermath of workers' revolution as a transitional political state in which the working classes would govern society in the interests of the masses. Famously, they described this transitional state as a "dictatorship of the proletariat," a governmental form constituted in such a way as to oppose and dismantle capitalist control of society, which rules society in the narrow interests of a small economic elite, and to replace it with real democracy—political power in the hands of the masses and in service of their interests. "Look at the Paris Commune," wrote Engels in his introduction to an 1891 edition of *The Civil War in France*. "That was the Dictatorship of the Proletariat" (Engels 1891, *MECW* 27: 191).

The concept of revolutionary admiration is grounded in the attitudes that Marx expresses, through his writings, toward the Paris Commune and the revolutionaries who produced it. In the following section, I draw out some of the most salient features of this admiring attitude.

SIX KEY FEATURES OF REVOLUTIONARY ADMIRATION

One may admire a work of art, the stars in the heavens, the pattern on a leaf. Revolutionary admiration, however, is specifically an admiration of persons, as individuals but especially as social groups. This emphasis on admiring social groups is rooted in Marx's approval of the Commune's relative lack of any single leader with supreme and unaccountable control over the movement; he writes that this lack "shocks the bourgeois who wants political idols and 'great men' immensely" (Marx 1871, *MECW* 22: 478). This skepticism of idols and "great men" highlights a key distinction between revolutionary admiration and mere unseemly flattery and uncritical hero worship.

I also wish to give special (though not exclusive) attention to admiration of another for the choices that other makes—choices that might be instructive for an observer, as she considers what types of choices she too might make under similar circumstances. This is not, however, to suggest that revolutionary admiration is bestowed upon others only on the basis of their conscious choices. An object of admiration may be admirable because of a skill, capacity, or virtue she possesses that is, at least not obviously, one she has "chosen" to have, or most readily demonstrated in terms of the choices she makes.

"Revolutionary admiration" has six key characteristics, although I do not take these to be exhaustive of the attitude. We can say, however, that revolutionary admiration is *wholehearted, humanistic, choice-oriented, imitative* and *energizing* (drawing directly on the Aristotelian concept of *energeia* as "actuality" in the sense of an actualized potential), *enlightening*, and *critical*.

Revolutionary admiration is *wholehearted* in that it does not involve a conflict between what one admires and what one judges to be *worthy* of admiration. It is not reluctant or grudging.

Revolutionary admiration is *humanistic* in that it is admiration of a person, persons, or entity made up of persons, such as a union or a social movement. Though one can of course admire the grace of a cat or the gleam of a gem, revolutionary admiration is admiration of human beings. Where revolutionary admiration seems to extend to a human product—such as, for example, a revolution—it is an indirect expression of the direct admiration of the human beings whose labor is made manifest in it.

Revolutionary admiration is *choice-oriented* in the sense that it is directed at persons primarily (though not exclusively) on the basis of the conscious choices they make, especially when these are difficult choices made under difficult circumstances.

It is *imitative and energizing* in that it inspires the admirer not only to passively regard another human actor positively but also to seek to imitate those characteristics that one finds admirable, even if only at a relatively general level of description. Revolutionary admiration inspires one to act, and in this way it is *energizing*, in the sense that it is a psychological state that helps to make what is only potentially the case, actually so.

Closely related, revolutionary admiration is *enlightening*. When one regards the object of one's admiration, one is reminded, or perhaps newly informed, of what is truly possible for human beings. The object of admiration occupies a space of realized possibility, enlarging our conception of what forms human existence can take. In so doing, it enlightens and assists us in our efforts to make real that better world which is possible.

And yet, revolutionary admiration is not to be confounded with mere hero worship. Rather, it is *critical*. Marx was a notoriously avid practitioner of what he termed "ruthless criticism of all that exists," apprehending the world always with an eye toward how it might be otherwise.[3] This extends to the Commune, of which Marx made his criticisms known.

Marx's admiring attitude toward the Commune is *wholehearted*. He is unstinting in his praise and writes in such a way as to stress that this praise is deeply and sincerely meant. His admiration is in that respect very far from the "grudging" or "reluctant" admiration described earlier in this chapter. It is *humanistic*, in that his admiration is directed towards the individuals who created the Commune, the working class in Paris at the time, and at the social form of the Commune itself, as realized in the ruling bodies of which it was made up. It is *choice-oriented* in that what Marx admires in the workers of the Paris Commune is primarily the brave and costly choices they made under chaotic and demanding circumstances. It is *imitative* in that Marx takes the workers in the Commune to be human beings worthy of emulation. It is *energizing* in that in finding the Paris Commune admirable, one makes it more likely as a practical matter that the possibilities it reveals shall become actual. It is *enlightening*. This is perhaps the greatest and most admirable achievement of the Commune: that it concretely demonstrated the possibility of workers seizing political power. And it was, of course, *critical*. In particular, Marx faulted the Commune for failing to protect itself adequately from counterrevolutionary forces within France, a mistake that contributed to its demise and diminished its—admittedly still quite significant—historical impact.[4]

AN INSTRUCTIVE COMPARISON BETWEEN REVOLUTIONARY ADMIRATION AND CARTESIAN *ADMIRATION*

The account of revolutionary admiration that I offer here owes something to René Descartes's discussion of *admiration* in his *Passions of the Soul*.[5] Namely, revolutionary admiration and Cartesian *admiration* are both complex psychological states constituted by other simpler and causally interrelated psychological states. It is useful here to explore key features of Descartes's foundational and familiar account of admiration, in order to further detail how it is that revolutionary admiration figures into, and departs from, a tradition of philosophical thought about the moral psychology of admiration.

For Descartes, *admiration* is a passion, a manner in which the soul is affected by the external world. It is the result of two physical processes, between which there is a causal relationship. An extraordinary object causes "an impression in the brain," which in turn causes "spirits" to flow in two directions: to the brain, serving to help preserve the impression of the extraordinary object so that one remembers and does not forget it, and to the sense organs, allowing one to focus one's attention on the extraordinary object, so that one may more fully and accurately perceive the nature of object. The result of this is *admiration*: a kind of particularly and singularly engrossed attention to the extraordinary. He writes:

> Wonder is a sudden surprise of the soul which makes it tend to consider attentively those objects which seem to it rare and extraordinary. So it is caused first by the impression in one's brain that represents the object as rare and consequently worthy of being accorded great consideration, and then by the motion of spirits disposed by this impression to advance with great force upon the place in the brain where it is, to strengthen and preserve it there—as they are also disposed by it to flow from there into the muscles for keeping the sense organs in the same position they are in, so that if it has been formed by them it will still be maintained by them. (Descartes 1989, *Passions of the Soul*, p. 57)

On this picture, *admiration* occurs in the individual's perceptive faculties, and does not engage the capacity to issue judgements of value. Cartesian *admiration* produces desire, not of the object itself, but of knowledge about the object. It entails no normative evaluation, whether positive or negative, of that strikingly unusual object. "[N]ot having good or evil as its object," writes Descartes, "but only knowledge of the thing wondered at, it has no relation to the heart and blood, which all the good of the body depends on, but only to the brain, where the organs of the senses are that contribute to this knowledge" (Descartes 1989, 57).

Admiration remains, however, associated with a passive contemplation of that which is taken to be strikingly otherwise from that which is already known and understood. And thus while *admiration* breeds curiosity, Descartes did not take *admiration* to be an especially reliable incentive to scientific inquiry, concerned that by contenting us with a purely stunned and static contemplation of that which is deemed admirable, it might instead inhibit our drive to perform the hard task of coming to know the world (Kaposi 2011, 114–16). He warns:

> [I]t happens much more often that one wonders too much and is astonished, in perceiving things worth considering only a little or not at all, than that one wonders too little. This can entirely eradicate or pervert the use of reason. That is why, although it is good to be born with some inclination to this passion, since it disposes us to the acquisition of the sciences, we should still try afterwards to emancipate ourselves from it as much as possible. For it is easy to supplement a deficiency of it by a particular [state of] reflection and attention to which our will can always bind our understanding when we judge that the thing presented is worth the trouble. But to prevent excessive wonder there is no remedy but to acquire the knowledge of many things, and to apply oneself to the consideration of all those which may seem most rare and unusual. (Descartes 1989, 61)

Employing a turn of phrase that Dorottya Kaposi invokes in her reading of Descartes, we might call this moderate degree of wonder "*admiration* excellently used." It is the nexus between the ever-surprising world around us and the individual's capacity to know it. Or as Kelly McConnell observes, "As the passion that allows man to experience wonder and surprise about the world around him, that allows him to desire knowledge and to proceed to judgment, admiration is in fact the interface between the Cartesian metaphysical system and the physical world" (McConnell 2014, 76).

Cartesian *admiration* "excellently used" has in common with revolutionary admiration that it is a complex, compound state made up of constitutive states and that share an internal causal relation to one another. It similarly involves a desire to perceive and apprehend the object of admiration as fully as possible, a desire sparked and inflamed by the perception that the object is distinct from other objects in a striking and novel way. It is importantly distinct, however, in that it does not involve normatively evaluative judgement, whereas revolutionary admiration always does.

Revolutionary admiration differs further in that it is fundamentally grounded not only in the faculty of perception of the world, but also in active and transformative practical intervention into the world.[6] Admiration is an inherently other-regarding psychological state and as such presupposes the subjective experience of genuine encounter with a really existing object of admiration. As N. M. L. Nathan points out, "Her eyes are blue and I admire them. To admire them, I have to believe that they are there and blue" (Nathan 1997, 453). He goes on to note that direct realism seems "to be the doctrine of perception that fits most easily with our admiration of the world of ordinary objects" (Nathan 1997, 454). Admiration, grounded as it is in the experience of surprise and the contemplation of the extraordinary, raises familiar questions about the relationship between mind and world, about skepticism and scientific knowledge, and for the possibility of transforming the strange "other" into the known and familiar.

A theory of admiration that takes Marx's admiration of the Paris Commune as its inspiration cannot be identical with Cartesian *admiration* which, although also (at least under ideal circumstances) such as to inspire one towards greater understanding of its object, does so by promoting an ultimately still contemplative attitude towards the admirable. Descartes's worry about excessive *admiration* is that it manifests as stunned amazement at least as likely to arrest inquiry into the extraordinary as it is to encourage it. Yet what Descartes proposes as an alternative—a "special state of reflection and attention"—is still all too much like that limiting attitude of amazement. Even *admiration* "excellently used," as a combination of receptiveness to impression and a payment of attention, proceeds from the implicit assumption that one best comes to know an object through non-interfering observation of it. One's activity is still limited to arranging oneself to receive sense-impressions of the object.

Here it is illuminating to recall Marx's insight that "[t]he question whether objective truth can be attributed to human thinking is not a question of theory but is a practical question. Man must prove the truth, i.e., the reality and power, the this-worldliness of his thinking in practice. The dispute over the reality or non-reality of thinking which is isolated from practice is a purely scholastic question" (Marx and Engels 1846, *MECW* 5: 3). In his 1844 "Private Property and Communism," Marx wrote that the abolition of private property was "the complete *emancipation* of all human senses and qualities, but it is this emancipation precisely because these senses and attributes have become, subjectively and objectively, *human*," meaning that human senses could themselves emerge and be recognized as not only natural faculties but also the sociohistorical products of generations of conscious and unconscious collective human social activity (Marx 1844, *MECW* 3: 300).

Revolutionary admiration is an attitude taken up towards figures one recognizes to be practically engaged in a struggle that one shares, and in this way, it bridges a gulf between the admiring subject and the object of that admiration. It is rooted in praxis: one deepens one's understanding of the object of admiration not through passive contemplation of it but through practically taking up its projects as one's own and recognizing oneself as engaged in the same activity as the admirable object.

This need not be the *very* same activity at a highly fine-grained level of particularity. It is not that we must be standing on the very same picket line or revolting against the same oppressive government. The activity may be, rather, as broad as the project of human social emancipation, of human potential realized in such a way as to place human beings fully in possession of their own essential powers. In his first draft of *The Civil War in France*, Marx wrote, "Paris, true to its historical antecedents, seeks the regeneration of the French people in making it the champion of the regeneration of old society, making the social regeneration of mankind the national business of France!" (Marx 1871, *MECW* 22: 449). This demonstration of the real practical potential for unifying and coordinating particular human actions within one universal emancipatory struggle is, for Marx, the genius of the Commune. Part of what it is to exhibit revolutionary admiration for the Commune is to attend to it, to note its novelty and significance, to study, and to draw the attention of others to it, as well. But more than that: it is also to stand in a tradition with it, and to take up its aims as our own.

CONCLUSION

Revolutionary Admiration and Contemporary Political Questions

> The cause of the Commune is the social revolution, the cause of the complete political and economic emancipation of the toilers. It is the cause of the proletariat of the whole world. And in this sense it is immortal. (Lenin 1960–1967, *LCW* 17: 143)

An account of revolutionary admiration offers numerous applications to contemporary philosophical and political questions. Firstly, it offers a firm distinction between dull, stultifying worship of "great men," and an active, critical engagement with their legacies. Marx greatly esteemed the Paris Commune, while acknowledging that this short-lived revolutionary government also made mistakes, some of them quite grave. In this way, Marx's admiration of the Commune provides a model for a celebration of the heroism of social liberation movements, that does not uselessly collapse into mere uncritical flattery.

Secondly, it allows us to resist the oft-repeated narrative that Marx did not say very much about what a revolutionary communist society would look like. He was clear and specific about what he took to be some of the most admirable features of the Commune, indicating the kind of democratic egalitarian model that a future communist society might emulate.

Thirdly, the concept of revolutionary admiration offers a guide to unpacking the nascently political implications of contemporary psychological and neurological research into the nature of admiration. This is true, whether we take admiration to be inherently normative, as it is in the case of revolutionary admiration, or silent on judgements of value, as in the case of Cartesian *admiration*. It is perhaps relatively clearer how an account that takes admiration to always involve judgements of value, will have a political meaning. But there are political implications even of non-normative Cartesian *admiration*, as to note a phenomenon as extraordinary is to make an implicit statement about what phenomena are ordinary and everyday, and which ones merit our curious attention.

In their 2009 "Witnessing Excellence in Action," Sara Algoe and Jonathan Haidt argue that

> [w]itnessing and interacting with excellent individuals can create opportunities for enrichment of the self and society. Inspiring leaders, caring benefactors, and selfless saints do more than draw praise from emotionally-responsive witnesses; these exemplary others inspire people to improve themselves, their behavior, and their relationships. Elevation, gratitude, and admiration are not just flavors of happiness. They are a part of the human emotional repertoire that, until now has been largely unexplored, and whose potential remains largely untapped." (125)

They did not, of course, have socialist revolution in mind, but the point is nonetheless very well taken.

One might ask whether Marx's revolutionary admiration of the Commune is itself worthy of revolutionary admiration. I think it is, and so my aim here has been to analyze Marx's admiration of the Paris Commune, in the hopes that doing so would provide some model of how to highlight movements for human emancipation as worthy of our study, emulation, and admiration, without calcifying them into idols. Admiration is a matter of pressing concern for those who seek to transform relations among human beings; attending to extraordinary others, regarding them with curiosity and interest, opens the doors to ways of seeing that are unlikely to leave the world the same as one found it before.

NOTES

1. In the *18th Brumaire of Luis Napoleon Bonaparte*, Marx writes, "[M]en make their own history, but they do not make it just as they please; they do not make it under circumstances chosen by themselves, but under circumstances directly encountered, given transmitted from the past" (Marx 1852, *Marx Engels Collected Works* (hereafter *MECW*) 11: 103).

2. The passage from *The Civil War in France* that appears in the *Marx-Engels Werke* as "Das paßte aber nicht in Bismarcks Spiel, wie er, spöttisch und ganz öffentlich, den bewundernden Frankfurter Philistern bei seiner Rückkehr nach Deutschland erzählte" is translated into English in the *MECW* as "Such, however, was not the game of Bismarck, as he sneeringly, and in public, told the admiring Frankfort Philistines on his return to Germany" (Marx 1871, *Marx-Engels Werke* (hereafter *MEW*) 17: 328; Marx 1871, *MECW* 22: 320).

3. One is reminded here of Marx's insistence upon the "*ruthless criticism* of all that exists, ruthless both in the sense of not being afraid of the results it arrives at and in the sense of being just as little afraid of conflict with the powers that be" (Marx, 1843 Letter to Arnold Ruge).

4. Marx complained that in the face of counterrevolutionary "atrocious provocations," "the Commune has contented itself to take hostages and to threaten reprisals, but its threats have remained a dead letter! . . . The Commune has refused to soil its hands with the blood of these bloodhounds!" (*MECW* 22: 449).

5. In my discussion of Cartesian admiration, I invoke Descartes's own term, the French word, "*admiration*," in order not to sidestep or conceal the potential interpretive difficulties presented by translation. Descartes's *admiration* has been translated variously as "wonder" (as in the translation of Descartes's *Passion of the Soul* which I consult here) and as the English word, "admiration."

6. In his *Theses on Feuerbach*, Marx famously wrote that the philosophers had merely interpreted the world, while the point is to change it. It is tempting to read Marx here as advocating a turn away from theory and toward pure practice, but the lesson to draw, rather, is that one cannot accomplish either without pursuing these tasks simultaneously in praxis. As Dieter Turck notes in his "Action vs. Contemplation (on Marx's Conception of Philosophy)," "Reason, i.e., philosophy, is theoretical and practical and at the same time" (Turck 1972, 67).

REFERENCES

Algoe, Sara B., and Jonathan Haidt. 2009. "Witnessing Excellence in Action: The 'Other-Praising' Emotions of Elevation, Gratitude, and Admiration." *The Journal of Positive Psychology* 4 (2): 105–27.

Descartes, René. 1989. *Passions of the Soul*. Indianapolis: Hackett Publishing.

Duncan, Martha Grace. 1996. *Romantic Outlaws, Beloved Prisons: The Unconscious Meanings of Crime and Punishment*. New York: New York University Press.

James, C. L. R. (published under pseudonym as J. R. Johnson). 1946. "They Showed the Way to Labor Emancipation: On Karl Marx and the 75th Anniversary of the Paris Commune." *Labor Action* 10 (11): 4.

Johnstone, Monty. 1971. "The Paris Commune and Marx's Conception of the Dictatorship of the Proletariat." *The Massachusetts Review* 12 (3): 447–62.

Kaposi, Dorottya. 2011. "Descartes on the Excellent Use of Admiration." In *Philosophy Begins in Wonder: An Introduction to Early Modern Philosophy*, edited by Michael Funk Deckard and Peter Losonczi, 107–18. Cambridge: James Clarke & Co.

Lenin, Vladimir Il'ich. 1960–1967. *Collected Works*. Moscow: Foreign Languages Publishing House.

Marx, Karl, and Friedrich Engels. 1975. *Collected Works*. London: Lawrence & Wishart.

Marx, Karl. 1964. *Marx-Engels Werke*. Berlin: Dietz.

McConnell, Kelly. 2014. "Admiration at First Sight: The Act of Admiring in Seventeenth-Century French Literature." PhD diss., University of Virginia.

Miller, Richard W. 1983. "Marx and Morality." *Nomos* 26 (1983): 3–32.

Nathan, N. M. L. 1997. "Admiration: A New Obstacle." *Philosophy* 72 (281): 453–59.
Ross, William D. 1924. *Aristotle's Metaphysics: A Revised Text with Introduction and Commentary*. Oxford: Clarendon.
Thomas, Robert. 1997. "Enigmatic Writings: Karl Marx's *The Civil War in France* and the Paris Commune of 1871." *History of Political Thought* 18 (3): 483–511.
Turck, Dieter. 1972. "Action vs. Contemplation (On Marx's Conception of Philosophy)." *Southwestern Journal of Philosophy* 3 (2): 63–70.
Whelan, Frederick G. 1983. "Marx and Revolutionary Virtue." *Nomos* 26 (1983): 54–75.

Chapter Eight

Judging in Times of Crisis

Wonder, Admiration, and Emulation[1]

Marguerite La Caze

This chapter distinguishes wonder and admiration, and both from emulation, in order to understand the role they can play in our ethical lives, especially in times of moral crisis when we cannot rely on our social and political context. There is quite a literature on wonder, and the beginning of growth in research on admiration with Linda Zagzebski's work and this volume. I argue that wonder should be understood in René Descartes's (1649/1989) sense, as a response to something unfamiliar that is based on the object, prior to our judgements about it. In contrast, in admiration, we must judge the objects as admirable, that they have some valuable traits. In ordinary times, it may be immoral acts that stand out as unfamiliar and so provoke wonder. However, I will focus on the importance of wonder in times of crisis, to recognise the unfamiliar, when many or most are treating the immoral as normal, as Hannah Arendt (2003) describes it.[2] Then admiration is the response that can enable us to take the unfamiliar moral actors as valuable moral exemplars and to emulate them.

Nevertheless, I will argue *contra* Zagzebski that we can admire a person, action, or character trait without necessarily being motivated to emulate them. Also, I contend that we can have ambivalent feelings mixed with our admiration and still be moved to emulate others in ethical ways. The complexity of the relation between these three emotions and attitudes—wonder, admiration, and emulation—means that while they can contribute to resistance to immorality in times of crisis, they are not completely trustworthy. I will begin by distinguishing wonder from admiration and emulation.

DESCARTES, WONDER, AND EMULATION

Wonder and admiration are closely related etymologically in some languages and further apart in others; in any case we can separate them conceptually. For example, the German words for wonder and admiration are very similar; they are *Wunder* and *Bewunderung* and admire is *bewundern*. Likewise, the one word in Latin—*mirabilis*—means both admirable and wonderful. I argue that wonder needs to be followed by admiration for our emotional responses to lead us to act ethically, especially in cases where a moral exemplar is our guide to action in a context where social norms are not moral. Furthermore, there needs to be a link between admiration and emulation, as I will show. Wonder has to be linked to a positive feeling towards the object before it can start to be regarded as admiration, which we can see if we look at Descartes's account of the passion of wonder.

In *The Passions of the Soul*, Descartes makes a series of distinctions, first between wonder and other passions, as "the first of all passions" (Art. 53, 1989, 52) and later a distinction between wonder and emulation, which maps onto the distinction between wonder and admiration. He uses the French *admiration* for wonder; however, I believe this is a "false friend" if we translate it as "admiration" in English in this particular case, even though that is how it normally is and should be translated. "Wonder" does better in conveying his sense of wonder at an object that we have not made a judgement about yet.[3] For him it is related to surprise and astonishment at something that is new and unfamiliar. It has no opposite, like desire, according to Descartes. Further, wonder is a kind of foundation for all the other passions, as we need some element of wonder to be moved by what we experience at all.[4] This sense of wonder allows a special place for an emotional response that is not predetermined by our liking or disliking for things, or our desires or aversions to them. Wonder allows us to be moved by others, prior to judgement, and is the first step to admiration and moral emulation of exemplars.

Descartes maintains that emulation (*l'émulation*) is a species of courage, which for him is "a certain fervor or agitation which disposes the soul to be exceedingly inclined to the execution of the things it wills to do, whatever their nature may be" (1649/1989, Art. 171, 113). Emulation then "is nothing but a fervor which disposes the soul to undertake things it hopes it may succeed at because it sees others succeed at them" (1649/1989, Art. 172, 114). The example provided by others is the external cause, and the needed additional internal cause "consists in having one's body disposed in such a way that desire and hope have more power to propel a great quantity of blood to the heart than apprehension or despair has to hinder it" (1989, Art. 172, 114). The object of emulation will be the thing we want to achieve, for

Descartes, which will require boldness if it is dangerous (1649/1989, Art. 171, 113).

This view of admiration, if we understand emulation to be admiration here, is quite limited, as it does not really focus on moral qualities as we think of them. However, for Descartes, the things we want to "succeed" at and the good or moral life are quite closely connected and thus could include ethical characteristics. The fact that we can distinguish between admiration and emulation makes the situation more complicated, and explains why we can think of them independently, as admiring someone, but not wishing to emulate them, and admiring them *and* being moved to emulate them, as I will discuss. However, thinking of emulation as a passion or something that we experience passively does not enable us to understand properly how admiration might be connected to motivation, although by linking emulation to courage, Descartes tries to build in a feature of motivation, that of our being inclined to do something. Furthermore, his reference to desire and hope suggest passions that will assist our actually acting on the passion, as long as that hope is not simply a passive view that things will somehow turn out for the better.[5]

I argue that we need a threefold distinction between wonder, admiration, and emulation in order to make sense of the complexity of our ethical experience in this regard. This is partly because wonder by itself does not involve a judgement and because admiration does not necessarily involve action. This threefold distinction will also enable us to tease out some of the complications in Zagzebski's account concerning the relation between emotion and judgement and between admiration and envy, and other negative feelings towards moral exemplars. The process of developing ethical and political judgements Arendt describes helps us to see how our experiences of admiration can be reflected on, while Zagzebski gives us a greater sense of admiration as an emotion. So first I will show how wonder still plays a role in relation to admiration by looking at Arendt's account of moral exemplars and their relation to judgement in "dark times."

JUDGEMENT IN TIMES OF CRISIS

Wonder is important in times of crisis, as it allows us to recognise the unfamiliar and see that it requires our judgement, when the immoral becomes familiar. In her essay, "Personal Responsibility under Dictatorship," first published in shorter form in 1964, Arendt sees a kind of reversal of normality towards criminality or "honest overnight change of opinion" in dictatorships, where what was before thought to be moral is what stands out for us. Her primary examples of dictatorships are the totalitarian dictatorships of the Nazi regime (1933–1945) and the Stalinist regime (1929–1941, 1945–1953)

(Arendt 2003, 24, 43). Following the norms of such societies can mean an acceptance of immorality. So wonder could operate in two important ways in these contexts: either by alerting us that what is taken for granted in dark times should not be or as a response that sees the ethical actions in that context as standing out. In *Eichmann in Jerusalem*, Arendt recounts witness testimony concerning a German soldier, Anton Schmidt, who had assisted Jewish partisans in Poland, someone she sees as an exception (1963/1992, 230–31). Then admiration is the response that can move on from wonder and enable us to take the unfamiliar actors, such as Anton Schmidt, as valuable moral exemplars and to emulate them. Arendt develops her idea of moral and political judgement in her lectures on Kant's political philosophy, given in 1964 and 1970 (Arendt 1982). In her sense, aesthetic judgement takes the place of Kant's categorical imperative in both the moral and political realms. She sees aesthetic judgement and imagination as able to take this role due to their recognition of human plurality, the *sine qua non* of genuine politics. Arendt applies Kant's work in *The Critique of the Power of Judgement* and his political essays to ethical and political judgement by developing an inter-subjective account of that judgement, so retaining a concern with the particular, while using the notion of intersubjectivity to explain the possibility of impartial judgement.

Arendt is critical of Kant's reliance on reason, and instead argues that his account of aesthetic judgement can be used to describe the process of forming political judgement, through "enlarging our mentality" or thought by imagining how I might think and feel if I were in others' places (Arendt 1968, 241).[6] She contends that right and wrong can be determined by intersubjective judgements of taste, since politics is primarily the art of judgement.

Kant's idea that the imaginative capacity to represent something not present to us shows how we can make judgements that are disinterested and impartial. The first kind of judgement is that of the actor, who is concerned with fame, the opinion of others, and the future (Arendt 1982, 57). The actor or agent is engaged in making practical forward-looking judgements within the political realm, prior to action or speech. The other kind of judgement is the judgement of the spectator, who stands apart from action, like that of a philosopher, historian, or poet, such as Homer, and is backward-looking (Arendt 1982, 66–67).[7] While the spectator's judgement is supposed to be more impartial, the actor can make judgements even though they are involved in events, and I will focus on the actor's judgement. In admiring exemplars, we could appeal to the past, such as the Norwegian king's refusal to cede his country's sovereignty to the Nazis, recently portrayed in the film *The King's Choice* (2016), or to the suffragists who fought for the vote for women, to help us face the future. King Haakon VII's action and its portrayal show the importance of honour, both in standing up to an overwhelming aggressor and in not usurping the democratically made decision to do that.

There are two reasons Arendt believes Kant's account of judgement can be useful in this way. The first is that judgement relies on others, a question of sociability, that we need company even in thinking.[8] The second reason is that the faculty of judgement deals with particulars. This is because we are concerned with a thing as representation, not whether it exists or not—judgement arises from "a merely contemplative pleasure or inactive delight." (Kant 1996, 212; Arendt 1982, 15). Thus, Arendt believes that considering questions of right and wrong from a distanced, aesthetic standpoint is the way to ensure the proper impartiality that we need, and we communicate and try to persuade others of our view. She is struck by Kant's claim that the fact human beings are affected by beauty means that "we are made for and fit into this world" (Arendt 1982, 30). Everyone can evaluate life with respect to pleasure and displeasure. An issue that arises from this description, however, is how such contemplation and delight could be translated into action, as it sounds quite passive? We have to consider how the pleasure that we take in moral exemplars could lead us to imitate them, a question I consider in the following section. Also, Arendt is considering the judgement of the spectator, who is not involved in the action, so when we are amidst action, such pleasure will have a different, more effective valence.

Arendt changes Kant's account of intersubjective judgement by making the universal standpoint into a general one (2000, 5: 179–80). The particular for her could be a fact, an event, or a person. A good moral exemplar, such as Oskar Schindler, must help us to judge events and make decisions, when our conscience does not tell us what to do. Schindler would have had to contend with competing claims on his decisions, as well as temptations not to act on his conscience. He was a member of the Nazi party and engaged in espionage for the Nazis for years, so he had to have had some change of heart and different judgement to become a rescuer.[9]

In Arendt's view, the horrors of the twentieth century required a development of this kind of judgement, and our contemporary sense of crisis may make similar demands. She takes the stress on publicity in Kant's moral philosophy in conjunction with her view of the plurality of political actors. Reflection on a moral exemplar makes it possible for us to make decisions about what to do. In order for this reflection not to reinforce the norms of society or to imply we must make pointless sacrifices we need to compare a range of exemplars in a range of situations and see our own situation in its particularity.

What enables us to make judgements of taste is the *sensus communis*, "[a]n extra mental capability . . . that fits us into a community" (Arendt 1982, 70).[10] This is how we can communicate the ineffable experiences of art or what we see in someone we admire. Taste is "community sense" and sense is "the effect of a reflection upon the mind," according to Arendt (1982, 71). She then claims that this community sense, the faculty of judgement and discriminating between right and wrong, is based on our sense of taste: "The most surprising aspect of this business is that common sense, the faculty of judgement and of discriminating between right and wrong, should be based on the sense of taste" (Arendt 1982, 64). Sight, hearing, and touch deal directly with objects and can be shared with others, whereas smell and taste give private and incommunicable sensations, she claims. Aesthetic "taste" is being used by Arendt as an analogy for the ability to make discriminatory judgements concerning ethical and political questions. A concern here is what happens to this community sense when our actual community, perhaps including our family and friends, is not something that we can or should fit into. Then our appeal to moral exemplars may have to link to a more limited community or an imagined community.[11]

Arendt argues that sight, hearing, and touch are more objective, and are capable of representation "of making present something that is absent" (1982, 64). In imagination I can remember an admirable person or a time that someone helped others. I can withhold judgement from what I see, hear, or touch but, Arendt says, in taste and smell, the "discriminatory senses," I am often overwhelmed by my sense of whether it pleases me or not. Furthermore, we cannot recall them, we can only recognise them when we experience them again, she argues. For her, taste and smell relate to the particular *qua* particular, whereas objects of the objective senses are not unique and are more easily communicable. Taste and smell are subjective and inner, I am directly affected, so we cannot discuss whether they are right or wrong, on Arendt's account. So how can judgement be based on a private and individual sense of taste?

Arendt argues that taste has to be transformed and first describes the "operation of reflection" on the representation of an object. Her idea is that imagination makes the objects of the objective senses of hearing, sight, and touch into "sensed" objects, as if they were objects of an inner sense, when we reflect on its representation. Then the *represented object* pleases or displeases, not the object of perception (Kant 2000, 5: 294). Imagination transforms an object into something internalised, so I can reflect on it and judge it as right or wrong, or admirable or contemptible—not Arendt's terms, but important for this discussion. She distinguishes between the action of imagination and the action of reflection, which is the actual judging (Arendt 1982, 68). Her view is that once the object is represented, we will have the disinterestedness, the lack of involvement, needed for evaluating something impartially. She says that aesthetic, ethical, and political judgement is based on withdrawal from involvement and partiality of my own interests and the interests of others (Arendt 1982, 43).[12]

The second step is to link our subjective sense of taste with the taste of others through the *sensus communis*. We may approve or disapprove of our own feelings of pleasure and displeasure in an object and approval of our feeling is based on its communicability. In terms of crises, we may not be able to communicate directly with those around us so then we would need to appeal to moral exemplars. Arendt argues for the importance of intersubjectivity in judgement: the "nonsubjective element in the non-objective senses is intersubjectivity" (1982, 67).

Judgements of taste take the judgements of others into account; we care what they think. Judgements of pleasure in the beautiful or what is admirable are based on the common and sound intellect that must be presupposed in everyone. In cases where those who surround us are not acting morally, we might need to think of others distant in time or place or even fictional, and the beautiful must be distinguished from the admirable.[13] The represented particular may become an exemplar.

In the ethical and political realm, such an example, between a general rule or norm and one case, allows us to judge right and wrong. Ethical and political judgement can take place through judging examples, as Arendt explains it, "the faculty to judge *particulars* without subsuming them under those general rules which can be taught and learned until they grow into habits that can be replaced by other habits and rules" (Arendt 2003, 189). This kind of judgement is reflective, as in Kant's aesthetics, in contrast to the determinant application of a rule to a particular that characterises judgement in Kant's first *Critique*. Achilles stands for her as an exemplar of courage, Solon as an exemplar of insight (Arendt 2003, 144). Another exemplar for Arendt is Socrates, who stands out as a moral figure, with his precepts of "it is better to suffer wrong than to do wrong" and not to "be out of harmony with myself" (Arendt 2003, 181–83; 1982, 37). Similarly, in *Men in Dark Times*, Arendt describes the lives of exemplars of moral taste, by which she primarily means judgement in her sense, such as Rosa Luxemburg and Karl Jaspers (Arendt 1968, 38, 40, 77, 79). Her biography of Rahel Varnhagen sets out the achievement of a life as a conscious pariah rather than a parvenu (Arendt 1997).

In times of crisis, these moral concerns come to the fore, as totalitarian regimes, for example, do not allow a space for the political. We are members of a human community in virtue of having a human existence we share with others around us and thus we at least have the potential to communicate with each other and so when we judge and act in political matters, we should use this idea as our touchstone. We would have to appeal to a wider or different community than our own, or to past examples like Schindler, if we are living in Duterte's Philippines, Trump's America, or Erdogan's Turkey. Arendt's suggestion is that we may have to communicate in thought, if we cannot communicate in our political context.

In my view, her approach to judgement is fruitful for understanding the process of identifying moral exemplars and deciding whether they should be emulated. Nevertheless, the emotional experience of admiration of moral exemplars, and its relation to emulation, requires a more detailed description, and I take Zagzebski's account, with some modifications, to be productive in this respect. So I will explore how her account of the moral psychology of admiration can be extended and linked to Arendt's view of moral exemplars in the following sections. We need to consider how we can bring our capacities for thought in relation to the moral exemplar, so we do not uncritically or globally imitate them.

ADMIRATION

In her paper on admiration and the admirable, and in her recently published book *Exemplarist Moral Theory* (2017), Zagzebski notes that admiration can misfire in two ways: when we do not admire what we should or admire what we should not.[14] When we are admiring, "the object appears admirable," and so questions of whether the emotion is fitting to its objects are relevant (Zagzebski 2017, 33). She assumes that "to be admirable just *is* to be good in a certain way" and that admiration's inclusion of a desire to emulate means that it is stronger than approval.[15] Furthermore, Zagzebski contrasts the admirable and the desirable, arguing that we do not admire such things as friendship, happiness, or health, and that we admire the virtues such as courage, self-control, and self-sacrifice even if we do not desire them (Zagzebski 2017, 30). So, for example, on this account we could admire courage but not desire it. Perhaps it is like Augustine's praying to be granted chastity and self-restraint but not yet (Augustine, *Confessions*, 8: 17). Perhaps I admire you but I do not want to be like you. How she puts it is that you need to argue to convince someone that the virtues are desirable.

Zagzebski contends that what is admirable is more basic than what is desirable, and the connection between what we admire and what is admirable is more trustworthy than that between what we desire and the desirable (Zagzebski 2017, 31).[16] She takes her lead from Aristotle in considering how we should understand these terms, because of its importance to understanding virtues and moral exemplars, for her heroes, sages, and saints. According to Zagzebski, moral exemplars play a foundational role and we can identify them even if we cannot describe them. "Narratives of fictional and non-fictional persons" can help us to identify exemplars, she says (Zagzebski 2017, 15). Narratives can also lead us to mis-identify exemplars, an issue Zagzebski notes. However, she argues that a conscientious Nazi should have discovered inconsistencies in their tendencies to admiration (2017, 47). Arendt's discussion of reflection on exemplars can help in this identification, as can consideration of "dark times" where we have to appeal to an imagined community, rather than the "common tradition" Zagzebski relies on.

For Zagzebski, admiration has a typical feeling, although there are two kinds, and it is at least "potentially motivating" (Zagzebski 2017, 33). The two kinds of admiration are that for natural talents or gifts and acquired excellences, whereby we admire acquired traits such as kindness in a different way from inborn talents (Zagzebski 2017, 38).[17] This distinction appears to be too strong, since we are unlikely to admire someone who *enjoys* being kind less than someone who struggles with the effort to be kind, unless we think that the disinterested, cold-hearted, or melancholy benefactor is more admirable than the happy benefactor, as is often thought to be Kant's view (Kant 1996, 4: 398). Zagzebski does admit that "the line between natural talent and acquired excellences is not easy to draw and there are probably many mixed excellences," such as those of the Dalai Lama (Zagzebski 2017, 39). One reason for taking Zagzebski's view is that what is imitable in a person's actions and character may only be what is acquired.[18] Another difficulty is that we find ourselves in different circumstances and with different resources from those we admire.[19]

Zagzebski also maintains that something can appear admirable even when we do not judge it to be admirable. Her view is that "admiration is a state consisting of a characteristic feeling of admiring someone or something that appears admirable. Admiration need not include the judgement that the object of our admiration is admirable, but if we trust our emotion, we will be prepared to make that judgement" (Zagzebski 2017, 34). So she seems to think that a judgement is something made only after reflection on an emotion, not a feature of the emotion itself; whereas my view is that a person or quality can only appear as admirable insofar as we judge them/it to be admirable. One way to understand Zagzebski's view to make it compatible with mine is to think of the initial judgement that is made in an emotion as an implicit or prereflective judgement. Then the judgement Zagzebski is talking about is the revised or reflective judgement after we consider the appropriateness of our emotion of admiration.[20] This sense links her view to that of Arendt's, as we have an experience of pleasure related to a judgement.

Overall, she contends that admiration is quite trustworthy, once we have reflected on our admiration and then made the judgement, despite the fact that she argues the experience of emotions like admiration seems to exemplify a "thick affective *concept*."[21] Thus, Zagzebski defines admiration as "a state consisting of a characteristic feeling of admiring someone or something that appears admirable" (2017, 34). I can accept that, with the proviso that admiration involves at least an implicit judgement, as Arendt argues is central in relation to moral exemplars.[22] Furthermore, we may need to convince ourselves that an exemplar is worthy of admiration and is indeed a moral exemplar.

Indeed, Zagzebski adds that "if the agent trusts the emotion upon reflection, she will use it as the ground for a judgement of admirability" (Zagzebski 2015, 209). According to her, once we trust it, admiration will typically have these features of pleasant feeling, judgement, and action together but they may separate so that it does not feel good to admire someone and admiration does not necessarily lead to emulation.[23] Admiration will be felt towards heroes like Leopold Socha, who protected Jewish people in Poland during the Shoah, saints like Jean Vanier and the members of L'Arche who create communities for people with mental illness and disability, and sages like Confucius (Zagzebski 2017, chapter 3). In the next section I discuss how Zagzebski sees the relation between admiration and negative moral emotions, such as envy, spite, and *ressentiment*.

ADMIRATION AND ENVY

While Zagzebski allows that emulation is not a *necessary* component of admiration, she describes the object of admiration as "imitably attractive" in order to stress the link with moral motivation (2017, 35). The exemplar, such as Confucius, is seen to be attractive rather than repulsive or neutral, we are likely to copy them, and the feeling of admiration is pleasant. Zagzebski explains how Aristotle, in the *Rhetoric*, distinguishes between emulation (*zēlos*), which can be of moral goodness such as courage or wisdom, and envy or *phthonos*, which may lead us to try to stop others having things (Aristotle 1984, 1388a30–35).[24] He says that emulation will prompt us to try to attain the good qualities we lack and feel that we deserve to have. People that we do not emulate are objects of contempt (*kataphronesis*) (Aristotle 1984, 1388b22–4). Zagzebski takes admiration to be like Aristotle's emulation, which aligns with Descartes's use of emulation, because it motivates us to imitate others in trying to attain certain goals, although Descartes does not say that it is painful. Aristotle finds emulation to be painful, whereas Zagzebski thinks it is pleasant, perhaps because Aristotle stresses the lack of the good quality or thing we admire, while Zagzebski stresses the good that the other person has (Zagzebski 2015, 210; 2017, 52). Nevertheless, as I will argue, these feelings could be painful without being hostile.

The other way that Zagzebski's view differs from Aristotle's is that for her emulation is a form of behaviour rather than an emotion; nevertheless, she believes that their views are close enough to talk about admiration in both cases. *Zēlos* or emulation is between admiration and envy, but closer to admiration, Zagzebski argues (2015, 212). This view follows because she links *Zēlos* as painful admiration with admiration proper; and envy with spite, by arguing that admiring or emulative envy should be grouped with admiration, whereas envy mixed with negative feelings is connected to spite and *ressentiment* (Zagzebski 2015, 213–14). Citing Kristján Kristjánsson (2006), Zagzebski argues that there are two kinds of envy, one that is admiring and one that is spiteful, where we want "to deprive the other of the good, and we do so without any good moral reason" (Zagzebski 2017, 52). Furthermore, the two are different enough they should be treated as distinct emotions, one admiring and the other spiteful envy.

Her idea is that two people might see the same just or heroic act, but one would be moved to emulate it, whereas the other would be pained by it. One person is delighted to learn of Swedish student Elin Ersson's protest against deporting an asylum seeker to Afghanistan, another painfully reminded of how little they do. Zagzebski allows that we may envy something another person has without wishing them to be deprived of it—the thought is that once we gain the same thing, the envy goes away (2017, 54). A difficulty here is that Zagzebski uses the example of a car rather than a moral quality, which makes it harder to see whether it makes sense for moral qualities. She makes a further distinction between ill will or hostility and spitefulness, spitefulness being the desire to deprive a person of something they have, presumably when it does not mean that we gain that thing.[25] Because Zagzebski does not know of any studies of benign envy of *moral* traits, or what she describes as "a negative (painful) feeling that leads to emulation" (2017, 53), she leaves that aside and turns to hostile envy towards a person's moral traits.

Zagzebski's strongest claim in the original article, and the one I wish to contest, is that "I cannot emulate someone if I have hostile feelings towards that person" (2015, 213). Her view is that admiring envy cannot coexist with hostile feelings, but if we are hostile we are also spiteful and do not want to become like that person or acquire their qualities. However, such hostility can also be a self-deceptive cover for a desire to be more like them, or coexist with admiration, as I argue. The largest problem Zagzebski sees is that we might distrust admiration altogether and move from admiration to envy and on to *ressentiment*. These problems are more serious, she contends, than disagreement about what to admire or our tendencies to admire people because of their good looks or influence (2017, 52). Soon I will discuss this problem as a genuine phenomenon, but here I want to challenge her view that all negative feelings mixed with admiration prevent emulation and that emulation is tightly linked to admiration.

ADMIRATION AND "MIXED FEELINGS"

The problem with this view is that the hostile feelings toward a morally exemplary person would seem to arise through a shallow judgement about appearance and reputation, rather than a deep one about the value of the ethical qualities the person has. As Zagzebski notes, moral qualities cannot be seen as mere "advantages" and moral qualities must be something we can gain (Zagzebski 2017, 54). Nevertheless, she allows we can have true (hostile) envy of a morally admirable person

> when the envious person cares more about how he measures up to the other person than about acquiring the good the other person has. Whether or not Jim can become as courageous (kind, just) as some other person, Mary, he knows he is now morally inferior in that respect. If he really hates to be morally inferior to someone else, he can feel envy of a moral quality as much as for the neighbour's new car—in fact, more so if he thinks that rating high on the moral scale is a measure of how he rates as a person. (Zagzebski 2017, 55)

What Zagzebski conjectures is that if we envy a person for their virtuous qualities, the envy "prevents, or at least inhibits, the acquisition of the virtue" (2017, 55). This is a qualified version of the earlier claim, yet still one I believe it is important to contest.

Furthermore, Zagzebski's argument that we cannot emulate a person we envy appears to be circular. She says that "envying someone's courage counteracts the motives that would lead me to become courageous because it makes emulation of a courageous person impossible" (Zagzebski 2017, 55). Unpacking slightly further, her view is that having hostile feelings towards a person prevents us from emulating them, and since we are prevented from emulating them, we will instead be spiteful and wish that they lose their good quality of courage, for example, or we will rationalise that they do not really have courage. But we need a reason for thinking that painful or hostile feelings prevent imitation or for following all of the steps in this argument. Another distinction Zagzebski makes to shore up this view is between regarding others as competitors or ideal selves. She claims we may feel pained if we concentrate on our lack of a moral quality, but if we see it as possible to acquire, then we are feeling benign envy or a kind of admiration (2017, 56). For her, seeing someone as an ideal self "is the key to emulating motives" (2017, 136). However, we could see someone as both a competitor in terms of their acts *and* an ideal self, particularly when we are talking about ethical qualities. This is in fact Aristotle's view: that with our friends, we compete *and* emulate (1984, 1162b6–12 and 1172a10–15).

So let's look at these ideas in more detail. First, if we properly recognise the qualities as moral qualities and intrinsically good, as distinct from being concerned with the reputational aspects, we will want to or hope to emulate them. We could have ambivalent feelings or hostile feelings towards the person, but they might be able to be quashed if we considered we had equal moral worth. For example, if we unexpectedly have an opportunity to demonstrate similar courage to another person, we might not be able to rise to the occasion if we did not have the example of our acquaintance. Imagine someone speaking out against racism in a meeting while we ourselves were silent. While it is possible that we would feel "shown up" immediately after, on reflection the example could inspire us to speak up next time.[26]

Zagzebski's dichotomous view is only achieved by ruling out the possibility of painful admiration that leads to emulation and the possibility of a benign envy directed towards moral traits. In my judgement, there needs to be more acknowledgement of ambivalence towards those we admire, an acknowledgement that could assist with what must be the goal of research on moral exemplars, encouraging people to imitate them. We could be hostile but emulate, and conversely be full of goodwill but not emulate because we think that the trait suits the other person but not us. Gore Vidal's famous quotation "Every time a friend succeeds, something inside me dies" does not necessarily imply that Vidal never emulated any of his successful friends (Parini, 2015). One of the reasons that Zagzebski may not see the possibility of conflicting emotions at work is that she believes that judgements are made after we reflect on the emotion of admiration, rather than as a component of it. These conflicting emotions may not only be envy, but there could be other more serious conflicts.

Admiration of moral traits or virtues seems different from material goods, as Zagzebski notes, as there is not a competition for ethical qualities, at least understood as intrinsic qualities—one could cultivate those traits, or at least some version of them. If we are competing for such traits, then we would be seeing the moral traits as external, being concerned with how we appear to others, or rivalrous about the other person being superior to us. Another possibility is that we see the differences as a zero-sum game, which appears unlikely when we are talking about moral traits, in contrast to material goods, non-moral traits, or awards. Some of the ways in which good deeds are rewarded, such as by honours or sainthood, may encourage such attitudes. But if our primary focus is the competition and besting others, then our focus is not on the moral. Furthermore, there might be some moral characteristics that we could not acquire, for example, if it was too late in our lives, as Aristotle thinks could be the case (1984, 1105a34), or a personal problem we had prevented us from developing a virtue such as courage, like agoraphobia. Perhaps if we thought we could not acquire some moral quality for those kinds of reasons, we might be more likely to feel a spiteful envy rather than an emulative envy.

Moreover, there is no reason to think that the same person could not be both moved to emulation and pained by the original action or quality in the sense of feeling made small by it. However, at least some of the time feeling small is an impetus to improve. Part of the goal of seemingly ineffective actions such as attempts to stop individual deportations of asylum seekers is to send a message and inspire others. It seems that something must be added to sheer admiration, sheer pleasure in others' goodness, whether that be envy, as Sara Protasi argues (2016), or ambition, as Kristjánsson believes (2006).[27] Given that we are considering the ethical realm, we can take seriously the thought that we also have appropriate desires to become a better person, which do not need to be understood in such terms.

Conversely, must admiration include the desire for emulation (Zagzebski, 2015, 205)? We might not be moved to emulate people we admire for practical reasons—we cannot achieve those traits, they do not suit us, or we do not have the means. Or we might think that while a person's life is admirable, it is not imitable, because it is too extreme or because what they have done is supererogatory, or the context is so different. The idea of emulating Nelson Mandela almost does not make sense, unless we split his life up into abstract qualities. Many exemplars are as mixed as our feelings about them, a phenomenon that Zagzebski acknowledges (2017, 154). We often admire only aspects of individuals, although I think it is important that we admire that quality in them, such as Mandela's ability to bring people together.[28] Lastly, I will discuss the important point that Zagzebski does bring out concerning our difficulties with admiring moral exemplars.

SPITEFUL ENVY OF THE ADMIRED

Zagzebski tries to rule out the possibility of truly mixed feelings towards moral exemplars by adding another condition, which is that the person desires to be equal to the other person *more* than they admire them. Even this point is a simplification, as desires may be in conflict and shifting over time, so no one desire can be said to be the dominant one. But for the time being let's just accept that sometimes spiteful envy "wins" over admiration. In relation to the question of the serious problem that Zagzebski identifies with admiration, that of a general cynicism about anyone being admirable, she has delineated something important here that we need to understand, which may be connected with spite (2017, 45).

Zagzebski uses Søren Kierkegaard's work to explain envy as a distortion of admiration, where what we admire is denigrated or the admired person is ostracized (Zagzebski 2017, 56–58). Furthermore, she admiringly cites Nietzsche's account of *ressentiment* as a general refusal to accept that the morally superior person's virtues are really virtues. As examples, she refers to our delight in debunking moral exemplars and exposing them as hypocrites. Our admiration turns to envy, like a common response to celebrities, or the well-known "tall poppy syndrome." Moral exemplars are often put down, as in discussions of whether anyone acts from altruistic motives; Mother Teresa's name used to come up as the first example of someone who acted from self-interested motives. Still, it seems odd to suggest that students envy Mother Teresa or feel *ressentiment* towards her. The phenomenon Zagzebski describes is one we see in relation to oppressors or perpetrators and victims, whereby the oppressors try to cast themselves in the role of victim when that is morally valued. It is possible that when we talk about popular public figures like Mother Teresa or Nelson Mandela, their status as "celebrities" and therefore the reputational aspects come into play. This claim was often made of Barack Obama.

Yet Kierkegaard also focuses on our ambivalent experience of admiration. In *Fear and Trembling*, he shows how Johannes de Silentio both admires and is appalled by the knight of faith, exemplified by Abraham, in his willingness to obey God's command to sacrifice his only son, Isaac. He writes, "While Abraham therefore arouses my admiration, he appalls me as well" (Kierkegaard 2006, 53). Whether we should imitate the knight of faith is an open question, and we might not wish to emulate the fanaticism of Abraham. Nevertheless, we can take from Kierkegaard a detailed description of admiration profoundly mixed with other emotions. In times of crisis, this mixture should not prevent us from reflecting on our admiration and making a judgement that could help us to make decisions about resistance and aid to others.

CONCLUSION

We can link Descartes's view of wonder to Arendt's account of moral exemplars to see how both play a role in assisting our judgement when we cannot rely simply on current moral norms. I have examined Zagzebski's discussion of admiration and moral exemplars as it seems to me a promising line of thought in ethical theory that should be investigated further, and that extends aspects of Arendt's account of moral and political judgement as pleasure in beauty. Conversely, Arendt's idea of judgement as enlarged thought and how an exemplar works supplements Zagzebski's notion of the feeling of admiration.

Wonder is our first response to the unfamiliar, before it is linked to specific judgements, and then we may judge and emotionally respond to a person, quality, or action as admirable, and finally may or may not be moved to emulate them. To develop these ideas, I have argued that Zagzebski has over-simplified our moral motivations and that we need to have conceptual room for mixed feelings about exemplars that do not prevent emulation and pure feelings of admiration that do not inspire us enough. So, while admiration is not entirely reliable, it can play an important role in enabling good moral judgement in times of crisis when other supports are absent.

NOTES

1. Arendt referred to many crises: in culture, in education (Arendt 1968), in the U.S. Republic (1972), the totalitarian regimes (1976), and to "dark times" (1983). I would like to thank Alfred Archer and André Grahle for the invitation to contribute to the workshop and volume, Sophie-Grace Chappell and André Grahle for their comments, the University of Tasmania for inviting me to present the Henri Martineau public lectures on this topic, audiences there and at the Australasian Association of Philosophy conference for helpful feedback, and to the Australian Research Council and School of Historical and Philosophical Inquiry for supporting my research.
2. The work of Arendt and Zagzebski may seem an unlikely combination; however, they share an interest in judgement that they trace back to Aristotelian *phronesis* (Zagzebski 2017, 119; Arendt 1968, 221; Beiner in Arendt 1982, 134–45).
3. A range of terms in French are used to convey this kind of wonder, for example, "une sensation d'émerveillement" or "penser" or "songer á" for to wonder about something.
4. The six basic passions are wonder, love, hatred, desire, joy, and sadness, and Descartes argues that all the other passions are built up from these (Art. 69, 1989, 56).
5. For Hepburn, wonder is linked to compassion, gentleness, and humility, rather than dread or a sardonic attitude (Hepburn 1984, 145–46; Sherry 2013, 348). When we admire someone we look up to them, so in that sense we consider ourselves humble, but capable of improvement, as in Descartes's emulation.
6. Arendt takes into account Kant's view that we must follow the maxims of thinking in an unprejudiced (maxim of enlightenment), broad-minded (maxim of enlarged mentality), and consistent (be in agreement with oneself) way (Kant 2000, 5: 294–45), that is, understanding, judgement, and reason.
7. See, for example, Beiner in (Arendt 1982), Dostal (1984), Bernstein (1986), Vila (1999), d'Entreves (2000), Yar (2000), and Degryse (2011) on this distinction.
8. The rules of the third *Critique* are valid only for human beings, not reasoning creatures in general.
9. Schwartz and Comer make the additional point that Schindler had to hide what he was doing and its purpose from others (2013).
10. This distinguishes human beings from animals and gods; it is specifically human because speech needs it. See Borren (2013) for a discussion of *sensus communis* understood in the context of Arendt's hermeneutic-phenomenological method.
11. Thus, I am using this term in a more literal sense than that of Benedict Anderson, who thinks our sense of ourselves as part of a nation is an imagined community (2016).
12. I have argued elsewhere that a sense of others' difference from ourselves is needed for a more complete ethics (La Caze 2013), but I am focusing on the idea of "enlarged thought" as a crucial factor in difficult times.
13. This kind of admiration must be distinguished from the "public admiration" or status Arendt criticises in *The Human Condition* (1998, 56–57).
14. See her discussion of people who admired Hitler (Zabzebski 2017, 47).
15. For Zagzebski, an action that is admirable is not *necessarily* morally right. Something may be morally right, such as taking one's life rather than face certain death, but not admirable, or admirable, such as More's refusal to sign Henry the Eighth's oath of allegiance, but we might still consider there were enough reasons to sign the oath (2015, 206). Here she concedes we can admire someone without wishing to emulate them.
16. In her book, she also links the morally admirable and exemplars with right acts and duties (Zabzebski 2017, 21–22). A practically wise person will do the right act, and an exemplar would feel guilty if they did not do a duty.
17. Zagzebski claims that we admire intellectual virtues in the same way that we admire moral virtues, and a sage like Confucius mixes the two, a view dependent on her understanding of intellectual virtues that I cannot go into here (2017, 39).
18. Zagzebski also argues that we can imitate saints, in the sense of using them as a model and becoming more like them (2017, 24, 39).
19. So constitutive and circumstantial moral luck play a role.

20. Zagzebski does not intend for her account of the emotions to prevent scholars with different views of emotions from taking other aspects of her theory seriously (2017, 32).
21. The other positive moral emotions Zagzebski finds trustworthy are sympathy, compassion, and indignation (2017, 46).
22. Zagzebski discusses the work of Jonathan Haidt et al. (2003a and 2003b; Algoe and Haidt 2009; Haidt and Seder 2009; Vianello, Galliani, and Haidt, 2010). Following Thomas Jefferson, they distinguish between "admiration" for other-praising emotion in response to the non-moral excellences of others and "elevation" for other-praising emotion in response to *moral* excellences. "Elevation" involves the object that evokes it, such as generosity or honesty displayed, physical feelings of the chest opening, the feeling of elevation, and emulation, the motivation to act in the same way (2015, 208). However, Zagzebski questions the use of a different word for our response to the moral excellences, compared to non-moral ones. It seems an artificial division, not to mention the difficulties of getting people to use the word "elevation." Furthermore, she questions their view that we only feel elevation for acts that do not benefit ourselves, since we can feel both admiration and gratitude for good deeds done to us (2017, 42).
23. The antonym of admiration is contempt for Zagzebski and disgust for Haidt. I think Zagzebski is right to pose contempt, or perhaps scorn or disdain, as the antonym of admiration, as it is more evidently moral (2017, 31, 43).
24. Zagzebski observes that Greek philosophy has the idea of the fine or noble, the *kalon*, but not a verb form or emotion that corresponds exactly to admiration. Irwin queries this claim about Greek philosophy, and Aristotle's work, arguing that *thaumazein* should in some contexts be translated as "admire" rather than "wonder" (2015, 239). However, Zagzebski contends that this emotion lacks the emulative motivation of admiration (Irwin 2015; Zagzebski 2017, 51).
25. To be more precise, Zagzebski says that "[w]hat makes Jones hostile is the fact that Smith has something Jones wants and Jones does not have, the envy disappears if *either* Smith loses his Maserati or Jones gets one too" (2017, 54).
26. I have argued in a previous paper that envy can be a response to injustice and a spur to self-improvement, in contrast to spiteful envy or envy as a character trait (La Caze 2001). Protasi distinguishes further by arguing that there are four types of envy: emulative, inert, aggressive, and spiteful (2016).
27. Protasi argues that admiration, if thought of as purely pleasant, will not motivate us to act, whereas envy will (2016, 540). Kristjánsson, in contrast, contends that emulation (understood as an emotion) needs to be combined with ambition or zeal, a concern with great honours (megalopsychia) and small honours (2006, 44).
28. Even fictional characters, say from Shakespeare, could be the object of admiration and lead us to moral improvement, as Arendt believes (2003, 144).

REFERENCES

Algoe, S. B., and Jonathan Haidt. 2009. "Witnessing Excellence in Action: The 'Other-Praising' Emotions of Elevation, Gratitude, and Admiration." *The Journal of Positive Psychology* 4 (2): 105–27.
Anderson, Benedict. 2016. *Imagined Communities: Reflections on the Origin and Spread of Nationalism*. London: Verso.
Arendt, Hannah. 1968. *Between Past and Future: Eight Exercises in Political Thought*. London: Penguin.
———. 1972. *Crises of the Republic*. New York: Harcourt Brace Jovanovich.
———. 1992. *Eichmann in Jerusalem: A Report on the Banality of Evil*. London: Penguin.
———. 1992. *The Human Condition*. 2nd edition. Chicago: University of Chicago Press.
———. 1982. *Lectures on Kant's Political Philosophy*. Ed. Ronald Beiner. Chicago: University of Chicago Press.
———. 1978. *The Life of the Mind*. San Diego: Harcourt Brace.
———. 1968. *Men in Dark Times*. San Diego: Harcourt Brace.

———. 1976. *The Origins of Totalitarianism*. San Diego: Harcourt Brace
———. 1997. *Rahel Varnhagen: The Life of a Jewess*. Ed. Liliane Weissberg, Trans. Richard and Clara Winston, Baltimore: The John Hopkins University Press.
———. 2003. *Responsibility and Judgment*. New York: Schocken.
Aristotle. 1984. *Nicomachean Ethics* in *The Complete Works of Aristotle*. Vol. 2. Edited by Jonathan Barnes. Princeton: Bollingen.
Augustine. 2007. *Confessions*. Translated by F. J. Sheed. Indianapolis: Hackett.
Bernstein, Richard. 1986. "Judging—the Actor and the Spectator." In *Philosophical Profiles: Essays in a Pragmatic Mode*, 221–37. Philadelphia: University of Pennsylvania Press.
Borren, Marieke. 2013. "'A Sense of the World': Hannah Arendt's Hermeneutic Phenomenology of Common Sense." *International Journal of Philosophical Studies*. 21 (2): 225–55.
Degryse, Annelies. 2011. "*Sensus Communis* as a Foundation for Men as Political Beings: Arendt's Reading of Kant's *Critique of Judgment*." *Philosophy and Social Criticism* 37 (3): 345–58.
Descartes, René. 1649/1989. *The Passions of the Soul*. Translated by Stephen H. Voss. Indianapolis: Hackett.
Dostal, Robert. J. 1984. "Judging Human Action: Arendt's Appropriation of Kant." *Review of Metaphysics* 37 (4): 725–55.
d'Entreves, Maurice Passerin. 2000. "Arendt's Theory of Judgment." In *The Cambridge Companion to Hannah Arendt*, edited by D. Villa, 245–60. Cambridge: Cambridge University Press.
Haidt, Jonathan. 2003a. "Elevation and the Positive Psychology of Morality." In *Flourishing, Positive Psychology and the Life Well-Lived*," edited by C. L. M. Keyes and J. Haidt, 275–89. Washington: American Psychological Association.
Haidt, Jonathan. 2003b. "The Moral Emotions." In *Handbook of Affective Sciences*, edited by R. J. Davidson, K. R. Scherer, and H. H. Goldsmith, 852–71. Oxford: Oxford University Press.
Haidt, Jonathan, and Patrick Seder. 2009. "Admiration and Awe." In *Oxford Companion to Affective Science*, edited by D. Sander and K. Scherer, 4–5. New York: Oxford University Press.
Hepburn, R. W. 1984. *"Wonder" and Other Essays: Eight Studies in Aesthetics and Neighbouring Fields.* Edinburgh: Edinburgh University Press.
Irwin, T. H. 2015. "Nil Admirari? Uses and Abuses of Admiration." *Aristotelian Supplementary Volume* 89 (1): 223–48.
Kant, Immanuel. 2000. *Critique of the Power of Judgement*. Translated by Paul Guyer. Cambridge: Cambridge University Press.
———. 1996. *Practical Philosophy*. Translated and edited by Mary J. Gregor. Cambridge: Cambridge University Press.
Kierkegaard, Søren. 2006. *Fear and Trembling*. Translated by Sylvia Walsh. Cambridge: Cambridge University Press.
Kristjánsson, Kristján. 2006. "Emulation and the Use of Models in Moral Education." *Journal of Moral Education* 35 (1): 37–49.
La Caze, Marguerite. 2001. "Envy and Resentment." *Philosophical Explorations: An International Journal for the Philosophy of Mind and Action*. Vol. IV (1): 31–45.
———. 2013. *Wonder and Generosity: Their Role in Ethics and Politics*. New York: The State University of New York.
Parini, Jay. 2015. *Every Time a Friend Succeeds, Something Inside Me Dies: The Life of Gore Vidal.* London: Little, Brown.
Poppe, Erik [director]. 2016. *The King's Choice*. Film. Culver City, CA: Samuel Goldwyn Films.
Protasi, Sara. 2016. "Varieties of Envy." *Philosophical Psychology* 29 (4): 535–49.
Schwartz, Michael, and Debra R. Comer. 2013. "The Difficulty of Being a Moral Exemplar When a Moral Exemplar Is Needed Most: The Case of Oskar Schindler." *Moral Saints and Moral Exemplars*, edited by Howard Harris, 153–68. Bingley: Emerald Group Publishing.
Sherry, Patrick. 2013. "The Varieties of Wonder." *Philosophical Investigations* 36 (4): 340–54.

Smith, Richard H., and Sung Hee Kim. 2007. "Comprehending Envy." *Psychological Bulletin* 133 (1): 46–64.

Vianello, Michelangelo, Elisa Marisa Galliani, and Jonathan Haidt. 2010. "Elevation at Work: The Effects of Leaders' Moral Excellences." *Journal of Positive Psychology* 5 (5): 390–411.

Vila, Dana. 1999. "Thinking and Judging." In *Politics, Philosophy, Terror: Essays on the Thought of Hannah Arendt*, 87–106. Princeton: Princeton University Press.

Yar, Majid. 2000. "From Actor to Spectator: Hannah Arendt's 'Two Theories' of Political Judgment." *Philosophy and Social Criticism* 26 (2): 1–27.

Zagzebski, Linda. 2015. "Admiration and the Admirable." Supplement, *Proceedings of the Aristotelian Society* 89 (1): 205–21.

———. 2017. *Exemplarist Moral Theory*. Oxford: Oxford University Press.

Chapter Nine

Admiration as Normative Support

André Grahle

A paradigmatic way for human beings to relate to each other is emotional. We sometimes feel love, sometimes feel contempt for each other; we envy or mistrust, we hope for, or pity each other; we are jealous of each other, or happy on behalf of another's joy. The list of emotions through which we relate to each other is comprehensive, presumably even exceeding the amount of names we have for them. Here is another example: We *admire* each other for certain acts, feelings, ways of being, or even for their life as a whole. In this chapter I focus on admiration for another person. More precisely, I look at second-personal *expressions* of admiration and argue that they can amount to forms of normative support.

Though somewhat linked to the exceptional, admiration is not a feeling exclusively reserved for the heroic or the superlative genius as manifested in people like Albert Einstein or Martin Luther King. The heroic only provides for particularly striking examples of suitable objects of admiration. Here the emotion is felt with appropriately greater strength. Moreover, admiration for the heroic often comes with a greater amount of visibility, as it is publicly expressed in art, traditional and social media, or in city life. Public admirers tend to implicitly or explicitly confirm to each other *that* they admire their hero and *what exactly* they admire about her. The intensity and frequency with which they are doing this seems to indicate *how much* they admire her as well. They regularly celebrate, sometimes even worship their hero through collective practices that serve to attract even more admirers and can have an effect on the strength of one's admiration as well. In fact it can be said that the social practices of celebration can figure as a second source for one's admiration, besides reflection on or perception of admirable-making features of the hero as such. Last but not least, encounter with the heroic is often easier to memorize, precisely because of the intensity of admiration it is capable of eliciting in us. When making general claims about who is admirable, we will more quickly be able to recall instances of the heroic and potentially overlook that the range of the admirable is in fact much broader.

I endorse the view that admiration includes or presupposes a judgement, however subtle, of the person manifesting properties that are rendering admiration for her appropriate. I take this claim to imply that we might be justified or not in admiring a specific person, but not to imply that any right-making features are necessarily instances of the heroic. There are more modest and at the same time more pervasive forms of the normatively admirable: her discipline at learning another language in advanced age, that skateboarder's courage in jumping the stairs, your friend's reliability at cooking so extraordinarily well, that activist's firm commitment to a particular case of justice, or these people's sincerity in loving each other. Moreover, there is nothing odd about judging there to be *something* in a person that is to *some degree* admirable, so that feeling *some* admiration for *that particular part* of the person is warranted while holding another part of the same person in low esteem or feeling even disdain for it. There might be limits for two downrightly countervailing feelings to be experienced at the same time, but most people are capable of changing feelings, depending on which aspect of a person they focus their attention on.

Now, John Skorupski (2010, 288) maintains that feelings of admiration are characteristically expressed by acts of *support*. Support as an expression of admiration comes in different forms. As Skorupski puts it, it "may take the form of attention and applause" as well as "private or public patronage, relief from duties, defence against criticism, and so on" (2010, 288). But while it seems obvious that, say, paying out a stipend to an artist is a form of support, it remains (despite some intuitive plausibility) unclear how applause and other kinds of attention functioning as expressions of admiration can be supportive. What is the supportive element of speech acts such as "Alex, what a great dancer you are!" and "Martha, I admire how committed you are to this case of justice!"? What is supportive about applauding an instance of the admirable by clapping one's hands or by showing characteristic facial expressions, or by commenting "Wow!" underneath the video that your friend just posted and that is showing her in a wing suit passing just another crevice in a mountain area on the other side of the globe while you are having your morning cup of coffee?

In the case of what might be called *complex* expressions of admiration, the obvious element of support is one that directly aims at making an impact in terms of preserving or changing some state of affairs to a certain advantage of the admired person. Patronage is a good example: by paying out a stipend one intends to clear away financial burdens that hinder the artist in pursuing the kind of artistic activity that makes her admirable. But no attempt to make any such impact can be identified in the case of what might be called *basic* expressions of admiration, confined to speech, gestures, and mimics. At first glance, they amount to nothing more than conveying one's very feeling of admiration for what one perceives or believes to be admirable about the person.

Call the kind of support that makes for a complex expression of admiration *material* support. Basic expressions of admiration, if they are supportive, amount to non-material support. Perhaps complex expressions, like basic expressions, if they really qualify as expressions *of admiration*, must be understood as conveying the feeling of admiration as well. If so, then conveying the feeling of admiration is a necessary property of all genuine expressions of admiration, while being complex in the sense of amounting to material support is an additional contingent property of only some of these expressions. Consequently, if it turned out that basic expressions of admiration are indeed supportive in a yet to be explained non-material sense, then all complex expressions would be supportive in two regards (materially and non-materially) while basic expressions would be supportive in but one regard (non-materially).

In this chapter I confine myself to the primary task of explaining the nature of non-material support, by focusing on basic expressions of admiration only. Moreover, as mentioned above, I shall concentrate on cases where one addresses someone with one's admiration second-personally. So for instance, when I say *to* Alex, "Alex, you are such a great dancer!" as against situations in which I talk to Liz merely *about* Alex, saying, "Alex is such a great dancer!" Or when I comment underneath the wing suit pilot's post, "Wow! I seriously admire you for your courage!," rather than communicating the same content somewhere else on the internet, in a different speech context, where my expression refers to the pilot only third-personally. While I do think that my argument has at least some bearing with regard to cases where the admired person becomes the *witness* of relevant third-personal expressions, I must leave the analysis of such cases for another occasion.

In the first section of this chapter, I briefly describe two forms of non-material support—*epistemic* and *innervating* support—that I think many readers will be inclined to accept rather easily. I only mention them in order to distinguish them from *normative* support, which to illuminate in detail is the aim of the second section and, indeed, the main aim of this chapter. I argue that basic second-personal expressions of admiration can, under certain conditions, instantiate forms of normative support, in virtue of them conveying the very feeling of admiration. More precisely, basic second-personal expressions of admiration can endow the admired person with an additional reason (a reason over and above the reasons that might be present already) to maintain or develop further her admirable properties. If I am right, then an important aspect of the normative nature of expressing admiration for each other is that such expression bolsters the admired person's justificatory resources in favor of their admirable-making project to continue. This, I will suggest, can equip our admirable-making activity with a certain stability, insofar as the availability of such reasons can serve as instances of encouragement for one to carry on.

1. OTHER FORMS OF NON-MATERIAL SUPPORT: EPISTEMIC AND INNERVATIVE

To begin with, consider the possibility of *epistemic support* through admiration. Adam Smith (1759/2002, 397) famously argued that people do not only want admiration for the sake of it but like to be objects *worthy* of admiration. Confidence about the latter might, however, be more of a social achievement than many of us will be inclined to admit. Even a person who very clearly excels in a certain field of conduct, might still fail to believe that she is worthy of admiration and even cultivate an attitude of active denial of that fact, if no one around her is actually *expressing* their admiration for her. Conversely, where a person does believe in her admirable-making properties and is not affected by reoccurring self-doubts, this confidence need not always be seen as an individual achievement but could in fact result from a steady supply of admiration delivered by that person's social context. As Smith (1759/2002, 133) puts it, "Their approbriation necessarily confirms our own self-approbation. Their praise necessarily strengthens our own sense of our own praiseworthiness." *Confirmation* of praiseworthiness is an epistemic matter. However, believing in one's praiseworthiness is also a necessary and typically sufficient condition for one to develop a healthy sense of pride. Here shows the potential practical impact of epistemic support. While a larger amount of self-doubt or downright denial of one's skills or competences, can make us hesitate to carry on, pride often activates us. Indirectly at least, epistemic support can help us get going and is therefore of practical relevance as well.

But now consider the possibility of *innervating support* through admiration. Imagine, you are aware of reasons for you to feel proud, so that to receive confirmation through admiration is epistemically redundant, but your awareness of there being reasons for you to feel proud, does not currently elicit the appropriate response in you. In other words, while sufficient confidence in one's skills and competences *typically* results in a healthy sense of pride, it sometimes does not. Perhaps you are going through some fatigue, but at the moment you simply do not feel much pride. Admiration can amount to what I call innervative support through bringing back that positive sense about yourself. Smith (1759/2002, 17–18) also argues that when you have lost your feeling of admiration for a book or a poem that you are still convinced manifests the same admirable properties as ever before, go read it to a friend for whom it is still novel. While you grew tired of it, it still has the potential of eliciting admiration in your friend. It is then through sympathy with your admiring friend that your own admiration can come back.[1] Likewise, since pride parallels admiration in that it is simply the first person response to admirable properties in oneself, it might be possible for you to regain pride from sympathizing with the admiration that you receive from others who are less familiar than you are with your own competences. By bringing back pride and its activating potential, innervating support can have the same practical value as epistemic support.

Now, what I call normative support differs from epistemic and innervating support in one crucial way. Normative support is a matter of *creating* reasons, which cannot be said about innervating support, nor can it be said about epistemic support, which is solely a matter of confirming reasons that were already in place. Through expressions of admiration for a person's admirable properties, others can provide that person with an additional reason to maintain, or to further develop, her admirable properties. To be sure, all three forms of support can, in principle, be delivered by the same expression. Yet it makes sense to distinguish them, as different respects in which second-personal expressions of admiration can be supportive. It may also be possible that an agent can benefit from normative support, while currently not needing much epistemic or innervating support.

2. NORMATIVE SUPPORT: ADMIRATION-BASED PETITIONARY REASONS

In developing my claim, I proceed in three steps. First, let me focus on a particular aspect of the unexpressed feeling of admiration. Admiration is a complex feeling, being composed of a number of diverse affective states. While all of the affective states that make up the feeling of admiration are intentional, they vary in terms of direction of fit. Admiration does not merely depict by way of feeling what is believed or perceived to be admirable. What has sometimes been identified as an element of *wonder* can be understood as having a mind-to-world direction of fit, but other elements of admiration clearly have a world-to-mind direction of fit including certain desires.

So far philosophers have focused on the admirer's alleged desire to emulate the admired (see, for example, Mendelssohn 1756/1838, 822–23 in a letter to Lessing; Smith 1759/2002, 234; Velleman 2009, 42, who mentions an alleged "disposition" of the admirer to emulate; as well as recently Zagzebski 2017). Others have been arguing that admiration comes with a kind of meta-desire for the very feeling of admiration to persist (de Sousa 1990, 178). I will not discuss these claims here. Instead I shall focus on another type of desire that strikes me as particularly worthy of attention. What philosophers (to my knowledge at least) have not yet paid sufficient attention to is a specific kind of desire that comes with admiration and entails an interest of the admirer for the persistence of the admired properties. I hold the following view (where "O" stands for "another person," "P" stands for the person who receives O's admiration, and "F" stands for the admired property of P):

1. *ADMIRATION-DESIRE*: If O admires P for F, then (among other things), O has some desire for F to be maintained or developed further, rather than to disappear.

I take it that (1) is primitively intelligible and that the postulated desire makes best sense of any further disposition to come to the support of an admired property. But let me say a few words to avoid misunderstandings.

Notice that this desire need not be an all-things-considered response. For instance, in admiring the extraordinary courage of the activist, I desire that she maintains this very property. However, due to another contingently related property such as her mental health, I might desire that she ends her struggle even on pain of losing what makes her courageous.[2] Moreover, (1) does not state that the desire that the admirable property be maintained has to be stronger than the desires the satisfaction of which requires acts that cause the admirable property to disappear. Thus my desire that the activist ends her struggle for the sake of her health might be stronger than my desire for her political courage to persist. (1) states that there must be *some* such desire, no matter its strength in relation to any other countervailing desires. Just if there is no such desire, O cannot justifiably be said to admire P for F.

However, one might object that weaker desires disappear in the light of stronger countervailing desires, at least in the minds of rational evaluators; and that the same rational evaluators uphold their admiration as long as the relevant admirable properties remain accessible to them. If so, it must be possible for O to admire P for F without desiring F's maintenance. But it is not true that rational evaluators lose their desire for F to persist, when such countervailing stronger desires emerge. The F-bound desire typically continues up to the point where one revises one's judgement of F being admirable. One way such continuation manifests itself is through the feeling of regret, experienced by the admirer on learning that the activist did what she ought to do and ended her struggle. It seems perfectly intelligible for the admirer to justify his regret by reference to what he recognizes as an eliminating threat to F: "I regret she had to stop, because she was such an courageous activist." In regretting, the continued desire for F's maintenance manifests itself in its transmitted form, as a desire for what happened not to have happened. One might say that regret here is not what *rational* evaluators would feel. But we should beware of conflating the standards of rationality with the more demanding standards of a quasi-stoic ideal that only certain people adhere to. It seems perfectly reasonable to feel at least some mild form of temporary regret in contexts of the above kind. Arguably, it would be somewhat suspicious for someone who does not visibly adhere to such an ideal not to feel *any* regret whatsoever in such a situation. It would suggest that former expressions of admiration were somewhat insincere.

However there may be a different worry concerning (1). Imagine an art installation consisting of an object that self-destructs ten minutes after it is first presented to an audience. Suppose a knowledgeable and sufficiently rational audience responds with admiration upon being presented with the object and suppose they do so for the very reason that it self-destructs ten minutes after it is first unveiled. Would not such a case constitute an exception to (1) because the audience feels admiration without desiring that the object of their admiration be maintained? I do not think so. For the intuition rests on confusions as to what is really the object of admiration here. *Ex hypothesis*, it is precisely not *just* the object that is admired, but its property of *being an object that self-destructs ten minutes after it is unveiled*. Hence, the disappearance of *just* the object can be desired in full coherence with (1), as it is precisely this object's timely self-destruction that is *needed* in order to preserve the property actually admired. In other words, the event of self-elimination of *just* the object is what maintains the property of being an object eliminating itself in ten minutes. Of course, maintenance must be understood widely here. In the case of an inherently finite property (a process of destruction), we can think of it as non-interruption of that process until fully realized.

Now, assuming that (1) is correct, I want to ask, second, how its truth is reflected in basic *expressions* of admiration, set into a second-personal mode. I shall focus on what is presumably the most explicit way such expressions figure in human communication: the case of using (whole) sentences to convey one's admiration. I do think though that my argument holds *mutatis mutandis* for the more implicit forms of expression through micro activities, most notably mimics and gestures. So what do we do in circumstances where we address the admiree with a sentences such as "Alex, you're such a great dancer!"? In accordance with what I have said before, we should not understand these expressions as merely asserting the representational content of our admiration, as a matter of merely communicating what we are *depicting* by way of feeling. Linking up with the idea stated by (1), we should say that expressions of admiration also carry the sense of saying something along the lines of "Alex, I wish you to continue to be such a great dancer!"[3] Notice, this is not a command, nor is it an instance of advice. Rather it amounts to a weaker form of approaching someone with a concern. We have to think of it as a form of calling on another by way of *petitioning* her, while petitioning need not be understood as making any premature claim about what the addressee of the petition ultimately has sufficient reason to do (both commanding and advising are, in contrast, all-things-considered notions). In this sense, we can say that

> (2) DESIRE-PETITION: If O expresses her admiration for P's F by addressing P with her admiration, then O addresses P with a desire to the effect that O *petitions* P to maintain or develop her F.

If petitioning is what such expressions of admiration amount to, does it evoke anything of normative relevance on the side of the addressee, the one *being* petitioned through another person's expression of admiration? I believe that under certain conditions petitioning must have a normative output. I propose the following basic normative principle the status of which I take to be *a priori*:

> (3) PETITION PRINCIPLE: If O petitions P to Φ through an expression of a justified attitude, and if P has both the ability as well as the opportunity to Φ, then P as the addressee of the petition receives from O a *petitionary reason* to Φ.

Of course, we do not only petition each other through expressions of admiration, but in various expressions of second-personal desires such as when I ask you for the time or to open the window, when I tap your shoulder to get your attention, or when I cheer on the team to win the game. Petitioning is a ubiquitous element in the way human beings (and to some degree other animals) live together. But given what I have said about the nature of admiration and what it means to express such is correct, then—via the petition principle—it follows in conclusion that

> (4) ADMIRATION-REASON: If O expresses her admiration for P's F by addressing P with her admiration, and if P has both the ability as well as the opportunity to maintain or develop her F, then P receives from O a petitionary reason to maintain or develop her F.

To be sure, there will often be other kinds of reasons for an agent to maintain or develop her admirable properties. Someone might even want to argue that admirable properties in a person constitute a *sui generis* source of at least *some* reasons for maintenance. Yet the petition principle must be understood as formulating an independent source of reasons, so that petitioning through admiration does at least add extra reasons of its distinct kind to the scene, contributing to the normative weight in favour of maintaining the properties. Accordingly, these extra reasons would also add to (and presumably exceed the strength of) any reason that may be provided by the bare fact of the petitioner's desire that F persist, a desire that she would have had even if she had not expressed it. Arguably, the fact that another person has a justified desire that I can (and that possibly *only* I can) satisfy for her, already provides me with at least *some* reason to satisfy that desire. Epistemic worries aside (how am I to recognise such reasons, if the relevant desires are not communicated to me?), I take it that the sole fact of being petitioned adds an additional element to the scene, which, under the conditions specified, generates the kind of reasons I am interested in.

Not all instances of petitioning are reason-providing though. This brings me to the success conditions specified by the petition principle. First the point about ability and opportunity: if someone petitions a person to stop a train by hand, this cannot give him reason to do it if he does not have the ability to do so. And while I may have the intrinsic property of having the ability to do a thing that another petitions me to do, there might be no opportunity to do it during my lifetime. Opportunity here is understood as an extrinsic, relational property. Someone with the ability to explain to an ignorant adult one major difference between dogs and caterpillars could still lack the opportunity to do so in a world where no such ignorant adults currently exist. Petitioning the person to do so under these circumstances does not seem to generate a reason for him (nor even *pro tanto*).[4] Secondly, the petition principle requires the attitude of which the expression constitutes an act of petitioning to be supported by a reason in the first place. The admirable and that which is actually admired are distinct notions. Sometimes people come to admire a person who does not actually deserve to be admired. Usually they mistakenly *take* a certain property to be an admirable one, without realizing that they are doing so. It is unclear why petitioning through an expression of an unjustified response could ever provide the addressee of the petition with a practical reason to comply. An unjustified, hence intrinsically unreasonable, attitude is one that should not have come into existence in the first place. As such it reveals a disvalue that we would only wrongly appreciate with the response it formally requests from its addressee.[5]

Let me now say more about the distinct normative force that petitionary reasons can subject an agent to. First, it's worth pointing out that as petitionary reasons are reasons with which others address one, they resemble the notion of a second-personal reason recently advanced by Stephen Darwall (2006, 4). However, the *pro tanto* status of petitionary reasons also distinguishes them sharply from Darwall's notion. Darwall is primarily interested in understanding the nature of (rights-based) morality and thus reserves the notion for a remarkably narrow context. In Darwall, second-personal reasons have their normative source essentially in (*de jure*) authority relations that hold between people. These reasons are generated by commands and derive their normative weight from the commander's authority *qua* holder of moral rights, and Darwall argues that they are the basis of moral accountability. The person who is successfully addressed with second-personal reasons *must* comply with the command. If she does not, there is a sense in which she wrongs the commander (cf. Darwall 2010, 262). It is important to see that none of this holds regarding the normative impact of petitionary reasons. The second-personal standpoint clearly exceeds the domain of morality (and in particular of rights-based morality that is the main focus of Darwall's approach).[6] Although deciding against compliance with petitionary reasons will often transmit into reasons to explain one's non-compliance to one's petitioners, compliance is not *owed* to one's petitioners in any morally obligatory sense. Relatedly, we need no particular authority relation to endow each other with petitionary reasons. The petition principle describes an implicit rule of a more extensive phenomenon of responding to each other within a community of sufficiently rational beings.

3. THE SUPPORTIVE NATURE OF RECEIVING PETITIONARY REASONS

Pursuing one's admirable-making projects can be highly energy consuming, specifically if they belong to a wider field of excellences. It's difficult not just to become a great dancer, but also to keep going, to *stay* the great dancer one is, perhaps even to improve on one's competences. It's quite common for such agents to go through episodes of frustration and occasional despair, some of which are accompanied by a dissolution of will power, while others include the disempowering tendency of fearing one's effort's absurdity, a fear that often finds expression in the agent's wondering what it is that justifies her effort in the first place.

If my argument in the foregoing section is sound, then the fact that others' have addressed you with their admiration can contribute to the silencing of this worry. As I hope it could be shown, expressing one's admiration for an agent second-personally is a matter of bolstering that person's justificatory resources in favour of her admirable-making project to continue.

The idea invites, however, the following worry: bolstering somebody's justificatory resources must avoid a form of redundancy in reasons supplementation, which alas cannot be avoided in cases we are concerned with here. Consider what has been said before, namely that the mere fact of you manifesting admirable properties in your person and that fact that only you can cause their persistence, *already* is a reason for you to continue your admirable-making project; or that the mere fact of another person desiring (albeit not communicating her desiring) the persistence of your admirable properties *already* is a reason for you to continue your project. I have argued that the mere availability of reasons *pre-petitioning*, does not prevent the creation of *yet another* reason favouring the same activity, but the second worry is not silenced by such a reply. Rather it assumes that in order to amount to a form of "bolstering the agent's justificatory resources" that is worth its name, any practice of creating reasons must avoid redundancy. So even if we grant that receiving extra petitionary reasons is possible, the reasons must be superfluous, and therefore of no actual use to the agent. It is my aim of this last section to show that the worry is unfounded and that receiving petitionary reasons does indeed make a difference and benefit the agent in relevant ways.

My first reply corrects what I think is a false assumption about the way practical reasoning typically accounts for phenomena of reasons accumulation. Consider that in wondering, Why am I doing all this?, we are looking for what gives us *sufficient* reason to continue the pursuit of our admirable-making projects. This naturally requires us to take into account all considerations for and against our options, before judging which choice they favour *on balance* and there is little grounds to assume that a single *pro tanto* reason can settle the issue. Consider this alone: you should not assume the mere fact of you manifesting admirable properties that only you can cause to persist, to be a sufficient reason for you to continue your admirable-making project, as such continuation is specifically energy consuming. The fact that it is energy consuming provides at least *some* reason against such continuation (a strong one even if the consumption entails or imposes a risk to the agent's mental or physical health). However, in hoping to find clear justification for the continuation of our project, it makes sense for you to get an overview about the *many different* considerations favouring continuation. We know that by *collecting* reasons, the whole case for continuation can be gradually strengthened, up to the point where the reasons for continuation turn out to be jointly sufficient. The fact of having been petitioned provides for another reason adding to this collection. There is nothing superfluous here, which is why the act of addressing the other with one's admiration is a true case of bolstering that person's justificatory resources.

While this reply insists that redundancy, in the sense of receiving another reason favouring the same, does not prevent the incoming reason's strengths from counting overall; there are two additional replies that urge us to shift focus from the basic question of whether petitionary reasons count at all, to questions related to the special nature of petitioning as such. By stressing different aspects of this nature, each of the following replies suggest that petitionary reasons must be particularly beneficial to the agent.

First, the fact of having been petitioned is not only what *provides* one with a reason. Petitioning also calls on the addressee's *attention* for the reason it provides. It does so in virtue of being a communicative act. By contrast, many other considerations favouring the same activity are not, or not necessarily, communicative acts. To be sure, an act of petitioning typically does not explicitly introduce itself as reason-providing. You do not say (nor are you likely to be trusted on the mere basis of saying), "I admire you, and that I told you means I have just given you another reason to continue your admirable-making project." In this regard, petitionary reasons are on par with all other reasons, as even petitioning can remain completely unnoticed *qua normative event*. But an agent who has been petitioned by you and is endowed with some general knowledge about the normativity of petitioning, benefits from the latter's communicative character. For that kind of agent, petitionary reasons are not just waiting there to be taken up for weighing (or be possibly overlooked). In some sense, petitionary reasons *weigh in* to the effect of mitigating the risk of being omitted. They come with increased epistemic accessibility, which renders them more likely to be accounted for by the agent's reasoning and motivational capacities.

Secondly, apart from their increased epistemic accessibility, receiving petitionary reasons has a distinct phenomenology. Their weight is experienced to some degree as *pressurizing*. Suppose I have expressed my admiration for you and hence have endowed you additional reason to continue your admirable-making project. Knowing this, I have *some* rational expectation of you taking that reason into account. You, in turn, knowing that I have reason to entertain this expectation, feel at least mildly pressured by the presence of your petitionary reason. To make this thought more tangible, compare how children (sometimes adults) try to punish each other by way of unliterary deciding to ignore the other's attempt to communicate with them. Perhaps you remember from your own experience how difficult it is to actually *stick* to such a decision. If the others continue to petition you by way of calling on your attention, it is likely you will give up in some way or the other.

Arguably, what one experiences in these cases is petitionary reasons' *pressure*. In a similar, though clearly more moderate sense, this pressure can be felt, when being petitioned through others' admiration as well. It might be barely noticeable in these cases, if petitioning remains a one-time event caused by only one admirer. But any such pressure can increase in strength with the number of people expressing their admiration, in the sense that the multiple issuing of petitionary reasons gives rise to a more magnificent kind of *social* expectation. The latter can cause the agent to experience the presence and weight of her petitionary reasons more intensely and make it both more difficult for her to discount these reasons, as well as easier to actually act on them, where such acting is appropriate.

CONCLUSIVE REMARKS: A CASE FOR JUSTICE

As I hope it could be shown, addressing somebody with one's admiration can, under certain conditions, endow the admired person with petitionary reasons to continue her admirable-making project. On top of the normative weight brought in that way, the special nature of petitioning likely results in increased epistemic accessibility of the reasons it creates. Moreover, petitionary reasons are endowed with the experiential quality of a certain pressure. I have argued that all this renders the possession of petitionary reasons, as part of a diverse pool of other reasons favouring the same activity, specifically valuable for the agent. It can help her to get going, which can be a very good thing.

It can be a bad thing also, a very bad thing indeed, if neither the admirers nor the one who is petitioned by their admiration realizes that to feel admiration is unjustified in the first place. Under these conditions, the whole game of giving petitionary reasons can at worse encourage activity that is morally problematic or downright evil, by providing the agent with what they will in quite the same way perceive as extra-reason for doing what they are involved with. To be sure, they falsely *take* the fact of having been petitioned to be another reason to carry on with their project, but practically that is irrelevant. For the receiver of petitionary reason will not perceive her taking the fact of being petitioned as erroneous but as perfectly valid.[7] As with other social practices of mutual expression of sentiments to the effect of influencing other people's behaviour, most notably perhaps moral blame, whether good or ill is being promoted is "troublingly contingent," to use Miranda Fricker's (2016, 181) way of putting it.

I believe that this speaks once again for the urgent need for good social critique, including a form of ideology critique that aims at systematically unveiling the social causes of distorted perceptions, prejudiced assumptions, and ill-guided practices of collective valuing in contemporary societies. Admiration should never fully be treated as an entirely subjective sentiment of taste. Instead, admiration practices must be rendered the objects of permanent scrutiny. It must always be possible to ask, *why* are people—why am *I*, as a part of this society, given my social position—admiring a certain object (person or group). It must be asked whether we really *should* admire the object, or whether what we take to be good reasons are causes that we better try to resist. Surely, some people receiving admiration today, receive it as a result of the way racism and sexism has had an impact even on the sentiments that people remain capable of experiencing today. Moreover, and far from being necessarily unrelated to problems of sexism and racism, admiration might also be the mere result of some of the deceitful means of capital to manipulate our feelings for the sake of exploiting them economically (most notably, of course, by advertisement). Unveiling and communicating these mechanisms is a prerequisite for these forces to be changed or abolished.

Last but not least, if what I have said about admiration and support in this chapter is true, expressions of admiration become subject to considerations of just distribution.[8] In other words, the question whether what we admire is in fact admirable is important to ask. Yet, the challenge of a just distribution of our expressions of admiration persists, even in a counterfactual world in which everything we admire is admired rightfully so. Normative support (and the same could be said about epistemic and innervating support) is a good that some can have more of than others. It is possible for such unequal distribution to persist even in the unlikely case of people being equally admirable, and even if they had the same amount of people *feeling* admiration for them. This said, I did not claim that the availability of sufficient reasons to admire a person implies that there are sufficient reason to *express* admiration for that person. Rather, I feel inclined to accept that the normativity of feelings translates into the normativity of *expressing* feelings in less direct ways. I accept that if there is sufficient reason for one to feel admiration for *x*, then there is at least *pro tanto* reason to address *x* with an expression of that emotion.[9] It follows that it's possible for one to appropriately admire a person while lacking sufficient reason to *address* the person with one's admiration. The considerations that may speak against expressing it can be manifold, but one important consideration seems to be one of justice.

If we admire somebody who already receives *loads* of applause, do we really still have to join in the choir, and to provide that person with *even more* of what they already have? Suppose further, there is a person who is clearly admirable in certain respects but is frequently unnoticed and is not often addressed with admiration as others are. Knowing that such lack of response increases the risk of that person not carrying on with a great project, why not prefer *this* person instead? This consideration becomes specifically weighty, of course, when the reason for unequal distribution goes deeper, insofar as the causes for getting ignored is again based on sexist or racist ideology, or are sourced in unjust distribution of capital, with the consequence that, say, a certain (even genuinely admirable) artist can effort advertisement campaigns that another artist simply cannot and consequently secure an extra amount of normative support as well. Thus, it is important to see that, in the end, it is up to us whom to address with our admiration and where to better hold it back.[10]

NOTES

1. Compare Goldman (2006, 17) who takes up Smith's point.
2. Compare Gaut (2007, 214) on the possibility of conflicting desires.
3. Conversely, admiring Alex as a great dancer right before adding that one has no desire whatsoever for her to maintain her dancing skills, constitutes a case of *insincerity*. For parallels see Austin (1962, 51).
4. For extensive arguments in favour of the major intuitions behind my point, see Streumer (2007). See Heuer (2010) for criticism.
5. Notice, a reason *to bring it about* that one admires the person (a reason that, for instance, is provided by a threat) would not fulfil the reason requirement as stated by the petition principle. It would, strictly speaking, not be a reason for the expressed attitude. It would be a practical rather than an evaluative reason.
6. See Skorupski (2010, 373) who argues that second-personal expressions amounting to acts of "calling on" another or "summoning" another usually evoke the desire of the summoned

to comply, which in turn generates reasons via his Bridge Principle. I take the petition principle to be an interesting alternative and a more direct line in defence of such reasons.

7. I am assuming reasons for action to be external.

8. I think the same holds even if all that expressions of admiration amount to are forms of epistemic and innervative support.

9. This assumption could be made sense of by referencing Skorupski (2010, 264ff.).

10. I would like to thank audiences at the Universities of Sheffield, St Andrews, Osnabrück, Munich, Basel, Konstanz, and Bonn for helpful discussions of earlier drafts of this chapter. Moreover, I am grateful to the participants of our annual Munich-Erlangen ethics workshop, as well as to the following individuals for valuable input: Alfred Archer, Monika Betzler, Susanne Boshammer, Nikola Kompa, Jörg Löschke, Imke von Maur, James Camien McGuiggan, Martin Sticker, Joe Saunders, and Anna Wehofsits. Vanessa Wills has provided very helpful written comments on a penultimate version of this chapter.

REFERENCES

Austin, J. L. 1962/1995. *How to Do Things with Words.* Second Edition. Cambridge, MA: Harvard University Press.
Darwall, Stephen. 2010. "Authority and Reasons: Exclusionary and Second-Personal." *Ethics* 120 (2): 257–78.
Darwall, Stephen. 2006. *The Second Person Standpoint.* Cambridge, MA: Belknap Press.
de Sousa, Ronald. 1990. *The Rationality of Emotion.* Cambridge, MA: MIT Press.
Fricker, Miranda. 2016. What's the Point of Blame? A Paradigm Based Explanation. *Noûs* 50 (1): 165–83.
Gaut, Berys. 2007. *Art, Emotion, and Ethics.* Oxford: Oxford University Press.
Goldman, Alvin. 2006. *Simulating Minds—The Philosophy, Psychology, and Neuroscience of Mindreading.* Oxford: Oxford University Press.
Heuer, Ulrike. 2010. "Reasons and Impossibility." *Philosophical Studies* 147 (2): 235–46.
Mendelssohn, Moses. 1756/1883. "Brief an Lessing." In *Sämmtliche Werke,* 822–24. Wien: Verlag von Mich.
Skorupski, John. 2010. *The Domain of Reasons.* Oxford: Oxford University Press.
Smith, Adam. (1759/2002). *The Theory of Moral Sentiments.* Edited by Knud Haakonsen. Cambridge: Cambridge University Press.
Streumer, Bart. 2007. "Reasons and Impossibility." *Philosophical Studies* 136 (3): 351–84.
Velleman, J. D. 2009. *How We Get Along.* Cambridge: Cambridge University Press.
Zagzebski, L. T. 2017. *Exemplarist Moral Theory.* Oxford: Oxford University Press.

Chapter Ten

Admiring Animals[1]

Amanda Cawston

"The admired other embodies an ideal and encourages the admiring individual to similarly strive for this ideal by showing that this is possible and how it can be done." (Schindler et al., 2013, 110)

How can we ground the moral status of animals, or help to guide moral interactions with them? One strategy is to appeal to empathy, which has enjoyed a central place in animal ethics and is often cited as a useful alternative or supplement to rights theories. Empathy is thought to provide the means by which we perceive animals' moral status (via their capacity for suffering) and the motivational profile that can prompt appropriate action. However, relying on empathy has also come under criticism. Jesse Prinz (2011) notably argues against the view that empathy is integral to moral judgement. Not only is empathy not necessary for moral judgement, it is subject to biases that undermine its moral credibility. Similar concerns have been raised about empathy specifically in the domain of animal ethics and in grounding the moral status of animals. Curtin (2014), for instance, argues that while the capacity to empathize makes morality possible, on its own it is fragile and limited, and susceptible to empathy fatigue.[2] Others, such as Francione (1996) and Harvey (2017), worry that the focus on welfare that can result from grounding moral concern for animals in empathy remains compatible with the utilization of animals for human benefit. Finally, Kasperbauer (2015) draws on empirical research to show that while empathy may play a supporting role in moral concern for animals, there is little support for assigning it a central or necessary role. In light of this demotion of empathy, both Prinz and Kasperbauer advise turning to other emotions such as anger, disgust, guilt, and admiration to ground moral judgement.[3]

In this chapter, I take up this advice and explore the potential for admiration to ground the moral status of animals and to promote their ethical treatment. In particular, I explore the potential of Linda Zagzebski's exemplarist moral theory (2006, 2017) to ground the moral status of admirable animals, and Alfred Archer's Value Promotion Account (forthcoming) of admiration's motivational profile to support the moral treatment of animals. I argue that Zagzebski's view does offer important resources for grounding ethical concern for animals (though this result does not imply replacing the role of empathy). In exploring this potential, I will also raise some issues concerning our understanding of admiration and suggest a modification to Archer's Value Promotion Account.

The chapter will proceed as follows: in section 1, "Admiration," I outline the main features of Zagzebski's exemplarist moral theory, including her characterization of admiration in terms of emulation. This is followed by an introduction to Archer's critique of Zagzebski and alternative Value Promotion Account of admiration's motivational profile. Section 2, "Admiration and Animal Ethics," explores the ways in which admiration can ground the moral status of animals or promote their moral treatment in ways that are conducive to the aims of animal ethics. Finally, section 3, "Revisiting Admiration," revisits the notion of admiration and suggests an important clarification brought to light via consideration of its role in motivating the moral treatment of animals. I conclude with some speculative remarks concerning future research in this area.

ADMIRATION

I begin by introducing two approaches to defining and characterizing admiration. The first, termed the Emulation View, is advanced by Linda Zagzebski as part of her exemplarist moral theory.[4] For Zagzebski, admiration is an important moral sentiment for it both reveals moral value (what is good) and motivates its pursuit.[5] In other words, Zagzebski turns to admiration to answer two fundamental meta-ethical questions, namely "What grounds the moral?" and "Why be moral?" (2006, 53). On the first question, Zagzebski eschews a wholly conceptual grounding for ethics and instead draws on the direct reference approach to defining natural kind terms. For direct reference theorists working in philosophy of language, terms such as *gold* or *water* are defined indexically, that is, water is "whatever is the same liquid as *that*" (2006, 57).[6]

Zagzebski proposes extending this theory to moral concepts where it can define our key terms through the study of exemplars. Exemplars "anchor each moral concept," writes Zagzebski, where "[g]ood persons are persons *like that*, just as gold is stuff like that" (2006, 59). Importantly, we are able to identify exemplars via the experience of admiration, which Zagzebski characterizes minimally as an emotion of imitable attraction (2006, 62) with the "power to move us" (2006, 60). Perceived via admiration, these exemplars "collectively set a standard for the admirable life" (2006, 62).

Zagzebski turns to admiration again to answer the second question, why be moral? She interprets this question as one about the *desirability* of the "good life." She notes first that exemplars not only provide the reference for "good person," but also for the "good life." This is because she thinks our admiration for exemplars is closely tied to our admiration for their exemplary life. Thus, as admiration consists of an imitable attraction, the life of the exemplar, that is, a life that exemplifies a moral virtue or goodness, is desirable. To avoid the problem of exemplars' lives not going well due to bad luck, Zagzebski refines the claim to the idea that the life desired by the admirable person is the desirable life. "A desirable life is a life desired by an admirable person. Admirable persons desire an admirable life, so the admirable is desirable" (2006, 66).

Zagzebski develops this line further in her more recent work (2017) wherein she spells out admiration's role in moral development as tied to admiration's connection with the motivation to *emulate* an exemplar. As Archer notes, Zagzebski previously characterized this connection as a necessary one such that admiration is equated with a desire to emulate the admired. She later weakens the tie, acknowledging that not all instances of admiration will be paired with a desire to emulate. Importantly, she restricts her focus to admiration for acquired excellences, which theoretically could be developed by the admirer, rather than of natural talents, which are impossible for the admirer to develop (via emulation). Moreover, the admirer is motivated to emulate the admired in the respect in which they are admired (2017, 33). For example, if an exemplar is admired for her kindness, the admirer desires to become more kind (Archer, forthcoming, 5). As Zagzebski writes, admiration "gives rise to the motive to emulate the admired person in the way she is admired" (2017, 43). In his analysis of Zagzebski's account, Archer defines the Emulation View as follows: "In prototypical cases of admiration for acquired talents, an agent who experiences admiration will be motivated to try to emulate the object of their admiration in the way in which she is admired" (Archer, forthcoming, 8).

Archer proceeds to level three objections against the Emulation View. These objections aim to show that Zagzebski's approach is overly limited and unduly omits important objects of admiration and variants of its motivational character. First, Archer takes issue with Zagzebski's limited focus on acquired excellences. It seems possible, thinks Archer, to admire non-human animals, landscapes, and works of art (Archer, forthcoming, 9), yet it is difficult to comprehend how one could desire to emulate these objects of admiration. Recognizing these examples as cases of admiration without emulation undermines the idea that emulation is a prototypical feature of admiration. Second, Archer offers further evidence for thinking that admiration (frequently) comes apart from emulation. While Zagzebski thinks this happens only in cases where it is impossible to acquire the admired excellence, Archer thinks this restriction is too strong. He points to examples in which one does not feel motivated to emulate the admired not because doing so is impossible, but because the "way of life [is] quite different from one's own whilst being perfectly happy with the life one is leading" (Archer, forthcoming, 13). For example, I may admire a moral saint and consider it possible to acquire her qualities, but not feel motivated to pursue the life of a moral saint.[7] Third, Archer surveys a range of other motivational responses besides emulation that seem related to admiration. He points to empirical studies that associate admiration with desires to honor or acknowledge the admired (Algoe and Haidt 2009), or to affiliate with them (Schindler et al. 2015).[8] Other responses could include desires to praise the admired, support their cause, or defend or protect them from harm or damage (Archer, forthcoming, 15–16). Archer concludes that while insufficient to reject the connection between emulation and admiration, these objections show that the Emulation View at best describes only some instances of admiration. This result means the Emulation View fails as a general account of admiration that acknowledges its varied objects and motivational responses.

In its place, Archer offers his *Value Promotion Account*. For Archer, admiration is fundamentally a positive evaluation (or appraisal) tied to a desire to promote the admired value(s). He states the account as follows (forthcoming, 20):

> The Value Promotion Account: In prototypical cases of admiration, an agent who experiences admiration will be motivated to promote the value(s) that she admires in the object of their admiration

This account expands the range of admirable objects beyond acquired excellences to include non-human animals, inanimate objects, and natural talents. Moreover, as promoting the admired value can take many forms, including emulation, this account will better accommodate the varied motivational responses seemingly associated with admiration. For example, one may promote a value by trying to develop it in oneself, or one could try to encourage its development in another (Archer, forthcoming, 23).

I intend to draw on two points from the above discussion. The first is Zagzebski's appeal to admiration to ground her meta-ethics and the second is Archer's expanded characterization of admiration. It may be possible, I will argue, to build on these foundations to support additional grounds for animal ethics.

ADMIRATION AND ANIMAL ETHICS

How can *admiration* help ground the moral status of animals, or help guide moral interaction with them? One obvious strategy might be to observe that some of our existing moral exemplars demonstrated concern for non-human animals and desired to live lives that did not inflict suffering on other creatures. Zagzebski mentions Buddha, for instance, as a paradigmatic moral exemplar (2006, 56), a figure widely recognized as one who aspired to prevent animal suffering.[9] Thus, if we admire such figures and take their lives as definitive of the good life, we can consequently derive the goodness of moral concern for animals. This strategy however is disappointingly derivative, grounding moral concern for animals only through admiration for human exemplars. I would like to pursue a more ambitious strategy grounded in the admiration directed towards animals themselves.

Such a strategy is promising in part because there seem to be ample cases of humans admiring animals. Some animals are admired for their aesthetic features, for instance the plumage of a peacock, or for their physical capacities, like the speed of a cheetah. Some have also been admired for exhibiting recognizable moral virtues such as tenacity, bravery, gallantry, devotion, and generosity. For example, in her essay on the depiction of horses in Western films, Jennifer McMahon writes:

> Horses are striking animals. Their fluid elegance, elasticity of movement, and natural grace are captivating. Moreover, in a country where the national symbol could as easily be a horse as an eagle, horses embody other powerful ideals including freedom, grace, and community. To the extent that we aspire to these qualities, we admire horses for having them. (McMahon 2010, 336)

After observing a pack of wolves, renowned naturalist and author Farley Mowat describes one wolf's mothering as "inspirational," and expresses respect for her partner, George, whom he describes as follows:

> His dignity is unassailable, yet he was by no means aloof. Conscientious to a fault, thoughtful of others, and affectionate within reasonable bounds, he was the kind of father whose idealized image appears in many wistful books of human family reminiscences. . . . George was, in brief, the kind of father every son longs to acknowledge as his own. (Mowat 1979, 61)

Moreover, we are familiar with cases of individual animals being formally honored, including dogs used in the military or in the police. The dog Lucca, for example, was awarded the Dickin Medal for her bomb-detection work in Afghanistan, work that cost her one of her legs. She was described as heroic and displaying "conspicuous gallantry and devotion to duty" (Mosbergen 2016).

What can we draw from these expressions of admiration? First, we can further support Archer's claim that a general theory of admiration ought to include admiration of animals. Second, as the above examples indicate, animals can be admired as *moral* exemplars. In her argument for the possibility of friendship with animals, Cynthia Townley similarly recognizes the potential for moral exemplarism in animals:

> Moral exemplars may achieve their influence without reflecting on and verbally recounting what they are doing and why. So animals are not in principle excluded from this role. Our connection to, close observation of, and caring about nonhuman animals can teach us about important values and virtues. Animals exhibit compassion, bravery, and loyalty, as well as joy, tolerance, and forgiveness. . . . We can admire qualities we could share, and those that are beyond us, in other humans and in nonhuman friends. (Townley 2017, 32)

If we return, then, to Zagzebski's claim that exemplars set the meaning of "the good" and of "the good life" and recognize that animals are similarly identified as exemplars via admiration, we can conclude that admirable animals also collectively set the standards of the good. We are looking, though, to ground the moral status of animals, which calls on us to read further into Zagzebski's view: she does not suggest that it is the exemplars themselves who have moral value. However, her comments do suggest there is room to build such a claim. On her view, we point to exemplars as examples of "the good." Moreover, she thinks in pointing to the person, we also implicitly point to their life as an example of "the good life." She writes, "I doubt that we define 'good life' independently of the way we define 'good person'. . . . [a] person is not independent of her life" (Zagzebski 2006, 62). Admirable traits, persons, and lives, then, are interconnected and not neatly separable.[10] Moreover, given Zagzebski's direct theory of reference, exemplars are not merely examples of the good, but are instances of the good. In this way, we must in some sense take the life that exhibits the good to be itself part of the good, including when exhibited by an animal life. Admiration thus seems capable of providing some grounds for including animal lives in our definition of the good and thus as having moral value.

One could argue further that it is precisely that *kind of life* that has moral value. It may be the case that we get only partial glimpses into the nature of courage from a particular exemplar and gain a more complete picture from observing courage in a variety of lives. If so, the particular shape that courage takes in Lucca's life as a dog, for instance, lends specific value to her life in particular.[11] I stress this point in part to help stave off a particular worry about ascribing virtue to animals. This worry is helpfully brought out in John Berger's essay "Why Look at Animals?" Here, Berger tracks the increasing division humans introduce between themselves and other animals, and the gradual receding and marginalization of animals. This is contrasted with an earlier relation wherein humans drew upon observations of animals to characterize the human. He cites, for instance, Aristotle's easy attribution of shared qualities between species:

> [S]o in a number of animals we observe gentleness and fierceness, mildness or cross-temper, courage or timidity, fear or confidence, high spirits or low cunning, and, with regard to intelligence, something akin to sagacity. Some of these qualities in man, as compared with the corresponding qualities in animals, differ only quantitatively. (Berger 1980, 10)

Berger credits Descartes's separation of soul and body and mechanistic view of animals with dealing the decisive blow that divided the human from the animal, and that led to the disappearance of animals from human life (Berger 1980, 11). One result is our modern "uneasiness" with Aristotle's description, which would be criticized today as pejoratively anthropomorphic (Berger 1980, 11). A further result, and one that marks the complete erasure of the animal, is the imposition of human qualities and desires on animals. That is, rather than looking to animals to provide metaphors for understanding the human, "they are being used *en masse* to 'people' situations" (Berger 1980, 19).

Berger's analysis suggests there are two points to note when pursuing this approach to grounding moral value: one is to not balk at ascribing virtues to animals, there is no need to keep these reserved for humans, and the second is to refrain from thinking of virtue in a totalizing, human way. That is, we ought to avoid thinking there is only one form of the virtue, and that form is most ideally expressed in the human. Again, I think this provides additional support for the idea that admirable animals have particular moral value. They exhibit forms of virtue that cannot be reduced to, or subsumed by, the human.

This point could be leveraged to argue for another way in which animal exemplars are valuable. That is, the different ways that they might exhibit or embody a virtue could itself be valuable for prompting critical reflection on our moral systems. As Freya Mathews writes, "Emotional involvement with creatures who do not share our human goals and aspirations, our system of values, enables us to gain an external perspective on those values. It enables us to appreciate how odd or arbitrary our human priorities might appear to non-human observers" (quoted in Townley 2017, 32). Thus, admiration of animals could be instrumentally valuable given the project of revising and reflecting on morality. While potentially fruitful, note that this strategy lends value to animals only derivatively, so I would caution against giving it a central place in the grounding of animal ethics.

I pause here to consider a possible objection. Specifically, one might object that I have not shown that human and animal exemplars necessarily have *equal* moral status. I acknowledge this issue and the dominance of this sentiment in popular thought. Some people may be willing to grant that animals have some moral status, and thus are owed some consideration, but that they do not bear the same moral status as humans and, specifically, they have *less* status such that the duties we owe to animals may be overridden by those we owe to humans. I will not be able to fully deal with this issue here but offer the following as a way to proceed.

I suspect that an account of moral value that incorporates admiration may be more resistant to the idea of allotting more or less status to agents than other approaches, for instance those based on suffering and empathy. There is nothing in Zagzebski's account upon which to build the idea that one exemplar has *more moral status* than another, both simply define the good and the good life. There is room however to feel *more admiration* for one exemplar than another. Rather than greater admiration conferring greater moral status, however, I contend it is better understood in terms of possessing stronger motivation on behalf of the admirer. This could translate into greater desires to emulate, or on Archer's Value Promotion Account, into greater efforts to promote, honor, or defend the admired.

This brings us to the topic of motivation as it relates to the *moral treatment* of animals. While the above may go some way to grounding the moral status of animals, or at least of those whom we admire, more needs to be said about how admiration could lend support for their moral treatment. This could be compared to Zagzebski's "why be moral" question. Recall Zagzebski read this question as asking about the *desirability* of the exemplary life, which she tied to the emulative nature of admiration. But as Archer argued, Zagzebski's characterization of admiration's motivational profile is too narrow. Admiration can be associated with the desire to emulate, but it can also prompt desires to honor, defend, affiliate with, or promote the admired. To my mind, this expansion does not undermine Zagzebski's view, but rather allows us to interpret desirability more broadly. As Archer notes, we may admire a life that we do not want to take up ourselves, or in other words, the admirable life may not be desirable *for me* to live, though I am nevertheless motivated to promote its value in some other way(s). I contend we can retain the idea that admirable lives are desirable, where this can include that it is desirable for me to live that way, but also that it is desirable that there are such lives and that this desire motivates one to promote and support their existence.

If this is correct, then admiration may provide motivational resources for the moral treatment of animals. Admired animals exhibit desirable lives that we are motivated to promote in various ways. Importantly, it seems likely that such promotion would go beyond a simple concern for animal welfare. Protection of an admirable life requires more than basic provision for survival, but conditions that allow such excellences room to develop and be celebrated. For example, admiring a horse's natural grace and community may motivate one to campaign against the keeping horses segregated in box stalls that restrict movement and social interaction. An excellence that could be expressed and enjoyed by others is denied. Such treatment jars against the desire to honor their grace. It may not always be obvious how best to promote an admirable animals' life, in particular because it may not be the same as a human instantiation. This approach thus also demands that admirers carefully and attentively observe animal lives with the aim of learning what the admirable life consists in.

REVISITING ADMIRATION

There are two objections to discuss concerning the above discussion. The first concerns the observation that some excellences are exhibited in moments of danger or adversity. For example, matador Coleman Cooney admires the power of the bullfight, claiming that "a portion of these animals are truly courageous" (Morin 2015), where this courage primarily becomes visible when the fearful bull is brought in to a ring to be killed. Or, Lucca's celebrated gallantry was evidenced in her response to the dangerous and traumatic situation of war. It seems a failure of the account if admiring animals was compatible with, and even called for this sort of treatment. That is, there is reason to reject the view if to promote these virtues, we must subject animals to trauma, abuse, and death. In response, I note that admiring the animal lives that exhibit virtue does not require that we ought to create challenges and traumas to provide opportunities to exemplify courage and resilience. As Archer notes (forthcoming, 20), admiration does not call for *maximizing* the admired value. So, honoring or promoting courage does not entail creating situations that call for courage. Moreover, recall Zagzebski's observation that the actual life of an exemplar may, for reasons of bad luck, fail to be a flourishing life (2006, 62). This is why she distinguishes between the desirability of the exemplar's actual life, and the desirability of the life that the exemplar desires, meaning the life she would want to be able to lead and through which to express her excellences. The same move can be made in the case of animal exemplars. We are motivated to promote the life the animal would want rather than the life they may happen to have. This leads to stronger demands for moral treatment and precludes many of the uses to which animals are currently put. It would certainly preclude activities such as bullfighting, which co-opts the language of admiration without taking note of the life the admired would like to live.

The second objection takes issue with how the above discussion on desirability is framed. Specifically, the discussion concerns the desirability of *lives* which are then the subject of honor and promotion. Archer's Value Promotion Account, however, which allowed us to attribute a wider motivational profile to admiration, is cast in terms of promoting *values*. That is, it is the values you admire *of* a person or animal that you are motivated to promote. This shift in focus could cause problems for my account and current project. Specifically, as stated, it seems possible to admire and promote a particular value independently of its exemplar. For example, one could in principle admire Lucca's gallantry and work to promote *gallantry* without promoting or honoring *Lucca*. Lucca merely provides the form for gallantry to be observed. This separability is likely overlooked when focused on cases of admiring humans, but its problematic implications become distinctly salient in the case of animals. This is because we are readily familiar with this very strategy and the worrisome actions it enables. That is, some ascriptions of admiring animals come paired with distinctly unethical treatment or non-promotion of animal lives. For instance, trophy hunters may celebrate the strength and power of the lion or cunning of the fox and thus describe hunting as promoting these values, but as removed from their animal lives.[12]

One first response might be to insist that these cases are better described as examples of envy rather than admiration. Envy describes a negative reaction to others' excellences and can motivate one to try to "level-down" (Schindler et al. 2013, 104). While I do not doubt that some cases of trophy hunters who profess admiration may in fact be cases of envy, more needs to be said to clarify the difference and, in so doing, solidify an important aspect of admiration.

As just mentioned, envy is taken to reflect the desire to respond to one's perceived inferiority by bringing the other down, that is, losing their enviable excellence. This is contrasted with admiration wherein one's inferiority motivates one to self-improve and thus "level-up." But on Archer's Value Promotion Account, admiration need not necessarily motivate self-improvement, but only some desire to promote the admired value. It seems possible, therefore, to imagine that some fox hunters find they can promote the value of cunning and stamina through preservation of the fox hunt, which does not require preservation of the specific fox and thus satisfy Archer's definition of admiration.[13] How can this result be avoided?

I suggest that self-improvement accounts of admiration and Archer's Value Promotion Account problematically underplay its relational dimension. When considering envy, the relation between the excellence and the other remains at the fore; it matters *where* the excellence lies, that is, in the other (and not in me). But this relation seemingly, and wrongly to my mind, drops out of our idea of admiration. This is particularly so for Archer's Value Promotion Account. In focusing on values rather than lives, Archer's view loses track of where the excellence lies, and that admiration ought to promote its *located* value. However, this relation between a virtue and its location seems fundamentally important, precisely to avoid such problematic results. This point holds for human exemplars and inanimate objects as well: it would seem odd to admire Confucius for his sagacity, and yet feel that it did not matter that sagacity was part of Confucius.[14] Or, to draw on an example from Archer, it would seem strange for William Wordsworth to admire the English Lake District (Archer, forthcoming, 16) for its beauty and yet feel it did not matter that such beauty took *that* particular form. There is a sense in which it is important that the beauty is of the Lake District, and Wordsworth is motivated to protect its specific instance rather than the ideal of beauty in other forms.[15] Recognizing the locatedness of a value matters is thus an important dimension of admiration. I think such recognition is compatible with the Value Promotion Account, though does call for its reformulation. I propose the following as an initial attempt to reformulate the view:

> *The Located Value Promotion Account*: In prototypical case of admiration, an agent who experiences admiration will be motivated to (1) promote the value(s) that she admires in the object of her admiration (2) in ways that are compatible with admiring the object itself.

This formulation retains the expanded characterization of admiration's motivational profile (i.e., to include diverse ways of promoting a value) but aims to preclude the problematic separation of value and object. Moreover, this revised notion provides resources for rejecting the trophy hunter, the matador, and the fox hunter's claims to admire their quarry. Lacking concern for the location of courage, strength, and cunning in their animal forms, their sentiments cannot be described as admiration. This is a useful result for clarifying the nature of admiration, but also for providing grounds for discrediting appeals to admiration as a way to humanize or elevate their actions.

CONCLUSION

I have explored some of the initial resources that admiration offers for grounding key notions in animal ethics. I argued that if you accept Zagzebski's exemplarist moral theory and her application of the direct theory of reference to moral terms, it is possible to partly ground the moral status of admirable animals. As with human exemplars, admirable animals constitute instances of "the good" and of "the good life" and are thus imbued with foundational moral status. I also argued that admiration could provide the motivation for treating animals well. I drew on Zagzebski's claim that the admirable life is desirable in virtue of admiration's power to provoke emulation. I then incorporated Archer's broader account of admiration's motivational profile to argue that the admirable life is indeed desirable, though its desirability can provoke other forms of value promotion besides emulation. Thus, we can assert that an admirable life is desirable and that we desire to promote it, without it being the case that the life must be desirable *for me*.

Finally, I explored two objections to my analysis, both of which dealt with the question of whether admiring animals might be compatible with immoral treatment. In responding to these objections, I offered a modification to Archer's Value Promotion Account to better keep the location of a virtue at the fore. In this way, we can avoid the separation strategy that permits the promotion of value independently of the animal life.

In addition to the above analysis, appealing to admiration does promise to avoid or mitigate two of the worries associated with building an ethical approach on the basis of empathy. First, it not obvious that our capacity to admire is limited in the same way that empathy may be. It is unclear, in other words, that admiration will be susceptible to something like "admiration-fatigue." Importantly, admiration is cast as a positive emotion, whereas empathizing may provoke negative feelings or suffering in the empathizer. While the weight of caring about numerous others may prove to be overwhelming and thus unable to reliably ground animal ethics, the inspirational dimension of admiration seems capable of expanding our ethics without the cost.

This chapter, however, does not represent a full examination of admiration's potential contribution to animal ethics, nor a complete review of how thinking about animals might call for revisions to our understanding of admiration. More empirical work needs to be done on the experience of admiring animals, as well as a broader survey of philosophical approaches to admiration and meta-ethics. Moreover, I do not claim that the above provides full and complete grounds for animals' moral status. There are problems with relying on admiration for animal ethics, in particular, that not all animals are considered admirable (e.g., rats, spiders, snakes, etc.). Consequently, this approach ought to be coupled with existing theories that appeal to empathy or compassion. There may also be reasons for trying to promote or develop capacities for admiring animals. Deane Curtin (2014), for instance, introduces a distinction between emotions (as basic cognitive judgements and motivations) and feelings that are cultivated, reflective emotions and mark "the paradigm in human experience of the integration of reason and feeling, thinking and doing" (46). There may be potential in exploring how this distinction could apply here and support the idea of a cultivated feeling of admiration.

NOTES

1. I have chosen to use the term "animal" in this chapter for simplicity (rather than nonhuman animal) but this choice should not be taken to imply any substantive notions on differences between humans and other nonhuman animals, nor as dismissive of the impact language can have in these debates.

2. Curtin argues that our natural capacity for empathy can be cultivated into compassion, which is a more mature moral capability that better grounds moral practice (2014, 44–45).

3. Kasperbauer (2015) suggests moral concern for animals is more productively grounded in anger, while Prinz (2011) points towards guilt, anger, disgust, and admiration as alternative foundations for moral judgement.
4. See Zagzebski 2017. The term "Emulation View" is drawn from Archer's (forthcoming) analysis of Zagzebski's position.
5. See Zagzebski (2017, 31–32; 2006).
6. Zagzebski refers here to Kripke, Putnam, and Donnellan (2006, 57) as proponents of the direct reference theory.
7. Archer refers to Susan Wolf's work on moral saints to support this point (forthcoming, 14).
8. For further support, see Schindler et al. (2013) who show that admiration is associated with a number of motivational desires including desires to praise, credit, or honor those exhibiting the admired ideal, as well as to affiliate with the admired, and internalize or imitate the ideal. Importantly, Schindler et al. note that the desire to emulate need not focus on the specific admirable act, but can extend to "wanting to do good deeds or to excel more generally" (2013, 104). Moreover, they associate admiration with the desire to pursue long-term development rather than "immediate behaviour change" or internalization understood as "firm commitment to or increased valuation of an ideal" (2013, 105).
9. Zagzebski also mentions the Dalai Lama (a noted vegetarian) as an exemplar (2017, p. 19, 35).
10. I acknowledge others will disagree on this point, that is whether admiration is a globalist emotion (i.e., directed at the person as a whole), or is directed at specific, divisible traits. I will not settle this debate here, though agree this issue does relate to the general point I am gesturing at. However, my purpose here is to explore the potential of Zagzebski's account, and to that end, I maintain that such a claim is compatible with her position. See Calhoun (2011) for more on globalist attitudes including admiration.
11. This point suggests there may be epistemic value to observing a variety of lives, including animal lives. I will not develop this thought further here, but reiterate the focus on the moral value of this variety.
12. See for instance Marvin (2003) who records fox-hunters' admiration for foxes including for their "skills of deception . . . and for their bravery, strength, drive and stamina when under pressure" (2003, 55–56).
13. I am assuming for the sake of argument that the fox hunters are honestly reporting on their emotions and not falsely claiming to experience admiration for the fox's cunning.
14. Confucius is another of Zagzebski's (2017) paradigmatic "sage" type exemplars.
15. He may also be motivated to protect beauty in general, but it would seem odd if he was motivated to protect the general ideal but not the specific Lake District.

REFERENCES

Algoe, S. B., and J. Haidt. 2009. "Witnessing Excellence in Action: The 'Other-Praising' Emotions of Elevation, Gratitude, and Admiration." *The Journal of Positive Psychology* 4 (2): 105–27.
Archer, A. Forthcoming. "Admiration and Motivation." *Emotion Review*. DOI:10.1177/1754073918787235.
Berger, J. 1980. "Why Look at Animals?" In *About Looking*, 1–28. New York: Pantheon.
Calhoun, C. 2011. "Globalist Attitudes and the Fittingness Objection." *The Philosophical Quarterly* 61 (244): 449–72.
Curtin, D. 2014. "Compassion and Being Human." In *Ecofeminism: Feminist Intersections with Other Animals and the Earth*, edited by Carol J. Adams and Lori Gruen, 39–57. New York: Bloomsbury.
Francione, Gary. 1996. "Animals as Property." *Animal Law* 2: i–vi.
Freeman, Dan, Karl Aquino, and Brent McFerran. 2009. "Overcoming Beneficiary Race as an Impediment to Charitable Donations: Social Dominance Orientation, the Experience of

Moral Elevation, and Donation Behavior." *Personality and Social Psychology Bulletin* 35: 72–84.
Harvey, J. 2017. "Companion and Assistance Animals: Benefits, Welfare Safeguards, and Relationships." In *Pets and People: The Ethics of Our Relationships with Companion Animals*, edited by Christine Overall, 3–20. New York: Oxford University Press.
Kasperbauer, T. J. 2015. "Rejecting Empathy for Animal Ethics." *Ethical Theory and Moral Practice* 18 (4): 817–33.
Marvin, G. 2003. "A Passionate Pursuit: Foxhunting as Performance." *The Sociological Review* 51(2): 46–60.
McMahon, J. 2010. "Beating a Live Horse: The Elevation and Degradation of Horses in Westerns." In *The Philosophy of the Western*, edited by Jennifer McMahon and Steve Csaki, 329–50. Lexington: University Press of Kentucky.
Morin, R. 2015. "The Beauty and Moral Ambiguity of Bullfighting." *Vice*, February 6, 2015. Accessed September 3, 2018: https://www.vice.com/en_us/article/gq87ax/the-exquisite-moral-ambiguity-of-bullfighting-205.
Mosbergen, D. 2016. "Lucca, Hero Marine Dog Who Lost Her Leg in Afghanistan, Awarded Top Honor for Valor." *Huffington Post*, June 4, 2016. Accessed on October 1, 2018: https://www.huffingtonpost.com/entry/lucca-hero-military-dog-dickin-medal_us_57048c0ce4b0b90ac2709fa9.
Mowat, F. 1979. *Never Cry Wolf*. New York: Bantam.
Prinz, Jesse. 2011. "Against Empathy." *The Southern Journal of Philosophy* 49 (September): 214–33.
Schindler, I., J. Paech, and F. Löwenbrück. 2015. "Linking Admiration and Adoration to Self Expansion: Different Ways to Enhance One's Potential." *Cognition and Emotion* 29 (2): 292–310.
Schindler, I., V. Zink, J. Windrich, and W. Menninghaus. 2013. "Admiration and Adoration: Their Different Ways of Showing and Shaping Who We Are." *Cognition and Emotion* 27 (1): 85–118.
Townley, C. 2017. "Friendship with Companion Animals." In *Pets and People: The Ethics of Our Relationships with Companion Animals*, edited by Christine Overall, 21–34. New York: Oxford University Press.
Zagzebski, L. T. 2006. "The Admirable Life and the Desirable Life." In *Values and Virtues: Aristotelianism in Contemporary Ethics*, edited by Timothy Chappell, 53–66. Oxford: Oxford University Press.
———. 2017. *Exemplarist Moral Theory*. Oxford: Oxford University Press.

Part IV

Admiration and Moral Education

Chapter Eleven

Is It Morally Good to Admire?

Psychological Perspectives on the Potentials and Limits of Admiration and Elevation

Ines Schindler

> [E]very thing is useful which contributes to fix us in the principles and practice of virtue. When any signal act of charity or of gratitude, for instance, is presented either to our sight or imagination, we are deeply impressed with its beauty and feel a strong desire in ourselves of doing charitable and grateful acts also. . . . Now every emotion of this kind is an exercise of our virtuous dispositions; and dispositions of the mind, like limbs of the body, acquire strength by exercise. But exercise produces habit; and in the instance of which we speak, the exercise being of the moral feelings, produces a habit of thinking and acting virtuously.
> (Jefferson 1771)

This quote by Thomas Jefferson repeatedly has been cited to point to the uplifting powers of witnessing virtuous behavior and the associated emotion that Jonathan Haidt called "moral elevation" (in short "elevation") to separate it from other instances of admiration (Haidt 2003a; Pohling and Diessner 2016; Thomson and Siegel 2017). While psychologists have conducted several studies on elevation, the fact that Jefferson was referring to the emotional effects of great fiction, which he considered to be as powerful as those of real episodes, has not been discussed in much detail (but see Aquino, McFerran, and Laven 2011; Palmer et al. 2013).

Taking this quote as a point of departure, I will first provide an overview of two lines of research on admiration within psychology. Subsequently, I will discuss the potentials and limits of admiration and elevation and the associated question of whether both qualify as moral emotions. I will further offer some thoughts on why stories might be even more potent elicitors of admiration and elevation than personal encounters with exemplars.

TWO LINES OF RESEARCH ON ADMIRATION: ADMIRATION FOR SKILL AND ELEVATION

There are two uses of the term "admiration" in the psychological literature. First, the term can refer to all instances of admiration regardless of their elicitor (see review by Schindler, Zink, Windrich, and Menninghaus 2013). Second, "admiration" can refer to admiration for skill (see review by Onu, Kessler, and Smith 2016) as distinguished from elevation, defined as admiration for virtue (see reviews by Pohling and Diessner 2016; Thomson and Siegel 2017). In the following, I will use "admiration" in the first, encompassing sense and refer to admiration for skill and elevation when this distinction is important to make.

Research on admiration and admiration for skill has focused on its role in social learning, social comparison, and intergroup relations and behavior (cf. Onu et al. 2016; Schindler et al. 2013). Elevation is one of the emotions at the focus of the positive psychology movement and is considered as important to explaining human morality (e.g., Haidt 2003a; Pohling and Diessner 2016; Thomson and Siegel 2017).

COMMONALITIES AND DIFFERENCES OF ADMIRATION FOR SKILL AND ELEVATION

All instances of admiration are positive affective responses to witnessing excellence in another person. She or he intentionally represents an ideal or value, which is of personal importance to the observer, through a specific action or characteristic. The observer appraises it as rare to see this ideal or value embodied in such an outstanding way, but nevertheless as a signal that it is possible to live up to it. Associated subjective feelings include appreciation and liking of the target person, wonder, and inspiration. There still is a dearth of studies on objectively measured physiological responses during admiration. Self-reports of chills/goosebumps have been obtained for both admiration for skill and elevation (Algoe and Haidt 2009); other candidates for bodily symptoms common to all instances of admiration include self-reported increased heart rate and feelings of warmth in the chest. Admiration has both interpersonal and personal consequences. The admiring individual seeks to praise, affiliate with, and cooperate with the admired other. The admiring individual further desires to uphold and to strive for the embodied ideal, promoting the internalization of ideals and the emulation of the admired other.

Differences between admiration for skill and elevation are closely linked to the emotions' different elicitors. As people might feel intimidated by another's superior talent,[1] the cognitive appraisals giving rise to admiration for skill have been spelled out in greater detail than appraisals characteristic of elevation. As I will discuss in a subsequent section, admiration depends on perceptions of legitimacy of the other's superiority and absence of direct competition. Studies on the consequences of admiration have focused on emulation, personal growth, and self-expansion (Schindler 2014; Schindler, Paech, and Löwenbrück 2015; Van de Ven 2017). Intergroup admiration was studied as an emotion that helps people to accept the social order (Sweetman et al. 2013) or to benefit from an out-group (Onu, Smith, and Kessler 2015).

Research on elevation mainly focused on demonstrating its prosocial effects and associated subjective feelings and bodily symptoms. Reports of feeling uplifted, moved, or touched as well as warm, open feelings in the chest, a lump in the throat, moist eyes, and actual shedding of tears (e.g., Algoe and Haidt 2009; Aquino et al. 2011) are much more frequent in or even limited to the literature on elevation as compared with admiration for skill. Several studies have reported evidence of prosocial consequences of elevation (cf. Pohling and Diessner 2016; Thomas and Siegel 2017).

CLASSIFICATION OF ADMIRATION FOR SKILL AND ELEVATION AS MORAL AND SELF-TRANSCENDENT EMOTIONS

It might be surprising that *both* admiration (in general and when limited to skill) and elevation have been considered as "other-praising moral emotions" (Algoe and Haidt 2009; Haidt 2003a, 2003b) or "self-transcendent emotions" (Shiota, Thrash, Danvers, and Dombrowski 2014; Stellar et al. 2017). Given these classifications, it seems that all instances of admiration are moral emotions.

However, the designation of admiration (for skill) as a moral emotion sometimes rests on a rather general understanding of what makes an emotion moral. For instance, if moral emotions are defined as emotions that are considered "right" rather than "wrong" to have (cf. Weiner 2007), admiration is a moral emotion insofar as it is directed at a target worthy of admiration. Similarly, if one adopts a broad notion of self-transcendence (cf. Shiota et al. 2014), every emotion that responds positively to something that exceeds one's expectations or prior knowledge is self-transcendent.

More narrow conceptualizations of moral and self-transcendent emotions focus on the respective emotions' action tendencies (the intentions and actions they motivate). An emotion can be considered as a prototypical moral emotion to the degree that it makes the individual want to benefit others, care about others' welfare, or uphold the social order. Haidt offered a preliminary definition of moral emotions as "those emotions that are linked to the interests or welfare either of society as a whole or at least of persons other than the judge or agent" (Haidt 2003b, 853). Similarly, the motivation to enhance others' welfare is central to self-transcendent emotions, which ultimately function to bind individuals together and to reduce self-interested motivations (Stellar et al. 2017). When addressing the question of whether admiration is morally good, I will adopt these more narrow definitions of moral/self-transcendent emotions.

Importantly, these definitions rest on the emotion's action tendency and associated intentions. It is well possible that the individual ends up not acting on her or his intention or that the actions taken do not lead to the desired outcomes—good intentions do not necessarily lead to good outcomes. Alternatively, a person may be motivated by selfish concerns but still her or his actions may benefit others (e.g., a scientist who is motivated by a desire for prestige discovers a new medicine that will save the lives of many people). While these issues are important and can make it tricky to judge the morality of certain actions and outcomes, they are not relevant to defining moral emotions. A person can be considered as having a moral emotion to the extent that this emotion makes her or him want to act prosocially, care for others, or otherwise uphold the social order or conform to social norms.

WHEN, WHAT, WHAT FOR, AND FOR WHOM: POTENTIALS AND LIMITS OF ADMIRATION

In light of the central function of admiration—the social transmission of ideals and values—it is noteworthy that psychologists have largely neglected it as an emotion that plays a role in education (see Weiner 2007). In contrast, some philosophers have pointed to the usefulness of admiration and the associated desire to emulate for moral education (Croce and Vaccarezza 2017; Engelen, Thomas, Archer, and van de Ven 2018; Kristjánsson 2006; Zagzebski 2017).

Current psychological research on admiration further is limited to adults, which contrasts with the beginnings of empirical research on admiration. In 1919, Moore published probably the first large-scale study on children's admiration (Moore 1919). This research ties in with a line of research on children's ideals that started around 1900 (see Hawkes 1973). The major conclusions of these studies were that children with increasing age were less likely to nominate admired/ideal persons from their immediate environment (e.g., parents, other relatives, teachers) and more likely to select persons from the remote environment (e.g., historic and public persons, literary characters). The reasons for their nominations included bravery, goodness, kindness, power, possessions, cleverness, and prettiness (Hawkes 1973; Moore 1919). These findings already revealed that the targets of and reasons for admiration change with age (and historical time) and show considerable variation in terms of whether they would be considered as worthy of admiration from a moral standpoint. Starting with the question of when an individual is likely to experience admiration, I will now discuss moral implications of admiration and elevation.

When Do People Admire Others?

The social comparison literature has highlighted that exposure to excellence in others, that is, an upward social comparison, can have positive or negative effects (e.g., Lockwood and Kunda 1997; Monin 2007; Smith 2000). The resulting comparison-based emotions include admiration, inspiration, and optimism but also envy, resentment, and shame (Smith 2000).

Elicitors of Admiration Rather Than Envy

Admiration only results if another's excellence does not pose a potential threat to the observer's goals, resources, reputation, or positive self-regard (cf. Schindler et al. 2013). The other's superior outcomes or standing need to be appraised as deserved and legitimate (see also Onu et al. 2015). Furthermore, the person must perceive her- or himself as able to uphold the admired ideal or value in the future (cf. Schindler et al. 2013).

If these criteria are not met, the observer will likely envy and resent the other. Here, it is important to consider the distinction between malicious and benign envy (e.g., Crusius and Lange 2014; Van de Ven 2017; Van de Ven, Zeelenberg, and Pieters 2011). Both kinds of envy feel negative, but only malicious envy involves feelings of resentment and hostility towards the superior other and the motivation to pull her or him down to one's inferior level. In contrast, benign envy motivates the envious individual to pull her- or himself up to the level of the envied other, who is perceived to deserve her or his superior status. While benign envy feels frustrating, it helps increase attention to means for self-improvement (Crusius and Lange 2014) and motivates emulation of the envied other (Van de Ven 2017; Van de Ven et al. 2011).

Both benign envy and admiration thus are potential means to foster personal growth and depend on perceiving some similarity between one's potential future self and the other person. This perception is facilitated by comparing to someone who is supposed to be doing much better than oneself because of her or his greater experience and expertise. Children and novices in a specific discipline or profession, therefore, are in an optimal position to benefit from contact with exemplary role models. Initial evidence showed that admiration in the work sector was related to younger age and to less work experience (Botthof 2017). In our own study (cf. Schindler 2014; Schindler et al. 2015), we similarly found that the frequency of admiration decreased a little with increasing age across adulthood.

Experiencing admiration might become less likely for individuals who are grown up or highly advanced in a discipline or profession. Others excelling in domains central to oneself now might more readily elicit benign or even malicious envy. In contrast, admiration might be triggered most easily by excellence in domains that are not highly important to oneself, that is, domains which the person cares about but in which she or he does not have personal aspirations. Accordingly, there may be some developmental changes in admiration. During childhood it possibly starts out as an emotion driving the emulation of specific actions and ways of conduct of admired others within one's immediate social context (such as parents, siblings, and other relatives) that increasingly extends to outstanding role models in more remote social contexts. Admiration might also show developmental changes in its primary function from the social transmission of specific skills to the transmission of more encompassing and abstract values and ideals.

Exposure to Admirable Others as a Means of Education

The above considerations raise the question of whether educators should present students with excellent role models to induce admiration. The problem here is that it is possible to create situations, but impossible to exactly determine the emotions that individuals will feel in these situations. When the comparison with an admirable other lets the observer come off badly and the observer further sees no way to improve her or his own standing, what should have been an opportunity for admiration might turn out to be an elicitor of malicious envy. Even if the other person "objectively" deserves her or his superior status, the frustration evoked through being confronted with this person will likely make the observer seek to maintain a positive self-image by perceiving the other's status as undeserved. While this possibility has been considered for admiration for skill, it was largely ignored for elevation. This might be explained by a focus on envy as the most likely alternative to admiration. Who would truly be envious of the person sacrificing her or his own interest for someone else?

While not conducive to envy, unflattering comparisons in the moral domain nevertheless are highly problematic and painful. A series of studies showed that involvement in a morally relevant situation influenced how participants reacted to moral rebels (Monin, Sawyer, and Marquez 2008). If the behavior of a moral exemplar casts doubt on one's own morality, individuals will likely deny the virtue of the exemplar, trivialize the exemplar's moral behavior, or resent the exemplar (see also Cramwinckel and Monin, this volume; Monin 2007).

The resulting difficulty with trying to induce admiration for educational purposes is to present an admirable other who is relevant to observers and thus emotionally engaging, but who does not invite an explicit social comparison with the observers' current standing and behavior. One way to accomplish this is using examples of historical and fictitious persons presented in literature and film and other expressions of values in artworks (see, e.g., Engelen et al. 2018; Diessner et al. 2013; Smith and Smith 1970). Smith and Smith even maintained that "[i]t is the function of art, then, to make values vivid and persuasive as no other medium can" (Smith and Smith 1970, 49). This, however, raises the question of which values should be represented.

What Do People Admire?

In an online survey, we asked German adults to write down whom they admire (and whom they adore) and why they do so (Dubbel 2012; Schindler 2015). The most frequent reasons given for admiration were the other's competence/performance (e.g., skill, talent, mastery, and productivity), self-determination/self-regulation (e.g., perseverance, adaptability, ambition, and conscientiousness), and prosocial behavior/social virtues (e.g., altruism, helpfulness, generosity, and being a good person). A study comparing young adults from the United Kingdom, Iran, China, and Russia identified care/generativity, resilience/positivity, drive/determination, and intellect/education as the most frequent reasons for admiration (Robinson et al. 2016). Both studies thus show that admiration can be triggered by a broad range of values and ideals explicating the themes of skill and virtue.

Participants of our study subsequently did a longitudinal study for which they selected one target person whom they admire, adore, or hold in esteem (cf. Schindler 2014; Schindler et al. 2015). We were interested in the values participants associated with their target person and in participants' own values. Drawing on Shalom Schwartz's theory of basic human values (e.g., Schwartz et al. 2012), we studied values as trans-situational goals that serve as guiding principles in a person's life. Multiple values can be relevant to a single decision or action, some of which are compatible with each other and others' conflict. The relative importance of one value in comparison with other values that also are relevant in a situation guides actions. Within Schwartz's theory, values are organized in a circular structure that shows the pattern of relations among values, with values adjacent on the circle being congruent and values in opposing positions being in conflict. Schwartz further identified bipolar dimensions underlying the ordering of the values around the circle. One dimension distinguishes values with a personal focus (emphasizing concern with outcomes for oneself, i.e., self-direction, stimulation, hedonism, achievement, power, face, and personal security) and values with a social focus (emphasizing concern with outcomes for others, i.e., universalism, benevolence, humility, conformity, tradition, and societal security). Another more narrowly defined dimension contrasts self-enhancement (achievement and power) and self-transcendence (benevolence and universalism) values.

Admiration for skill most likely is linked to expressions of achievement and self-direction values, while elevation is linked to expressions of benevolence and universalism values. To study such associations, we asked participants to report on the frequency of feeling admiration (in general and for the target person), their own values, and the values their target person stands for (Schindler 2015). The results revealed overall value correspondence: if participants endorsed a value, they were more likely to also associate this value with their target person. We further found linkages between reasons for admiration participants had provided online prior to the longitudinal study and their value ratings for the target person. Participants associated values with their target person that match their reasons for admiration (Schindler 2015). For instance, if a participant had reported to admire prosocial behavior/social virtues, she or he perceived the target person to stand for benevolence values. In contrast, adoration of the target person was linked to associating this target person with social values (benevolence, tradition, and conformity), irrespective of the reasons provided for adoration. Moreover, adoration—but not admiration—was related to the overall correspondence between one's own and the target person's values: the values of participants who reported greater adoration of their target person showed greater alignment with the values of this target person. In line with our theorizing (Schindler et al. 2013), adored others thus were perceived as benefactors whose meaning-making system and associated values participants shared. In contrast, values associated with admired others did not necessarily have a social focus, and admiration of the target person did not lead to global alignment of one's own with the target person's values.

When looking at participants' own values, admiration (in general) was related to achievement, benevolence, and universalism values. Studies on dispositional elevation showed that elevation is associated with benevolence and universalism values, increased cognitive access to one's moral identity, agreeableness (in particular its facets altruism and tender-mindedness), and empathic concern (Diessner et al. 2013; Martínez-Martí, Hernández-Lloreda, and Avia 2016). Dispositional elevation further longitudinally predicted higher levels of moral identity internalization (i.e., greater importance of and desire for being a moral person; Pohling, Diessner, and Strobel 2017). Achievement values were unrelated to elevation, suggesting that the link between admiration and valuing achievement is accounted for by admiration for skill. This matches with the finding that inducing elevation led to desiring to be a better person and to do good for others, whereas inducing admiration for skill led to desiring personal success (Algoe and Haidt 2009).

What Is Admiration Good For?

In determining the functions of admiration, we found it helpful to compare it with adoration (also referred to as veneration, reverence, and worship; Schindler et al. 2013; Schindler et al. 2015). Both emotions are elicited by witnessing excellence, yet "admiration means to wonder at and try to figure out how excellence can be accomplished, whereas adoration means to relate to excellence that is beyond accomplishment and understanding" (Schindler et al. 2013, 110). Admired others show that it is possible to embody an ideal and how this can be done, whereas adored others represent an ideal state of being that others cannot accomplish themselves but share in and benefit from.[2]

Admiration Increases the Desire to Emulate Ideals Rather Than Idols

Based on this distinction between admiration and adoration, we argued that admiration has a selective influence. It leads to the internalization and emulation of a specific value or ideal represented by the admired other. This selective influence of admiration should help avoid uncritical conformity as a potential negative effect of role-model education. Students should learn to value and emulate a specific ideal embodied in a person rather than the person him- or herself (Kristjánsson 2006).

In contrast, adoration makes the adoring individual holistically internalize the set of values, ideals, and expectations that are attributed to the adored other. The previously reported finding of greater alignment between one's own values and those of a target person with greater adoration of the target person (Schindler 2015) matches this characterization. When others are adored, they become idols rather than models and exemplars. Rather than aspiring to become more like the other and to uphold the same value or ideal, adoring individuals seek to become adherents by affiliating with the adored other, the group of her or his followers, and their shared meaning-making system. Accordingly, we found that admiration and adoration were linked to self-expansion (i.e., increased potential efficacy due to the acquisition of perspectives, identities, and resources that facilitate pursuit of any goal that might arise) through different pathways: the link between admiration and self-expansion was mediated through emulation, whereas the link between adoration and self-expansion was mediated through affiliation (Schindler et al. 2015).

Overall, adoration likely is more effective than admiration when the goal is to achieve maximum social cohesion within a community. However, when the goal is to transmit a specific value or ideal through role-model education, admiration is much better suited than adoration. Admiration is easier to elicit and its effects are easier to anticipate and control, as they likely are limited to a specific value seen in the admired other. Nevertheless, this also raises the question of whether the benefits of exposure to admirable others in education will be evident in students' behavior. As stated by Bardi and Schwartz, "Unless there is a clear link between values and behavior, there is little point to efforts to establish and change values in daily conducts, such as in education and the mass media" (Bardi and Schwartz 2003, 1207).

Admiration Motivates Commitment to Values and Ideals Rather Than Immediate Action

Probably one of the most controversial issues in the literature on elevation and admiration concerns the question of whether these emotions motivate immediate action. While Algoe and Haidt suggested that elevation "may not lead to immediate altruistic action when such action is difficult" (2009, 124), Pohling and Diessner concluded that "elevation indeed does prompt immediate prosocial behavior" (2016, 414). This conclusion was based on findings linking elevation to the behavioral activation system (BAS; Van de Vyver and Abrams 2017) and the suggestion that feelings of elevation provide the motivational impetus to act on one's salient values (Schnall and Roper 2012). Moreover, some studies have shown that elevation leads to actual prosocial behavior (rather than prosocial intentions and attitudes), such as volunteering and charitable donations (for overviews see Pohling and Diessner 2016; Thomson and Siegel 2017). However, even if elevation predicts behavior in some situations, this does not mean that it primarily functions to spur action.

I will extend our previous argument that admiration serves to induce commitment to values (Schindler et al. 2013; Schindler et al. 2015) by characterizing this emotion as *abstract*. Emotion-eliciting events and the associated actions can be mentally construed on different levels of abstraction. These range from a concrete representation of details of the situation and specific acts to an abstract representation of the general meaning of the situation and actions. According to construal level theory (CLT; Trope and Liberman 2010), level of abstraction is linked to psychological distance (defined as the subjective experience that something is far away from the self in the "here and now"): mental construals become more abstract as psychological distance increases. This means that a low-level construal of an emotion-eliciting event ensues from little psychological distance from the event (it happens to me right here and now), while a high-level construal of an emotion-eliciting event ensues from greater psychological distance.

Admiration requires psychological distance: it is elicited by witnessing the actions of another person, who is dissimilar to oneself in some important way (social distance). Moreover, the admired actions often have taken place in the past (temporal distance), in another place (spatial distance), or even are fictitious (distance dimension of hypotheticality). Moreover, Linda Zagzebski has argued that when we say we admire *that*, "what we mean to be designating is not the acts themselves but whatever it is about the person that leads her to do such acts" (Zagzebski 2017, 60). That is, the observable acts serve as a basis to derive conclusions about some abstract aspect of the psychology of the admired person.

Assuming that psychological distance enables admiration, it is likely that not only the emotion-eliciting event but also the resulting states of action readiness will be construed on a high level of abstraction. This high-level construal contains information about an action's general importance and meaning and includes high-level goals such as values and ideals (e.g., McGregor et al. 2010; Trope and Liberman 2010; Vallacher and Wegner 1987). While conducive to reinforcing values, this abstract construal might simultaneously distract from specific actions that could be taken to exemplify these values. There is a tradeoff between meaning and manageability (cf. McGregor and Little 1998; Vallacher and Wegner 1987) such that individuals experience the eliciting situation of admiration as highly meaningful, but do not readily see how this apprehended meaning should inform their current behavior.

This problem was already discussed in 1927 by Werrett Wallace Charters, who viewed presenting abstract ideals through the lives and actions of persons portrayed in stories, songs, or pictures as a potent educational mean to arouse the desire for ideals (in part through the released emotions characterized as feeling touched, emotional warmth, and thrills). However, he also recognized that "[f]or those who have the ability to apply principles to specific situations the story is very useful in presenting general lines of conduct; but . . . this is an extremely difficult task for all children and most adults to perform with frequency" (Charters 1927, 282). Indeed, research has shown that children have difficulty abstracting principles from stories and films and are unlikely to be influenced by appeals to abstract principles (cf. Mares, Palmer, and Sullivan 2008). Thus, "outside of the restricted group of the abstract-minded" (Charters 1927, 284), it is important to make the moral of a story explicit and to apply it to specific situations (see also Mares et al. 2008).

It is now possible to reconsider the study by Van de Vyver and Abrams (2017) cited to support an influence of elevation on immediate action. They found an association between dispositional elevation and the BAS-reward subscale measuring the disposition to respond to the occurrence or anticipation of reward. Ideals and values, rather than more specific goals or actions, are a highly efficient focus for such approach motivation, because they can be approached by heightening imagined commitment to them (McGregor et al. 2010). This might mean that the link between dispositional elevation and reward seeking can be accounted for by a tendency to experience approaching ideals and values in thought—rather than through action—as rewarding.

The notion that admiration contributes to the formation of ideals and values as abstract, high-level goals is further supported by research comparing admiration with benign envy. While both admiration and benign envy can motivate emulation, the precise nature of the emulative tendency is different (Schindler et al. 2015; Van de Ven 2017). Emulative tendencies for admiration have been found with items that were formulated to express a general wish to obtain something seen in another person (Schindler et al. 2015; Van de Ven 2017), but not when emulation was measured as intentions to perform specific actions or in terms of actual task performance (Van de Ven et al. 2011). Van de Ven (2017, 197) concluded that "(t)he negative, frustrating experience of envy thus triggers direct action . . . , while admiration . . . makes one look for broader opportunities." In line with the suggestion that admiration has more long-term effects on motivation (Schindler et al. 2013; Schindler et al. 2015), Blatz, Lange, and Crusius (2016) presented evidence that inducing admiration as compared with inducing benign envy elicited more abstract goals with a longer-term focus. Thus, benign envy may be characterized as right now wanting what another person already has. As a negative emotion with high motivational intensity, benign envy is likely to narrow cognitive processing to allow to zoom in on the coveted object and ways to obtain it (Crusius and Lange 2014). In contrast, admiration is experienced as wanting something that matches the ideal or value seen in another person at some future time, which leads to broadened attention to future possibilities, approaching ideals in thought, and perceived self-expansion (Schindler et al. 2015).

Admiration Fosters Growth Rather Than Satisfaction or Success

Admiration increases commitment to values, but it does not increase opportunities to perform value-expressive behavior, ability to perform such behavior, and success of this behavior. Thus, if one seeks to demonstrate effects of admiration beyond an increased importance of a specific value, one needs to study behavior in situations that allow one to express this value and focus on the motivation to perform value-expressive behavior rather than on the successful execution of the intended actions.

While there is some correspondence between values and behavior, the size of the respective associations varies across values (Bardi and Schwartz 2003; Pozzebon and Ashton 2009), persons (Wojciszke 1987), situations, and cultures (cf. Roccas and Sagiv 2010). A longitudinal study revealed that associations between values and behavior at the transition from childhood to adolescence are reciprocal (Vecchione et al. 2016). For instance, self-enhancement values predicted later increases in behavior that expresses them (and decreases in behavior expressive of self-transcendence values). Behavior expressive of self-enhancement values, in turn, had an influence on later increases in self-enhancement values.

One important influence on the strength of relation between values and behavior is whether behavior in a domain is subject to normative pressure (Roccas and Sagiv 2010). For instance, self-reported benevolence values were related only weakly to the frequencies of value-expressive behaviors reported by romantic partners and peers (Bardi and Schwartz 2003; Pozzebon and Ashton 2009). Thus, people may conform to norms for prosocial behavior even when this behavior does not match their personal values.

The consideration of values and value-expressive behavior is further relevant to the question of whether admiration contributes to greater well-being. Buchanan and Bardi (2015) tested whether values or value-expressive behaviors were more strongly related to a broad range of well-being indicators. They found no direct link between values and well-being. Rather, personal and social values contributed to greater well-being only to the extent that they increased the likelihood of achievement and prosocial behaviors. This also matches the finding that not merely having goals but prospect of goal attainment is related to happiness (e.g., McGregor and Little 1998).

Given that values are not necessarily expressed in behavior and that most likely only successful behavioral expressions of values contribute to satisfaction, it is not surprising that admiration is not consistently linked to well-being. With the exception of one study reporting moderate associations of dispositional admiration for skill and elevation with life satisfaction (Martínez-Martí et al. 2016), the disposition to admire/feel elevated showed only small or no associations with satisfaction (Diessner et al. 2013; Peterson et al. 2007; Schindler 2014). In contrast, dispositional admiration and elevation were more strongly and consistently related with meaning (Peterson et al. 2007), personal growth, and purpose in life (Martínez-Martí et al. 2016; Schindler 2014).

Whom Is Admiration Good For?

Viewed from a social functional perspective on emotions, other-directed moral emotions signal to others whether an individual considers the conduct of an emotion-eliciting person as praiseworthy or blameworthy (Rudolph and Tscharaktschiew 2014). In the case of admiration, there are four parties that could potentially benefit from such an emotional signal: the admiring individual, the admired target person or group, the admiring individual's social in-group or society, and members of social outgroups and other societies. Admiration is a positive emotion that is enjoyable to the admiring individual and helps foster commitment to values and ideals. Expressing admiration and praise can make the admired other feel good and encourage her or him to continue in her or his exemplary conduct. Admiration may further help admired persons or groups to maintain dominance by engendering deferential behaviors in admiring individuals (cf. Sweetman et al. 2013). Admiration signals to other observers, including members of the social in-group and out-groups, that the admiring individual truly values the ideals expressed by the admired other. It thereby helps observers to tell whether the individual can be expected to engage in behavior linked to the admired ideal even in situations when there is no social pressure to show these behaviors.

Admiration for Skill Does Not Motivate Prosocial Intentions and Behavior

To qualify as a moral emotion, instances of admiration usually would have to yield benefits to others or to the upholding of the social order. Considering the four potential beneficiaries of admiration reveals that this assumption is not defensible. Admiration can occur for others who are not present in the situation or do not even exist (any longer; consider deceased and fictitious persons). Admired others thus often cannot benefit from being admired and praised. Similarly, individuals can experience admiration in privacy and, thus, admiration is not necessarily a social signal of value to other observers. This means that the primary question to ask is whether the values and ideals fostered by admiration have a social rather than personal focus (i.e., are concerned with outcomes for others and society). In the case of admiration for skill, it is possible to argue for admiration being a "selfish" rather than self-transcendent emotion. If admiration for skill increases the importance an individual places on achievement, this also means that this person is more likely to prioritize achievement over benevolence values when they are in conflict. Admiration for skill thus is an emotion that primarily serves an individual's own progress. Other findings from our research are in line with this interpretation. Persons who reported to more frequently admire provided higher ratings of their three most important personal goals as helping fulfil needs for self-esteem and personal growth (Schindler 2015). When including admiration and adoration as rival predictors, only adoration was linked to perceiving one's personal goals as helping to care for others and to assume social responsibility. Thus, while a person's self-improvement may also benefit others (e.g., consider artistic, athletic, or scientific achievements), such potential benefits likely were not the primary motivation driving the person to work hard to improve.

Admiration Has Evolved to Benefit the Social In-Group

Research on the role of admiration in intergroup behavior has shown that this emotion can help maintain or challenge the social hierarchy (Sweetman et al. 2013). While admiration for those of higher status serves to maintain the social order, admiration for subversive individuals can serve to challenge the prevailing social order.

It is important to consider that admiration has evolved to benefit the individual and her or his social group rather than out-groups (cf. Palmer et al.

2013). While admiration—when elicited by members of an out-group—may help reduce social conflict, it may also work to increase conflict. An extreme case is cited by Pohling and Diessner (2016, 418): Suicide bombers elicit elevation in members of their cultural group. This underscores that one social group's admired hero or martyr can be another social group's villain or terrorist (cf. Palmer et al. 2013, 92).

CONCLUSION: WHEN IS IT GOOD AND WHEN IS IT MORAL TO ADMIRE?

Answering the question "Is it morally good to admire?" has turned out to be complex. Admiration per se is not a moral emotion. It is neither morally right nor morally wrong to feel it—unless one were to consider acknowledging excellence or personal development and growth as moral obligations. The primary function of all instances of admiration is to create desire for and commitment to values and ideals to facilitate their social transmission and social learning of associated skills, knowledge, and ways of conduct (Schindler et al. 2013). Accordingly, psychologists have found it necessary to distinguish elevation defined as admiration for virtue from admiration for skill. Admiration for skill is linked to valuing achievement (and potentially self-direction and power). As such values with a personal focus are primarily concerned with outcomes for the self rather than for others, an emotion increasing commitment to personal values does not fit the definition of a prototypical moral emotion (Haidt 2003b)—even though striving for achievement can produce outcomes that are valuable to society.

In contrast, elevation generally is a moral emotion functioning to promote social values and emulation of prosocial behavior (Haidt 2003a; Pohling and Diessner 2016; Thomson and Siegel 2017). However, in circumstances that are not prototypical of instances of elevation, the moral righteousness of elevation might become questionable. For instance, elevation might get used to motivate attitudes and behavior that are harmful to a social out-group.

Outside of such extreme circumstances, there is merit in seeking to induce elevation and also admiration more generally in education to facilitate learning from virtuous, knowledgeable, and skilled others. However, it seems advisable to have modest expectations about the immediate effects of exposure to admirable others. Admiration does not readily translate into behavior. Contrary to what was suggested by Haidt's "inspire and rewire" hypothesis (Haidt 2003a, 286), it would be a very rare event that a single moral peak experience of elevation turns an individual's values and life around. Rather, I would assume that elevation and admiration have small, cumulative effects that serve to establish, maintain, and increase commitment to values and ideals over months, years, and an entire lifetime of repeatedly experiencing these emotions (see the "moral upward spiral" described by Pohling et al. 2017, 8). Given the many ways individuals might see fit to express, stand up for, and act on their values, it would be difficult to devise emotion-focused pedagogical interventions that reliably turn elevation and admiration into immediate emulative behaviors. Nevertheless, this should not lead to overlooking the potentials of elevation and admiration to foster commitment to values and ideals through (moral) education, especially when these emotions are experienced in situations that allow for abstract construals of the witnessed events. Such situations include reading fiction and other representations of excellent role models in media and artworks.

NOTES

1. See also Zagzebski (2017) for a distinction between admiring natural versus acquired excellence. Admiration for skill is more complex as it often entails admiration for natural (artistic, athletic, or intellectual) talent (which cannot be acquired or imitated) and admiration for acquired excellence (hard work, perseverance, and determination). In contrast, moral virtues are usually considered to be acquired, more readily imitable, and, thus, less intimidating.

2. Our distinction between admiration and adoration can be related to Croce and Vaccarezza's (2017) distinction between moral heroes and moral saints. While heroes display one virtue to an exceptional degree (leading to admiration), saints are supposed to possess all the virtues (leading to adoration).

REFERENCES

Algoe, Sara B., and Jonathan Haidt. 2009. "Witnessing Excellence in Action: The 'Other-Praising' Emotions of Elevation, Gratitude, and Admiration." *The Journal of Positive Psychology* 4 (2): 105–27. https://doi.org/10.1080/17439760802650519.

Aquino, Karl, Brent McFerran, and Marjorie Laven. 2011. "Moral Identity and the Experience of Moral Elevation in Response to Acts of Uncommon Goodness." *Journal of Personality and Social Psychology* 100 (4): 703–18. https://doi.org/10.1037/a0022540.

Bardi, Anat, and Shalom H. Schwartz. 2003. "Values and Behavior: Strength and Structure of Relations." *Personality and Social Psychology Bulletin* 29 (10): 1207–20. https://doi.org/10.1177/0146167203254602.

Blatz, Lisa, Jens Lange, and Jan Crusius. 2016. *Gain With and Without Pain? Upward Motivation in Admiration and Envy Differs in Abstractness and Long-Term Focus*. Poster presented at the European Association of Social Psychology Medium Size Meeting "Promoting a Social Approach to Emotions," Cologne, Germany, April 15–16, 2016.

Botthof, Alisia. 2017. "Positive Kontakte im Arbeitsleben: Skalenentwicklung zur Messung von Bewunderung und Verehrung am Arbeitsplatz." B.S. thesis, Friedrich-Alexander-Universität Erlangen-Nürnberg.

Buchanan, Kathryn, and Anat Bardi. 2015. "The Roles of Values, Behavior, and Value-Behavior Fit in the Relation of Agency and Communion to Well-Being." *Journal of Personality* 83 (3): 320–33. https://doi.org/10.1111/jopy.12106.

Charters, W. W. 1927. *The Teaching of Ideals*. New York: The Macmillan Company. https://babel.hathitrust.org/cgi/pt?id=ucl.$b67970;view=1up.

Cramwinckel, Florien M., and Benoît Monin. 2019. "Obstacles to the Admiration of Moral People." In *The Moral Psychology of Admiration*, edited by André Grahle and Alfred Archer, 217–32. London: Rowman &Littlefield International.

Croce, Michel, and Maria Silvia Vaccarezza. 2017. "Educating through Exemplars: Alternative Paths to Virtue." *Theory and Research in Education* 15 (1): 5–19. https://doi.org/10.1177/1477878517695903.

Crusius, Jan, and Jens Lange. 2014. "What Catches the Envious Eye? Attentional Biases within Malicious and Benign Envy." *Journal of Experimental Social Psychology* 55: 1–11. https://doi.org/10.1016/j.jesp.2014.05.007.

Diessner, Rhett, Ravi Iyer, Meghan M. Smith, and Jonathan Haidt. 2013. "Who Engages with Moral Beauty?" *Journal of Moral Education* 42 (2): 139–63. https://doi.org/10.1080/03057240.2013.785941.

Dubbel, Anneke. 2012. "Bewunderung und Verehrung: Eine vergleichende Analyse zu Begründungen." Diploma thesis, Westfälische Wilhelms-Universität Münster.

Engelen, Bart, Alan Thomas, Alfred Archer, and Niels van de Ven. 2018. "Exemplars and Nudges: Combining Two Strategies for Moral Education." *Journal of Moral Education*. Advance online publication. https://doi.org/10.1080/03057240.2017.1396966.

Haidt, Jonathan. 2003a. "Elevation and the Positive Psychology of Morality." In *Flourishing: Positive Psychology and the Life Well-Lived*, edited by Corey L. M. Keyes and Jonathan Haidt, 275–89. Washington, DC: American Psychological Association.

Haidt, Jonathan. 2003b. "The Moral Emotions." In *Handbook of Affective Sciences*, edited by Richard J. Davidson, Klaus R. Scherer, and H. Hill Goldsmith, 852–70. New York: Oxford University Press.

Hawkes, Thomas H. 1973. "Ideals of Upper Elementary School Children." *Psychology in the Schools* 10 (4): 447–57.

Jefferson, Thomas. 1771. "From Thomas Jefferson to Robert Skipwith, with a List of Books for a Private Library, 3 August 1771," *Founders Online,* National Archives, last modified April 12, 2018. http://founders.archives.gov/documents/Jefferson/01-01-02-0056.

Kristjánsson, Kristján. 2006. "Emulation and the Use of Role Models in Moral Education." *Journal of Moral Education* 35 (1): 37–49. https://doi.org/10.1080/03057240500495278.

Lockwood, Penelope, and Ziva Kunda. 1997. "Superstars and Me: Predicting the Impact of Role Models on the Self." *Journal of Personality and Social Psychology* 73 (1): 91–103. https://doi.org/10.1037/0022-3514.73.1.91.

Mares, Marie-Louise, Edward Palmer, and Tia Sullivan. 2008. "Prosocial Effects of Media Exposure." In *The Handbook of Children, Media, and Development*, edited by Sandra L. Calvert and Barbara J. Wilson, 268–89. Oxford, UK: Blackwell Publishing.

Martínez-Martí, María Louisa, María José Hernández-Lloreda, and María Dolores Avia. 2016. "Appreciation of Beauty and Excellence: Relationship with Personality, Prosociality and Well-Being." *Journal of Happiness Studies* 17 (6): 2613–34. https://doi.org/10.1007/s10902-015-9709-6.

McGregor, Ian, and Brian R. Little. 1998. "Personal Projects, Happiness, and Meaning: On Doing Well and Being Yourself." *Journal of Personality and Social Psychology* 74 (2): 494–512. https://doi.org/10.1037/0022-3514.74.2.494.

McGregor, Ian, Kyle Nash, Nikki Mann, and Curtis E. Phills. 2010. "Anxious Uncertainty and Reactive Approach Motivation (RAM)." *Journal of Personality and Social Psychology* 99 (1): 133–47. https://doi.org/10.1037/a0019701.

Monin, Benoît. 2007. "Holier than Me? Threatening Social Comparison in the Moral Domain." *Revue Internationale de Psychologie Sociale* 20 (1): 53–68.

Monin, Benoît, Pamela J. Sawyer, and Matthew J. Marquez. 2008. "The Rejection of Moral Rebels: Resenting Those Who Do the Right Thing." *Journal of Personality and Social Psychology* 95 (1): 76–93. https://doi.org/10.1037/0022-3514.95.1.76.

Moore, R. C. 1919. "The Emotion of Admiration and Its Development in Children." *Journal of Experimental Pedagogy* 5: 221–35.

Onu, Diana, Thomas Kessler, and Joanne R. Smith. 2016. "Admiration: A Conceptual Review." *Emotion Review* 8 (3): 218–30. https://doi.org/10.1177/1754073915610438.

Onu, Diana, Joanne R. Smith, and Thomas Kessler. 2015. "Intergroup Emulation: An Improvement Strategy for Lower Status Groups." *Group Processes and Intergroup Relations* 18 (2): 210–24. https://doi.org/10.1177/1368430214556698.

Palmer, Craig T., Ryan O. Begley, Kathryn Coe, and Lyle Steadman. 2013. "Moral Elevation and Traditions: Ancestral Encouragement of Altruism through Ritual and Myth." *Journal of Ritual Studies* 27 (2): 83–96. http://www.jstor.org/stable/44368897.

Peterson, Christopher, Willibald Ruch, Ursula Beermann, Nansook Park, and Martin E. P. Seligman. 2007. "Strengths of Character, Orientations to Happiness, and Life Satisfaction." *The Journal of Positive Psychology* 2 (3): 149–56. https://doi.org/10.1080/17439760701228938.

Pohling, Rico, and Rhett Diessner. 2016. "Moral Elevation and Moral Beauty: A Review of the Empirical Literature." *Review of General Psychology* 20 (4): 412–25. https://doi.org/10.1037/gpr0000089.

Pohling, Rico, Rhett Diessner, and Anja Strobel. 2017. "The Role of Gratitude and Moral Elevation in Moral Identity Development." *International Journal of Behavioral Development*. Advance online publication. https://doi.org/10.1177/0165025417727874.

Pozzebon, Julie A., and Michael C. Ashton. 2009. "Personality and Values as Predictors of Self- and Peer-Reported Behavior." *Journal of Individual Differences* 30 (3): 122–29. https://doi.org/10.1027/1614-0001.30.3.122.

Robinson, Oliver C., Abigail Dunn, Sofya Nartova-Bochaver, Konstantin Bochaver, Samaneh Asadi, Zohreh Khosravi, Seyed Mohammad Jafari, Xiaozhou Zhang, and Yanbo Yang. 2016. "Figures of Admiration in Emerging Adulthood: A Four-Country Study." *Emerging Adulthood* 4 (2): 82–91. https://doi.org/10.1177/2167696815601945.

Roccas, Sonia, and Lilach Sagiv. 2010. "Personal Values and Behavior: Taking the Cultural Context into Account." *Social and Personality Psychology Compass* 4 (1): 30–41. https://doi.org/10.1111/j.1751-9004.2009.00234.x.

Rudolph, Udo, and Nadine Tscharaktschiew. 2014. "An Attributional Analysis of Moral Emotions: Naïve Scientists and Everyday Judges." *Emotion Review* 6 (4): 344–52. https://doi.org/10.1177/1754073914534507.

Schindler, Ines. 2014. "Relations of Admiration and Adoration with Other Emotions and Well-Being." *Psychology of Well-Being: Theory, Research and Practice* 4 (14): 1–23. https://doi.org/10.1186/s13612-014-0014-7.

Schindler, Ines. 2015. "Selbsttranszendente Emotionen und Prosozialität: Wie Verehrung und Rührung das Eigeninteresse zurücktreten lassen." Vortrag im Forschungskolloquium des Fachbereichs 8: Psychologie, Universität Koblenz-Landau, 25.

Schindler, Ines, Juliane Paech, and Fabian Löwenbrück. 2015. "Linking Admiration and Adoration to Self-Expansion: Different Ways to Enhance One's Potential." *Cognition and Emotion* 29 (2): 292–310. https://doi.org/10.1080/02699931.2014.903230.

Schindler, Ines, Veronika Zink, Johannes Windrich, and Winfried Menninghaus. 2013. "Admiration and Adoration: Their Different Ways of Showing and Shaping Who We Are." *Cognition and Emotion* 27 (1): 85–118. https://doi.org/10.1080/02699931.2012.698253.

Schnall, Simone, and Jean Roper. 2012. "Elevation Puts Moral Values into Action." *Social Psychological and Personality Science* 3 (3): 373–78. https://doi.org/10.1177/1948550611423595.

Schwartz, Shalom H., Jan Cieciuch, Michele Vecchione, Eldad Davidov, Ronald Fischer, Constanze Beierlein, Alice Ramos, Markku Verkasalo, Jan-Erik Lönnqvist, Kursad Demirutku, Ozlem Dirilen-Gumus, and Mark Konty. 2012. "Refining the Theory of Basic Individual Values." *Journal of Personality and Social Psychology* 103 (4): 663–88. https://doi.org/10.1037/a0029393.

Shiota, Michelle N., Todd M. Thrash, Alexander F. Danvers, and John T. Dombrowski. 2014. "Transcending the Self: Awe, Elevation, and Inspiration." In *Handbook of Positive Emotions*, edited by Michele M. Tugade, Michelle N. Shiota, and Leslie D. Kirby, 362–77. New York: Guilford Press.

Smith, Ralph A., and Christiana M. Smith. 1970. "Justifying Aesthetic Education." *The Journal of Aesthetic Education* 4 (2): 37–51. http://www.jstor.org/stable/3331546.

Smith, Richard H. 2000. "Assimilative and Contrastive Emotional Reactions to Upward and Downward Social Comparisons." In *Handbook of Social Comparison: Theory and Research*, edited by Jerry Suls and Ladd Wheeler, 173–200. New York: Kluwer Academic/Plenum Publishers.

Stellar, Jennifer E., Amie M. Gordon, Paul K. Piff, Daniel Cordaro, Craig L. Anderson, Yang Bai, Laura A. Maruskin, and Dacher Keltner. 2017. "Self-Transcendent Emotions and Their Social Functions: Compassion, Gratitude, and Awe Bind Us to Others through Prosociality." *Emotion Review* 9 (3): 200–207. https://doi.org/10.1177/1754073916684557.

Sweetman, Joseph, Russell Spears, Andrew G. Livingstone, and Antony S. R. Manstead. 2013. "Admiration Regulates Social Hierarchy: Antecedents, Dispositions, and Effects on Intergroup Behavior." *Journal of Experimental Social Psychology* 49 (3): 534–42. https://doi.org/10.1016/j.jesp.2012.10.007.

Thomson, Andrew L., and Jason T. Siegel. 2017. "Elevation: A Review of Scholarship on a Moral and Other-Praising Emotion." *The Journal of Positive Psychology* 12 (6): 628–38. https://doi.org/10.1080/17439760.2016.1269184.

Trope, Yaacov, and Nira Liberman. 2010. "Construal-Level Theory of Psychological Distance." *Psychological Review* 117 (2): 440–63. https://doi.org/10.1037/a0018963.

Vallacher, Robin R., and Daniel M. Wegner. 1987. "What Do People Think They're Doing? Action Identification and Human Behavior." *Psychological Review* 94 (1): 3–15. https://doi.org/10.1037/0033-295X.94.1.3.

Van de Ven, Niels. 2017. "Envy and Admiration: Emotion and Motivation Following Upward Social Comparison." *Cognition and Emotion* 31 (1): 193–200. https://doi.org/10.1080/02699931.2015.1087972.

Van de Ven, Niels, Marcel Zeelenberg, and Rik Pieters. 2011. "Why Envy Outperforms Admiration." *Personality and Social Psychology Bulletin* 37 (6): 784–95. https://doi.org/10.1177/0146167211400421.

Van de Vyver, Julie, and Dominic Abrams. 2017. "Is Moral Elevation an Approach-Oriented Emotion?" *The Journal of Positive Psychology* 12 (2): 178–85. https://doi.org/10.1080/17439760.2016.1163410.

Vecchione, Michele, Anna K. Döring, Guido Alessandri, Gilda Marsicano, and Anat Bardi. 2016. "Reciprocal Relations across Time between Basic Values and Value-Expressive Behaviors: A Longitudinal Study among Children." *Social Development* 25 (3): 528–47. https://doi.org/10.1111/sode.12152.

Weiner, Bernard. 2007. "Examining Emotional Diversity in the Classroom: An Attribution Theorist Considers the Moral Emotions." In *Emotion in Education*, edited by Paul A. Schutz and Reinhard Pekrun, 75–88. Amsterdam: Elsevier Academic Press.

Wojciszke, Bogdan. 1987. "Ideal-Self, Self-Focus and Value-Behaviour Consistency." *European Journal of Social Psychology* 17 (2): 187–98. https://doi.org/10.1002/ejsp.2420170206.

Zagzebski, Linda Trinkaus. 2017. *Exemplarist Moral Theory.* New York: Oxford University Press.

Chapter Twelve

Admiration and the Development of Moral Virtue

Alan T. Wilson

Philosophers and psychologists have recently been focusing on the important question of how positive character traits are developed.[1] Within philosophy, these positive character traits are referred to as *virtues*. In this chapter, I examine one intuitively appealing proposal concerning virtue development—the idea that the path to moral virtue can begin with the experience of admiration for a moral exemplar. My aim is to provide a model of how this process might work by identifying the different stages that it would involve. I then highlight three ways in which admiration might nevertheless *fail* to result in the development of moral virtue. It is hoped that providing this model, and highlighting the potential problems, will be helpful for those interested in *encouraging* virtue development. With this in mind, I also provide a brief discussion of admiration in the context of virtue education.

I. PRELIMINARIES

Before setting out the proposed model of virtue development through admiration, I want to briefly provide some detail on the main concepts being used. Those concepts are (i) virtue, (ii) admiration, and (iii) moral exemplar.

As mentioned above, virtues are positive character traits, and philosophers typically follow Aristotle in dividing these traits into (at least) two categories. *Moral virtues* are thought to include traits such as compassion, courage, honesty, and justice. *Intellectual virtues* are thought to include traits such as inquisitiveness, intellectual rigour, and intellectual humility. In both cases, virtues can be conceived of as stable dispositions to react appropriately (both emotionally and in terms of behaviour) to the situation that one finds oneself in, and to do so for the right reasons. Being virtuous involves an agent's emotions, behaviour, and habits of reasoning.[2]

For example, the moral virtue of generosity involves more than simply the behaviour of giving time and resources to other people. Instead, the virtuously generous agent will give *appropriately*, in a way that is sensitive to relevant features of the situation (such as whether the recipient will be able to manage the increased resources, or whether those resources could be better used in some other way). Importantly, the virtuously generous agent will also be disposed to act in this appropriate way for the right reasons. That is, the virtuously generous agent can be expected to give appropriately out of a desire to help others, rather than out of a desire to receive favourable publicity. My focus in this chapter will be on the development of moral virtues, and on the idea that this development can be prompted by the experience of admiration for a moral exemplar.[3]

In recent work, Linda Zagzebski (2013; 2015; 2017) has developed an *exemplarist moral theory* based on exemplars who are identified through admiration. As explained by Zagzebski, admiration is an emotion and, as such, involves both a characteristic affective component and an intentional object.[4] To say that admiration has an intentional object is just to say that it is directed *at* something or someone. We do not feel admiration in general, but rather we admire *that* person or *that* action. This is similar to other emotions. Anger, gratitude, fear, and so on, are all directed at intentional objects in the same way. Just as admiration is directed towards admirable people, so anger might be directed at a friend's thoughtless comment, and fear might be directed at the large spider in the corner of the room. Of course, as Zagzebski acknowledges, the targets of our emotions are not always appropriate. The friend's comment, while thoughtless, may well be trivial, and so not warrant our anger. The spider, while large, may well be harmless, and so not warrant our fear.

Concerning the characteristic affective component, or the "feel," of admiration, Zagzebski discusses relevant work from Jonathan Haidt and colleagues. Haidt refers to the emotion of "elevation," which Zagzebski takes to be roughly equivalent to what she is interested in when discussing admiration.[5] According to Haidt, the characteristic feel of this emotion involves "distinctive physical feelings, including the feeling of dilation or opening in the chest, combined with the feeling that one has been uplifted or 'elevated.'"[6]

While this may be right, it will not be necessary to endorse Haidt's specific understanding of the characteristic feel of admiration/elevation. All that is required is to accept that admiring a person or an action feels different from experiencing other emotions in response to the same intentional object. It feels different to admire someone than it does to fear them, or to love them, or to be angered by them. That is what is meant by the claim that admiration involves a characteristic affective component, in addition to having an intentional object.

The final concept to be explained is that of the exemplar. One approach here would be to provide a list of putative moral exemplars to illustrate the general idea. Exemplars listed by Zagzebski (2017) include Leopold Socha, who risked his life to shelter and protect Jewish families during the Holocaust, and Jean Vanier, who set up a network of interfaith and intercultural communities that welcome and care for those with disabilities. William Damon and Anne Colby (2015, ch. 2) have identified exemplars including Eleanor Roosevelt, and Nobel Peace Prize winners Jane Addams and Nelson Mandela. We might also want our list to include exemplars that are less extreme, such as those who volunteer for charity in their spare time or who set a good example in more everyday situations.

A different approach would be to define exemplars in terms of either of the two concepts already discussed. For example, exemplars could be understood as those agents who are appropriate targets of the emotion of admiration. Alternatively, we could understand exemplars as those agents who possess actual virtues. Rather than relying on the exemplarity of specific individuals, I will here assume that a moral exemplar is someone who it is appropriate to admire due to the possession of moral virtue.

II. FROM ADMIRATION TO MORAL VIRTUE

There is a strong tradition of philosophical thought linking moral virtue with reflection on exemplars. Aristotle (1941, 1402–03 [1388^{a}30–^{b}20]) tells us that experiencing *zēlos* in response to those who possess something highly valued can drive agents to acquire the valued thing for themselves. And he lists the virtues among those highly valued possessions that we can be driven to pursue in this way.[7] Despite this tradition, however, a surprising lack of detail has been provided on the process by which recognising and admiring a moral exemplar can lead to the possession of moral virtue.

In the most recent attempt, Zagzebski (2017, 134–39) suggests that the developmental process importantly involves imagination. The idea is that an agent who admires someone will want to imitate that person, including the emotions that characteristically motivate them. The admiring agent will then imagine being motivated in the same way, and this will lead to the actual possession of such motivations. As Zagzebski (2017, 136) states:

> I think the model can work because even though imagining ourselves with a motivating feeling is not the same thing as having the feeling, imagining is very close to having, and an imagined feeling can cause an actual feeling, especially when we want to become a person with such a feeling. There are

many examples of this phenomenon. Women can sometimes fall in love with a man by spending a long time imagining themselves in love with him.

Zagzebski's suggestion is that we can come to be virtuously motivated by imagining ourselves as being like the virtuous exemplar. Of course, one worry here would be that such imagining will lead to complacency, rather than to virtue development. Zagzebski (2017, 137) ultimately presents her suggestion only as a hypothesis to be tested, while remaining optimistic that it is plausible. My focus here will not be on Zagzebski's imagination-based account. Instead, I will provide an alternative model of how the move from admiration to virtue might occur, and then use this model to identify ways in which the process can go awry.

In order to understand the process leading from admiration to moral virtue, it is important to first differentiate the distinct stages that this process involves. My proposal is that attention needs to be paid to (at least) the following four stages:

1. The Experience of Admiration
2. The Drive to Emulate
3. The Habitual Performance of Virtuous Actions
4. The Possession of Actual Virtue

Suppose that Anne is a moral exemplar due to her possession of the virtues of honesty and compassion.[8] It will be possible for another agent, Ben, to begin on the path to moral virtue by first experiencing admiration for Anne. That is, Ben will experience the characteristic affective component of admiration in a way that takes Anne as its intentional object. As Zagzebski (2017, ch. 2) has explained, admiring someone involves perceiving that person *as admirable*. In experiencing admiration for Anne, therefore, Ben will be perceiving Anne *as admirable* in some way.

An open question here concerns the extent to which Ben must be capable of articulating exactly what he is experiencing, and exactly which features of Anne are responsible for her admirability. It is unnecessary to demand that Ben be able to use the language of virtues and vices, or that he be capable of identifying the emotion that he experiences as "admiration." However, it is important that Ben's admiration be responsive to *Anne*. That is, Ben's admiration ought not to be focused solely on some subset of Anne's *behaviour*, be that moral behaviour (such as telling the truth), or non-moral behaviour (such as driving an expensive car or captaining the football team). If Ben only admires certain behaviours, then the intentional object of his admiration is plausibly understood as the behaviour itself. If Ben instead admires Anne, then he will admire Anne as a person, and not merely the behaviour that she engages in.

Having first experienced admiration for the exemplar, stage 2 involves the agent being driven to emulate the exemplar. On some accounts of admiration, there is thought to be a conceptual link between viewing a person as admirable and being driven to emulate them. This would mean that it is not conceptually possible to experience admiration without being motivated (at least to some extent) to emulate the admired person. If you are not motivated to emulate, then you are not experiencing admiration. At times, this looks to be Zagzebski's view, such as when she distinguishes admiration from other emotions by offering what looks like a definition: "admiration, a positive feeling with the desire to emulate" (2017, 58). However, Zagzebski clarifies elsewhere that the drive to emulate is merely the "typical response" to experiencing admiration (2017, 34). In section III, I will explore the possibility of admiration failing to result in a (sufficient) drive to emulate. But in cases where admiration successfully leads to virtue, the experience of admiration for a moral exemplar motivates the agent to be *like* the exemplar in question.

Consider again the example of Ben's admiration for Anne. If Ben is going to continue along the path to virtue, then it is important that his perception of Anne *as admirable* generates in him the drive to emulate her. That is, the affective component of Ben's admiration must motivate in him the goal of wanting to be like Anne. (Similar to how the affective component of fear can motivate in us the goal of avoiding the large spider in the corner of the room.) Given that Ben's admiration is responsive to Anne as a person, Ben will view emulating Anne as including those actions that are most expressive of her character. Anne's honest and charitable nature means that being like Anne involves engaging in actions such as telling the truth and donating to homeless shelters. By the time an agent successfully moves through stages 1 and 2, therefore, the experience of admiration for an exemplar will have led to a motivation to be like the exemplar, where this includes acting in certain ways.

With these two aspects in place, it ought to then be clear how an agent could progress to stage 3—the habitual performance of virtuous actions.[9] If Ben has the goal of wanting to be like Anne, and if Ben's view of being like Anne involves telling the truth and donating to homeless shelters, then this can be expected to lead Ben to act in these virtuous ways. As long as nothing changes, Ben can be expected to continue to act in these ways. Ben will have developed a habit of virtuous action. This ought to be viewed as a moral achievement for someone not previously inclined to act virtuously. And it may be that, in some cases, the performance of virtuous actions (or the avoidance of vicious actions) is our most pressing concern. Nevertheless, it is important to note that habitual virtuous action is not sufficient for the possession of actual virtue. If we are concerned with actually being virtuous, then more will be required.

Moral virtue requires not only performing right actions, but also performing those actions for the right reasons. Ben's admiration for Anne might lead him to perform actions such as telling the truth, but Ben will not possess the virtue of honesty as long as his motivation for doing so is simply to imitate Anne. Plausibly, the motivation to imitate an exemplar is not the appropriate motivation for performing virtuous actions. The problem here is not that Ben's motivation is *immoral*. But if the explanation for Ben's truth-telling is his desire to imitate Anne, then this reveals that Ben's values and reasons are not (yet) those that would be expected of a morally virtuous agent.

How, then, might an agent move from the habitual performance of virtuous actions (stage 3) to the possession of actual virtue (stage 4)? At this point, we move beyond the specific issue of how admiration is connected to virtue development, and on to a more general question in virtue theory. It is widely agreed that developing virtue requires acting virtuously (where this means acting as a virtuous agent would act). This widespread agreement follows on from Aristotle's well-known claim (1998, 29 [1103^{a}32–^{b}35]) that

> men become builders by building and lyre-players by playing the lyre; so too we become just by doing just acts, temperate by doing temperate acts, brave by doing brave acts.

Any account of virtue development that accepts this claim will owe an explanation of how the habitual performance of virtuous actions results in moral virtue. This question is not specific to the issue of whether *admiration* can lead to moral virtue. For that reason, my focus here will be on how admiration can get us to the point of habitually performing virtuous actions, and (in the next section) on how this process might go awry. At this point, I will simply highlight that any theorist who makes positive claims concerning the connection between admiration and virtue development will have a stake in the general task of explaining how acting virtuously results in becoming virtuous.

It is important to note, however, that virtue theorists have recently been working on this very question. For example, Nancy Snow (2018) has argued that acting virtuously can lead to moral virtue through a series of realisations about the value of being virtuous. According to Snow (2018, 73), it is possible for an agent to realise the instrumental, constitutive, and intrinsic value of being virtuous through habitual virtuous action, such as when a parent realises the intrinsic value of patience while interacting patiently with his child. Other theorists, such as Julia Annas (2011) and Matt Stichter (2007; 2011), have argued instead that virtue development occurs in a way that is similar to skill development, where this too requires a period of practice through virtuous action. In these ways, virtue theorists have been providing proposals on how virtuous action can lead to virtue possession.[10] Some such account will be required to complete the proposed model of how the experience of admiration for a moral exemplar can lead to moral virtue.

In this section, I have sought to provide a model for understanding the path from admiration to moral virtue. However, in clarifying the different stages involved, it becomes apparent that there is plenty of scope for things to go wrong. In the next section, I discuss three ways in which the path from admiration to moral virtue can go awry.

III. THREE POTENTIAL PROBLEMS

In addition to the question of how virtues are successfully developed, there is the related question of why virtues sometimes fail to develop. This related question is interesting both at the conceptual level, for theorists of virtue and vice, and at the practical level, for those interested in *encouraging* virtue development. Distinguishing the different stages involved in moving from admiration to virtue helps to identify potential problems.

(1) Inappropriate Admiration

The most straightforward way in which admiration can fail to lead to moral virtue is when it is directed towards an inappropriate intentional object. Of course, this will happen when an agent experiences admiration towards someone who is non-virtuous. An agent who experiences admiration while thinking about vicious agents cannot be expected to thereby develop moral virtues.[11]

A different problem case is when admiration is experienced for a moral exemplar, but where the admiration is not responsive to the exemplar's morally relevant characteristics. In the simple example used above, it was important that Ben admired Anne in a way that was inclusive of her honesty and her compassion. Admiring Anne only when she is driving an expensive car would not be sufficient. For our admiration to be appropriate, it is not enough to ensure that we admire actual moral exemplars. It is also important that our admiration encompasses those features that are responsible for the exemplar's admirability.

This complication raises a serious challenge for those interested in using admiration when attempting to encourage virtue development. It is not obvious how agents can be brought to experience admiration for moral exemplars, but one tempting option is to utilise fictional stories and narratives. Children's literature, for example, is replete with righteous and hardworking exemplars who overcome initial hardship to later achieve success and popularity. The difficulty, however, lies in ensuring that any admiration that is sparked for these exemplars focuses on the fact that they are righteous and hardworking, and not (only) on the fact that they are ultimately successful and popular. It is to be hoped that future work can provide insights on exactly how narrowly focused the experience of admiration tends to be, and on what factors tend to influence our admiration for others.

(2) Admiration Without the Drive to Emulate

A second problem concerns the worry that admiration might fail to result in a drive to emulate the admired exemplar. As mentioned above, it might be thought that the experience of admiration is conceptually tied to emulation. Even if we accept this, it is clear that the motivation to emulate will not always determine an agent's actions. This is because the motivation to emulate will be just one among the many, perhaps conflicting, motivations that are present. There is no reason to suppose that this one motivation will always be given priority. Whether we understand this as admiration failing to generate a drive to emulate, or as admiration generating a *pro tanto* drive to emulate that is then overridden, if agents ultimately fail to emulate the exemplar, then they will not continue on the path to moral virtue.

Consider the following three ways in which a (sufficient) drive to emulate might fail to develop. First, there will be cases where the agent believes that emulation is too costly. It is possible to admire someone who is risking her life by protesting a brutal regime while at the same time deciding that such behaviour is too dangerous to emulate. Similarly, we might admire those who donate a significant percentage of their earnings to support worthwhile causes, while at the same time deciding that that is not the life for us. In such cases, there is no need to stipulate that we must not *really* admire the agents in question after all. Instead, our admiration has failed to result in a sufficient drive to emulate the admired exemplar.

A second type of problematic case is where emulation is thought likely to be ineffective. This possibility is most obvious when we focus on non-moral attributes. I can admire Roger Federer's tennis ability and yet be in no way moved to emulate him, simply because I realise that no amount of emulation is likely to succeed. The thought here is not that it would be too difficult or too time-consuming. Rather, it is that becoming as skilled as Roger Federer is simply not going to be possible for me, even if I devote the remainder of my life to the task. Of course, I could make progress in becoming more like Federer than I am currently. But I could not attain the actual thing that I admire, which is not simply above-average tennis ability but truly exceptional, unprecedented skill. Believing that it will be impossible to match the exemplar's admirability can cause people to fail to develop a sufficient drive to emulate.

One option here is to distinguish different forms of admiration. Zagzebski (2017, ch. 2, section 3) argues that admiration differs depending on whether it is experienced in response to "natural" or "acquired" excellences. It might be thought that if we focus on the latter form of admiration, and if we assume that acquired excellences are always potentially attainable, then we will not need to worry about cases where emulating an exemplar is unrealistic. However, such a move is problematic. First, there is the problematic assumption that the characteristics we admire can be divided into those that are natural and those that are acquired. It is unclear, for example, where Federer's immense skill falls on this divide. But even if we ignore this, it is important to note that the crucial factor here is not whether the admired attribute *really is* attainable. Rather, what is important is whether the admiring agent *believes* it to be attainable. Suppose that, contrary to Aristotle, it is possible for everyone to become virtuous. Nevertheless, someone might believe that virtue is impossible *for her*. If so, sufficient drive to emulate the virtuous exemplar will fail to develop.

A third way in which admiration might fail to result in emulation is when admiring agents view the exemplar's positive features as lacking in relevance for their own lives. Even if an agent believes that it would be both possible and not too costly to acquire the positive features herself, she may nevertheless lack the drive to do so if she believes that those features are somehow irrelevant to her circumstances. Again, this possibility is most easily demonstrated by thinking about non-moral characteristics. Someone might genuinely admire the specialised navigational abilities of sailors and explorers, and yet view this skill as lacking relevance to the average person in an age of Google Maps and GPS. In such a case, sufficient drive to attain those navigational abilities is unlikely to develop.

Is this sort of example possible regarding moral virtues, as opposed to non-moral skills? Perhaps moral virtues are universally relevant, regardless of one's life circumstances. This will be the case if, for example, the possession and exercise of moral virtue is necessarily connected to human flourishing. However, this would not be enough to demonstrate that agents will always *believe* that the possession of moral virtue is relevant to their own circumstances. Again, the problem here is that the drive to emulate may fail to develop depending on what agents believe to be the case, and not on the facts of the matter. We have no reason to accept that it is impossible for someone who admires a morally virtuous exemplar to nevertheless view the virtues as lacking in relevance for her own life. This perceived lack of relevance is one further way in which an agent can fail to develop a sufficient drive to emulate a moral exemplar, even in cases where the agent correctly recognises the exemplar's admirability.

(3) The Drive to Emulate Without Habitual Virtuous Actions

An agent who successfully progresses through stages 1 and 2 will have experienced appropriate admiration for a moral exemplar and will have developed a sufficient drive to emulate the exemplar. In the simple example of Anne and Ben, Ben's admiration for Anne prompted him to want to be like Anne, in a way that included telling the truth and donating to homeless shelters. However, there is no guarantee that appropriate admiration plus a sufficient drive to emulate will result in habitual virtuous actions. Successful progression to stage 3 will fail to occur when the agent is unable to work out how the exemplar would act in different situations.

The problem here is that any agent's experience of an exemplar will be limited. While Ben knows that Anne often tells the truth, he will not have witnessed Anne in every possible situation, and so may be unsure whether Anne would tell the truth regardless of the circumstances. Similarly, even if Ben has witnessed Anne donating to homeless shelters, he may be unsure whether she would be willing to donate to all charitable causes. Therefore, even if Ben wants to emulate Anne, his limited knowledge of Anne may mean that he is unsuccessful when attempting to do so. If virtuous actions are those that a virtuous agent would perform, then even those who are driven to emulate might fail to perform virtuous actions in situations where they are unable to work out how their admired exemplar would behave.

This is one place in which Zagzebski's discussion of the importance of imagination could prove useful. Zagzebski's suggestion, following David Velleman (2002), is that agents can imagine themselves as already possessing the admired features of their exemplars, and that this can lead them to acquire those features. Zagzebski (2017, 137) compares this process to method actors who take on the emotions of the characters they portray.

A different role for imagination would be to help fill in any gaps in the knowledge of how an exemplar would act in different situations. Even if Ben has only witnessed Anne in a limited number of situations, it may nevertheless be possible for him to spend time imagining how she would act in unfamiliar circumstances. By doing so regularly, Ben may be able to prepare himself in advance for times when he is in an unfamiliar situation and would otherwise be unable to work out what being like Anne would involve. Imagining exemplars in a variety of situations might go some way towards reducing the number of cases in which agents are unsure how to emulate their exemplars. This strategy will, of course, be limited by the extent of agents' imaginations, and by the data that they have to work with. But it may reduce the likelihood of agents failing to act in virtuous ways despite having a sufficient drive to emulate their exemplars.

The idea that we can be prompted into virtue by our admiration for moral exemplars is intuitively appealing. However, once we identify the different stages that are involved in this process, it becomes apparent how difficult it will be to develop virtue in this way. Anyone looking to use admiration in the development of moral virtue will have reason to take steps to avoid the three potential problems highlighted in this section.

IV. EDUCATING FROM ADMIRATION TO MORAL VIRTUE

One motivation for setting out a model of the path from admiration to moral virtue is that this could prove useful for those interested in virtue education. Before concluding, I want to take some steps in a practical direction and briefly discuss the use of admiration in an educational context.

The character education movement is one of the most prominent approaches to moral education, and influential proponents of this approach have generally been in favour of the use of moral role models.[12] Proposals for an Aristotelian form of role-modelling have been provided by Kristján Kristjánsson (2006) and Wouter Sanderse (2013). Kristjánsson and Sanderse both argue that, in practice, the educational use of role models must involve more than simply exposing students to exemplars and hoping that they will copy the exemplars' behaviour. At best, this will result in mere imitation of positive behaviour. It may not result, using the language set out above, in the habitual performance of virtuous actions.

What is required instead is to combine the experience of exemplars with explicit teaching about the virtues and about moral reasons for action. For example, Sanderse (2013, 37–38) argues that teachers, as potential exemplars, "will have to explain to students how their actions and emotional reactions are related to an ideal of the virtuous life." He also suggests (Sanderse 2013) that the role-modelling process could be improved "by giving so-called 'meta-comments,' verbalising feelings and explaining to students which choices they [the role models] make and why." Similarly, Kristjánsson (2006, 48) argues that any use of exemplars for the purposes of moral education will need to "highlight *moral content*: the reasons why the given quality to be emulated is morally commendable, how it contributes to human well-being." The idea is that combining the experience of exemplars with an explicit discussion of the virtues—what the virtues are, why they are valuable, and how they are related to human well-being—will provide students with the understanding required to do more than simply imitate their moral role models.

This Aristotelian approach of combining role modelling with explicit discussion of the virtues may be helpful in dealing with one of the problems highlighted above. One problem was that an agent might both admire and want to emulate an exemplar, and yet be unable to work out what acting like the exemplar involves in different situations. By taking time to explain why the exemplar is virtuous, and to explain the exemplar's reasoning, those who are educating for virtue might provide students with the tools required to work out how to act when faced with unfamiliar circumstances. For example, if Ben knows why Anne told the truth on a particular occasion (rather than merely witnessing that she did), he will have a better chance of extending that reasoning to unfamiliar circumstances. In this way, the Aristotelian approach suggested by Kristjánsson and Sanderse may go some way in reducing the likelihood of one of the potential problems highlighted above.

However, explicit discussion of the virtues may exacerbate one of the other problems. As explained above, the experience of admiration for an exemplar can fail to result in a sufficient drive to emulate that exemplar. This can happen when agents view emulation as being either too costly or as unlikely to succeed. One possible downside of introducing students to, particularly Aristotelian, accounts of the virtues is that they might come to believe that developing virtues will be extremely difficult, or even impossible.

For example, Aristotelian accounts of the virtues emphasise the importance of *phronesis* (or practical wisdom) and follow Aristotle in arguing that it is not possible to be morally virtuous without also possessing *phronesis*. As explained by Hursthouse (1999, 12), *phronesis* is an ability to "reason correctly about practical matters." As we gain a more detailed understanding of what is involved, it becomes clear that *phronesis* requires a range of different cognitive skills, as well as a high level of understanding concerning things like the likely consequences of actions; the relative weight of different values; and the nature of the good life. In setting out just some of the elements of *phronesis*, Kristjánsson (2015, 88) tells us that

> the function of *phronesis* is to "deliberate finely" about the relative weight of competing values, actions and emotions in the context of the question of "what promotes living well in general." A person who has acquired *phronesis* has thus, *inter alia*, the wisdom to adjudicate the relative weight of different virtues in conflict situations and to reach a measured verdict about best courses of action.

If the Aristotelian position is correct, then the combination of cognitive abilities plus high levels of understanding that is involved in *phronesis* will be required in order for someone to possess moral virtues.[13] Upon learning that the development of any one virtue will require the development of *phronesis*, it would be unsurprising for students to conclude that virtue development will be too demanding, or even impossible, for them. If this happens, students may fail to develop a sufficient drive to emulate their virtuous exemplars.[14]

How might this worry be avoided in the context of virtue education? A first suggestion applies to those who advocate combining exposure to exemplars with explicit teaching about the virtues. In order to avoid students becoming disheartened and losing (or failing to develop) a sufficient drive to emulate, it may be necessary to avoid discussion of certain features of the virtues. That is, those who endorse a demanding account of the virtues may be required to conceal certain aspects of that account when teaching students about the virtues. At least in the initial stages of development, it may be better not to explain that being virtuous requires the complex skills and understanding involved in *phronesis*, for example. Even those who think that this is an accurate claim about the virtues will have reason to refrain from mentioning it when attempting to educate for virtue. This will reduce the chances of students believing that emulating exemplars will be overly demanding, or even impossible.

A second suggestion for avoiding this problem is more general. Those seeking to educate for virtue will have to choose which moral exemplars to provide as examples for discussion. When making this choice, it may be best not to select those whose level of virtue is extreme. Those who risked everything to protect strangers during the Holocaust, or who suffered from persecution for standing up to unjust regimes, are no doubt highly admirable. But their levels of virtue may also be daunting to the moral novice, in the same way that Federer's level of ability can be off-putting to the beginner at tennis. Instead, it will be better to select those exemplars whose virtue is more immediately relatable and attainable.[15] Local examples of people who volunteer to run after-school programmes, or who contribute in less eye-catching ways, may be more effective in terms of ensuring that emulation is perceived as an achievable goal. The, perhaps surprising, result of this brief discussion is that those interested in admiration in the context of virtue education may have practical reasons to de-emphasise certain important features of the virtues, and to select as exemplars those who are less than perfectly admirable.

This discussion of the relevance of the proposed model to virtue education has only addressed the problem of failing to develop a sufficient drive to emulate as a result of viewing virtue as overly demanding or impossible. The hope is that this initial discussion will prompt future work on both this and the other potential problems that were identified above. Such work will be valuable if we want to pursue virtue education in a way that appeals to role models and exemplars.

V. CONCLUSION

I have provided a model of how the experience of admiration for a moral exemplar might lead someone, through a series of progressive stages, to the development of moral virtue. One of the benefits of setting out this model is that it allows us to identify potential problems for the approach—ways in which the path to virtue can go awry. It is hoped that this discussion will be beneficial for those interested in conceptual questions about the development of virtues (and vices), as well as for those interested in practical issues concerning virtue education.[16]

NOTES

1. See, for example, Annas, Narvaez, and Snow (2015); Miller et al. (2015, part VII); and Snow (2014).
2. For a helpful outline of the Aristotelian conception of virtue, see Hursthouse (1999, 10–14). For an excellent introduction to virtue theory, see Battaly (2015).
3. For a discussion of the development of intellectual virtues, see Wilson and Miller (forthcoming).
4. The account of admiration outlined here is set out in Zagzebski (2017, 32–35).
5. Haidt uses "admiration" for the response generated by non-moral excellence and reserves "elevation" for the response generated by moral excellence. I will follow Zagzebski in using "admiration" for both. Kristjánsson (2017) suggests the need to make a further distinction. He describes "a kind of moral awe" for "transpersonal moral beauty."
6. Described in Zagzebski (2017, 41). See also Algoe and Haidt (2009, 106) and Haidt (2003)
7. The usual translation of "zēlos" is "emulation." For discussion, see Zagzebski (2015) and Ben-Ze'ev (2003).
8. The purpose of using a (somewhat thinly described) fictional example is to avoid unnecessary distraction. Those with firm views on who the moral exemplars are should feel free to substitute their own preferred example here.
9. I follow Swanton (2003) here in distinguishing virtuous actions and actions *from* virtue.
10. For discussion of the two proposals mentioned here, see Wilson and Miller (forthcoming).
11. One complicated case would be admiration in response to someone who *appears* virtuous, but who is actually vicious. Such a case may be more like experiencing admiration for a fictional exemplar than for a (real) vicious person.
12. Of course, other prominent approaches to moral education also discuss role models. This includes both Noddings's (2013) care ethics approach and the Kohlbergian approach, although the appeal to modelling is noted as the "least acknowledged of Kohlberg's methods of moral education." See Snarey and Samuelson (2014, 73–75). For an early character education theorist who discusses modelling, see Carr (1991).
13. For more on *phronesis*, see Hursthouse (2006) and Russell (2009, section 1.2).
14. This problem will be exacerbated if we add further elements of Aristotelian doctrine, such as the "unity of virtue" thesis on which the possession of any one virtue requires the possession of all virtues.
15. For a similar point, see Croce and Vaccarezza (2017, 14), where it is argued that "it is easier to imitate someone, when we discover that her moral exemplarity is not beyond our reach."
16. I am grateful to the editors for the opportunity to contribute to this collection. For comments on earlier drafts, I am grateful to Alfred Archer; Christian Miller; participants at the "Psychology of Admiration" conference in Munich; and members of the Beacon Project's work in progress group at Wake Forest University. Work on this chapter was supported by a grant from the Templeton Religion Trust. The opinions expressed here are those of the author and do not necessarily reflect the views of the Templeton Religion Trust.

REFERENCES

Algoe, Sarah B., and Jonathan Haidt. 2009. "Witnessing Excellence in Action: The 'Other-Praising' Emotions of Elevation, Gratitude, and Admiration." *The Journal of Positive Psychology* 4 (2): 105–27.

Annas, Julia. 2011. *Intelligent Virtue*. Oxford: Oxford University Press.

Annas, Julia, Darcia Narvaez, and Nancy E. Snow, eds. 2015. *Developing the Virtues*. Oxford: Oxford University Press.

Aristotle. 1941. *The Nicomachean Ethics*. Oxford: Oxford University Press.

——— 1998. *Rhetoric*. In *The Basic Works of Aristotle*, edited by Richard McKeon, 1325–451. New York: Random House.
Battaly, Heather. 2015. *Virtue*. Malden, MA: Polity Press.
Ben-Ze'ev, Aaron. 2003. "Aristotle on Emotions Towards to the Fortunes of Others." In *Envy, Spite and Jealousy: The Rivalrous Emotions in Ancient Greece*, edited by David Konstan and N. Keith Rutter, 99–121. Edinburgh: Edinburgh University Press.
Carr, David. 1991. *Educating the Virtues*. London: Routledge.
Croce, Michel, and Maria Silvia Vaccarezza. 2017. "Educating through Exemplars: Alternative Paths to Virtue." *Theory and Research in Education* 15 (1): 5–19.
Damon, William, and Anne Colby. 2015. *The Power of Ideals: The Real Story of Moral Choice*. Oxford: Oxford University Press.
Haidt, Jonathan. 2003. "Elevation and the Positive Psychology of Morality." In *Flourishing: Positive Psychology and the Life Well-Lived*, edited by Corey LM Keyes and Jonathan Haidt, 257–89. Washington, DC: American Psychological Association.
Hursthouse, Rosalind. 1999. *On Virtue Ethics*. Oxford: Oxford University Press.
——— 2006. "Practical Wisdom: A Mundane Account." *Proceedings of the Aristotelian Society (New Series)* 106: 285–309.
Kristjánsson, Kristján. 2015. *Aristotelian Character Education*. New York: Routledge.
——— 2017. "Emotions Targeting Moral Exemplarity: Making Sense of the Logical Geography of Admiration, Emulation and Elevation." *Theory and Research in Education* 15 (1): 20–37.
———. 2006. "Emulation and the Use of Role Models in Moral Education." *Journal of Moral Education* 35 (1): 37–49.
Miller, Christian B., R. Michael Furr, Angela Knobel, and William Fleeson, eds. 2015. *Character: New Directions from Philosophy, Psychology and Theology*. Oxford: Oxford University Press.
Noddings, Nel. 2013. *Caring: A Relational Approach to Ethics and Moral Education (Second Edition)*. Los Angeles, CA: University of California Press.
Russell, Daniel C. 2009. *Practical Intelligence and the Virtues*. Oxford: Oxford University Press.
Sanderse, Wouter. 2013. "The Meaning of Role Modelling in Moral and Character Education." *Journal of Moral Education* 42 (1): 28–42.
Snarey, John, and Peter L. Samuelson. 2014. "Lawrence Kohlberg's Revolutionary Ideas." In *Handbook of Moral and Character Education*, edited by Larry Nucci, Darcia Narvaez, and Tobias Krettenauer, 61–83. New York: Routledge.
Snow, Nancy, ed. 2014. *Cultivating Virtue*. Oxford: Oxford University Press.
——— 2018. "From 'Ordinary' Virtue to Aristotelian Virtue." In *The Theory and Practice of Virtue Education*, edited by Tom Harrison and David Ian Walker, 67–82. London: Routledge.
Stichter, Matt. 2007. "Ethical Expertise: The Skill Model of Virtue." *Ethical Theory and Moral Practice* 10 (2): 183–94.
——— 2011. "Virtues, Skills, and Right Action." *Ethical Theory and Moral Practice* 14 (1): 73–86.
Swanton, Christine. 2003. *Virtue Ethics: A Pluralistic View*. Oxford: Oxford University Press.
Velleman, J. David. 2002. "Motivation by Ideal." *Philosophical Explorations* 5 (2): 89–103.
Wilson, Alan T., and Christian B. Miller. Forthcoming. "Virtue Epistemology and Developing Intellectual Virtue." In *The Routledge Handbook of Virtue Epistemology*, edited by Heather Battaly. Routledge.
Zagzebski, Linda. 2015. "Admiration and the Admirable." *Proceedings of the Aristotelian Society Supplementary Volume* 89 (1): 205–21.
——— 2017. *Exemplarist Moral Theory*. New York: Oxford University Press.
———. 2013. "Moral Exemplars in Theory and Practice." *Theory and Research in Education* 11 (2): 193–206.

Chapter Thirteen

Obstacles to the Admiration of Moral People

Florien M. Cramwinckel and Benoît Monin

When people witness the extraordinary behavior of someone else, such as displays of unique physical prowess (e.g., Serena Williams winning her twenty-third Grand Slam tournament while being pregnant), or examples of rare kindness (e.g., a stranger offering to help an old lady shovel the snow from her driveway; Haidt 2000), they often experience admiration, or the "acknowledgement of the superiority of another person, as well as a sense of wonder at their excellence" (Onu, Kessler, and Smith 2016, 219). While this is often discussed in the context of skill and competence (as in the tennis example), in this chapter we focus instead on whether people look up to particularly moral others (as in the shoveling example), a phenomenon we call *moral admiration*.

While there are plenty of situations when do-gooders are indeed admired, recent evidence suggests that this is not always the case (Cramwinckel, Van den Bos, and Van Dijk 2015; Monin 2007), raising some interesting questions about the nature and workings of moral admiration. Witnessing the superior behavior of someone else can also lead to envy (Van de Ven 2017) or self-threat (Cramwinckel et al. 2015), and therefore trigger backlash. While this also happens in the competence domain, this is especially problematic in the moral domain because moral admiration can be an important source of inspiration for prosocial action (e.g., Algoe and Haidt 2009; Aquino, McFerran, and Laven 2011; Van de Vyver and Abrams 2015), while envy or threat often lead to the less productive motivation to pull down those who are better than us (Cramwinckel, Van Dijk, Scheepers, and Van den Bos 2013; Van de Ven 2017). Thus, while moral admiration has the potential to change the world for the better (e.g., Bashir, Lockwood, Chasteen, Nadolny, and Noyes 2013; Bolderdijk, Brouwer, and Cornelissen 2018), obstacles to moral admiration can by contrast lead to more dire consequences.

In this chapter, we first review the positive effects of experiencing moral admiration. Then, we identify several factors that hinder admiration. We focus particularly on factors that uniquely affect moral admiration rather than admiration more generally. Finally, we discuss relevant issues for future research and theorizing on moral admiration.

POSITIVE CONSEQUENCES OF MORAL ADMIRATION

Moral admiration can have positive effects. Witnessing someone portraying moral excellence can induce positive emotions sometimes dubbed "elevation" (Haidt 2000), increasing people's motivation to do good and become a better person (e.g., Algoe and Haidt 2009; Aquino et al. 2011). For example, watching someone displaying moral excellence in a video increases people's willingness to help others out, lengthens the time they actually spend helping others (Schnall, Roper, and Fessler 2010), and increases donation amounts (Van de Vyver and Abrams 2015). Remembering a situation where one felt moral admiration increases subsequent donations (Siegel, Thomson, and Navarro 2014); and reading about moral excellence is enough to increase the motivation to become a mentor (Thomson, Nakamura, Siegel, and Csikszentmihalyi 2014). Note that in most of these cases, participants are inspired to do something that is different from the good deed that inspired them, ruling out a simple conformity interpretation and favoring the notion that inspiration is mediated by some form of elevation. Overall, these studies suggest that moral admiration induces the willingness to become a better person and leads people to engage in more moral behavior. In other words, experiencing moral motivation can change the world for the better. However, it is worth noting that in most of the cases above, moral admiration is evoked by learning about strangers doing exemplary things. In experimental settings, moral admiration is thus often induced by describing actions by unknown, distant others that participants will likely never meet—and in many vignette paradigms, may not even believe really exist. This may lead to different reactions from when one is confronted with moral excellence displayed by a real person in one's immediate life (Tesser 1988), especially when it is exhibited by a similar other. As we will review in the rest of this chapter, in real-life situations where people are confronted with the moral excellence of proximal others, they may experience much less moral admiration than we have documented so far.

CONSTRAINTS TO EXPERIENCING MORAL ADMIRATION

Below, we will discuss several constraints that hinder the experience of moral admiration when confronted with moral excellence. First, we argue that morality is at the core of most people's positive self-regard (Aquino and Reed 2002; Dunning 2007), as evidenced by the fact that they will go to great length to preserve a moral self-image (Mazar, Amir, and Ariely 2008; Monin and Jordan 2009) and reputation (Vonasch, Reynolds, Winegard, and Baumeister 2018). Witnessing the moral superiority of others can therefore be especially threatening, compared to upwards social comparison in other domains. This should be especially pronounced when the moral behavior performed by the other is perceived to be unattainable, or it is performed by someone who is lower in the formal hierarchy.

Moral Excellence as a Threat to Positive Self-Regard

On dimensions that are important to the self-concept (such as morality), people frequently monitor their standing relative to others, and spontaneously compare themselves with salient others to determine their standing on this dimension (Festinger 1954). This means that witnessing a morally superior other can quickly be interpreted as evidence of one's moral inadequacy, and this suggestion is threatening to most people, which may motivate them in turn to reduce this threat by putting the other person down.

There is ample evidence in the non-moral domain demonstrating that people often resent superior others and punish them accordingly. In Taiwanese hair salons, for example, Campbell and colleagues (2017) found that as employees' relative performance increased, they experienced more undermining behaviors from their colleagues. These undermining behaviors were mediated by perceptions that the excellent employees threatened other employee's access to resources. In a different context, Jensen and colleagues (2014) found similarly that the higher the performance of employees, the higher the likelihood of these employees being victims of covert aggression by coworkers (e.g., sabotaging the other's work). This victimization, in turn, reduced performance of excellent employees in a later stage. Thus, people sometimes effectively undermine or exclude others to reduce differences between them and superior others.

Compared to these demonstrations in non-moral domains, superior behavior in the moral domain may have an even more pronounced effect on perceived threat and consequent behavior (Monin 2007). Research on do-gooder derogation has consistently shown that people derogate morally superior others because they fear that these others would look down on them (e.g., Minson and Monin 2012). Resentment against this *imagined moral reproach* seems to be what motivates people to derogate moral superior others. O'Connor and Monin (2016), for example, investigated how obedient participants responded to a rebel who had refused to partake in a racially prejudiced decision task. They demonstrated in two experiments that merely imagining moral reproach by the rebel was enough to lead people to derogate the rebel, even when the rebel would never be in a position to actually judge the participants (for similar findings, see Monin, Sawyer, and Marguez 2008). So the *idea* that morally superior others might look down on one's behavior is enough to trigger resentment. However, people do not necessarily explicitly need to think about how others will view their own behavior in order for them to respond negatively to moral superior others.

Exemplary behavior by others can signal that one's own behavior is not good enough, which can threaten a person's own identity. Therefore, people are reluctant to admire moral superiors or follow their example when (they fear) this will negatively affect their own identity or image (Cramwinckel et al. 2013). For example, Parks and Stone (2010) have found that people wanted to expel extremely generous people (who contributed a lot to the group's shared resources) from their group because these generous group members set an "undesirable behavioral standard." People do not appreciate moral superior others or the behavioral choices they make when their own moral standing is implicitly on the line by comparison. This was posited to explain the actor-observer differences in the admiration of moral rebels demonstrated by Monin and colleagues (2008): individuals who were new to the situation admired the rebels (and recognize the morality of their stance), but individuals who had faced the same choice but had gone along resented the rebel's refusal, presumably because of what their obedience implies about their own failing moral identity, and reinforced by the perception that the rebel would judge the participant and find him or her wanting.

Similarly, Bolderdijk et al. (2018) showed that moral innovators (who promoted the concept of "no-packaging grocery stores") were disliked by target people who had a chance to promote the same concept, and had chosen not to, but not by observers who did not have the prior opportunity to promote the stores. Thus, when people could directly compare their own failure to promote a moral concept with the potentially superior behavior of another person who did, they disliked the other person, as well as the concept they promoted. This was mediated by a threatened identity. However, when people's identities were not on the line, because they did not have a chance to promote the concept, they actually appreciated the morally motivated innovator, as well as the concept this person promoted.

The strongest evidence to support the claim that a threatened self-concept underlies negative reactions to moral others comes from research on do-gooder derogation (Cramwinckel et al. 2013; Monin et al. 2008). Monin and colleagues (2008) demonstrated that obedient participants who went along with a racist task disliked moral others who refused to perform the task.

However, when obedient participants first engaged in self-affirmation—an action where the self-concept is strengthened by explicitly valuing certain aspects of one's self—they did not derogate the moral others who refused. Apparently, people did not need to cope with a potentially threatening situation by derogating others when their self-concept was adequately buffered against threats.

Cramwinckel and colleagues (2013) went one step further by assessing the threat on a physiological level. They demonstrated that individuals experienced physiological markers of threat when they learned about the moral superior behavior of a peer. In their research, participants first tasted a sausage and later read about the behavior of a confederate who had refused to taste the sausage out of moral reasons (vs. out of non-moral reasons). Participants were then invited to engage in a videotaped "speech task" where they talked about their eating behaviors and believed that their speech would be shown to the confederate. During this speech, physiological markers of threat were assessed (e.g., blood pressure, heart rate), in line with the biopsychosocial model of challenge and threat (e.g., Blascovich and Mendes 2010). Results demonstrated that participants indeed experienced threat when they thought they were delivering a speech to the moral confederate (vs. a nonmoral confederate). So apparently, being faced with someone in the same situation as you are who expresses moral reasons for refusing to do what you did can be threatening. Thus, people are worried about being frowned upon by moral superior others, and this trepidation hinders their feelings of admiration for these superior others. Exemplifying this worry, one participant wrote that he/she "did not want the other person to think that [he/she was] a monster for eating meat."

Unattainability of Moral Excellence

Another obstacle to the admiration of moral others is the extent to which the individual perceives the excellence portrayed by the exemplar to be attainable with a reasonable amount of effort (Han, Kim, Jeong, and Cohen 2017). The question of whether attainability enhances or reduces admiration is debated in the literature (e.g., Onu et al. 2016). The social comparison literature (Festinger 1954; Tesser 1988) suggests that superior others are less threatening if they are not relevant comparison standards, either because they differ in different way from the self (e.g., older), or because they are so far ahead on the dimension of comparison that they are more an inspiration than a threat.

However, one crucial difference between moral ideals and other types of ideals (e.g., competence) is that because morality forms such a core aspect of people's identities (Aquino and Reed 2002; Cramwinckel et al. 2015; Dunning 2007; Monin 2007), the morality domain is chronically relevant to people. Because of that, moral superiority by others will almost always be relevant. Therefore, in the moral domain, unattainability may obstruct—rather than increase—admiration. This may be particularly the case when the moral superiority is expressed by proximal others because these people form more relevant comparison standards than distant or unknown others.

This notion is investigated by Han and colleagues (2017), who studied how college students responded to peers who engaged in either attainable moral behavior (e.g., tutoring disadvantaged children for one hour a week) or unattainable moral behavior (e.g., tutoring disadvantaged children for fifteen hours a week). They found that although both types of moral exemplars were perceived as demonstrating moral excellence (assessed by the question "Did you think that the persons presented in the stories were morally excellent and better compared to yourself?"), only those engaging in *attainable* moral behavior evoked moral elevation (assessed by the question "Did you feel morally elevated by the stories?"), which we argue is most akin to admiration here. Perhaps even more important, the influence of moral superior others on participants' own behavior was only heightened when people learned about the attainable behavior of moral superiors. More specifically, six weeks after the experiment, people who learned about the attainable superior behavior reported engaging in roughly seven hours more volunteer work per month than people who learned about unattainable superior behavior. Apparently, admiration of moral others and subsequent behavioral change is hindered when the discrepancy between a morally superior person's behavior and a target person's behavior is too large.

Moral excellence may even backfire and lower moral behavior in others when it is (perceived as) unattainable. Stouten and colleagues (2013) had employees report the ethical leadership of their supervisors, and coworkers reported the respondents' own engagement in organizational citizenship behaviors (OCB; i.e., the extent to which employees engage in voluntary behaviors that support others or the organization). Results showed that, although more ethical leadership by supervisors led to an increase in OCB by respondents, there was a tipping point where even more ethical leadership in fact *decreased* respondents' own OCB behaviors (but see Vianello, Galliani, and Haidt 2010, for research depicting a monotonic positive linear relationship between ethical leadership and OCB). So in sum, admiration for moral superior others may be obstructed when the behavior these others display is seen as unattainable by observers.

The Exemplar's Place in a Formal Hierarchy

Some research suggests that moral admiration may be more easily experienced in hierarchical contexts, where the admired person has higher formal rank or status than the admirer, and moral admiration may seem appropriate.

Wellman and colleagues (2016) showed that individuals disliked coworkers who stood up against ethical wrongdoing (relative to obedient coworkers) when these principled others were positioned lower in the hierarchy, but liked them more when they were located higher in the hierarchy. As a result, people reported more negative behavior (e.g., bullying) towards principled coworkers in lower positions, and less negative behavior towards principled others in higher positions. This suggests that people only acknowledge and admire exemplary behavior from others who hold higher formal positions and try to bring down exemplary others in formally lower positions by derogating them and devaluing them.

FUTURE DIRECTIONS IN MORAL ADMIRATION

Having presented obstacles to moral admiration, we now turn to discussing relevant issues for future research in this domain. First, we describe the difference between moral behavior that is obligatory or forbidden and moral behavior that is recommended, but not obliged. This difference has important consequences on the likelihood that the expressed moral behavior will be admired. Second, we discuss the difference between the intent and consequence of moral actions, and how this influences admiration of these actions. Finally, we reserve some room to discuss what is missing in the assessment of moral admiration in current research.

Proscriptive vs. Prescriptive Morality

Another aspect that is relevant for admiration is whether the moral behavior displayed is in the domain of proscriptive (i.e., "thou shalt not") or prescriptive (i.e., "thou shalt") moral norms. Janoff-Bulman, Sheikh, and Hepp (2009) showed that proscriptive morality tends to be more mandatory and concrete, whereas prescriptive morality tends to be more aspirational and discretionary. The distinctive features of proscriptive and prescriptive morality echo the long-standing philosophical distinction between Kant's perfect duties ("Thou shalt not kill") and imperfect duties ("It's nice to give to charity but you don't have to"). The former suffer no exception and always apply; the latter are desirable but not strictly necessary, a category termed supererogatory in theology and ethics. Thus, proscriptive moral norms dictate which behaviors are obligatory (e.g., being faithful to a spouse) and forbidden (e.g., murder). Prescriptive norms, however, cover behaviors that are desirable but optional (e.g., giving to charity, housing refugees). Similarly, Monin and Miller (2016) suggest that moral choices can be broken down into moral tests (where your morality is at stake if you do or do not engage in a behavior, and your moral identity takes a hit if you do the wrong thing) and moral opportunities (where a behavior is not required, but gives a boost to your moral identity if you choose to engage in it—potentially making up for a previously failed moral test).

This distinction between proscriptive (and required) and prescriptive (and more optional) moral behavior raises the question of the nature of moral admiration, and the possibility that we often reserve moral admiration primarily to reward non-required, supererogatory, good deeds (i.e., loose prescriptive morality for Janoff-Bulman et al. 2009; and a moral opportunity for Monin and Miller 2016).

By its very nature, compliance with the strict moral requirements of proscriptive morality tends to be more common and less distinctive, whereas displays of recommended behaviors suggested by prescriptive morality tend to be more elective, less common, and therefore more distinctive. You don't get a gold star for not killing people—it is assumed most people wouldn't; but taking in a refugee family under your roof is more distinctive, and likely to inspire more moral admiration.

The fact that required and optional behaviors are evaluated quite differently makes moral admiration complex: the basis for admiring others for not cheating on their spouses (an articulable strong *pro*scription) may be quite different from that for admiring people who donate money to charity (a looser and potentially supererogatory *pre*scription). Indeed, Wiltermuth, Monin, and Chow (2010) showed that people think of condemning negative behaviors very differently from praising positive ones, such that people who condemn the most are not necessarily those that conversely praise the most, and that while condemnation is related to Aquino and Reed's (2002) internalization dimension of moral identity, praise is related to symbolization. The strength of proscriptive moral norms, at least the ones that a majority of people agree upon in society, means both that most people abide by them (or pretend they do), and that respecting the norm comes across as the basic requirement to be a decent individual, and not a badge of any special virtue. Therefore, moral admiration is likely to be elicited less by people who meet these basic requirements (i.e., abide by proscriptive norms) than by those who demonstrate recommended moral behavior (i.e., prescriptive norms). This raises the possibility that moral admiration is most likely to occur in the domain of prescriptive morality.

Of particular interest in this context are cases of moral disagreement, and in particular about whether something is prescribed or proscribed. For example, many meat eaters consider a vegetarian diet to be laudable, but not necessary—a moral prescription. However, many vegetarians see their dietary choices as obligatory, and eating meat as forbidden—a moral proscription. This difference in perspective can give rise to resentment and tension, because whereas the prescribers (here, meat eaters) are ready to admire someone who manages to cut their meat intake, the proscribers (here, vegetarians) are ready to condemn someone who fails to do so—or be perceived to condemn, triggering resentment (Minson and Monin 2012).

Although vegans and volunteers may both demonstrate morally laudable behaviors, volunteers may be more likely to be admired than vegans. People who volunteer a great deal or give a lot to charity can be a threatening standard to compare oneself to, but they are likely to inspire less resentment—precisely because one doesn't assume they see volunteering as a proscription, and therefore there is less of an implication that they judge others who do not behave like them. This again raises the possibility that moral admiration is more readily elicited by displays of morality in the domain of prescriptive, rather than proscriptive, moral behavior—and that it helps to believe the exemplary actor is not proscribing either.

Intent vs. Consequences

Another complexity that may be interesting for future research is the importance of intent over consequences, which echoes to some extent the distinction between deontology (e.g., Immanuel Kant) and utilitarianism (e.g., John Stuart Mill). There is a potential tension between admiring how much good one is bringing to the world (or how much damage one is preventing) and how much effort or intention one put into the moral act. Are billionaires who endow hospitals in their name with large reputational and tax benefits to be less admired than parishioners who spend their weekends handing out meals at the soup kitchen? Are bank CEOs who become rich by providing microloans to small businesses in developing countries to be less admired than individuals who donate money to an inefficient charity that has no measurable impact in the field? In both cases, our intuitions tug to the latter, even though their impact is trivial relative to the former.

This suggests that moral praise can be quite disconnected with the good one's actions are actually bringing about. Indeed, morally motivated individuals can be admired even if their efforts are entirely fruitless, as long as one agrees with their values. The millionaire example above also brings to the fore the issue of motivation or intent. A focus on consequences should put little weight on motivation: even if a donation is purely prudential or self-interested, it should inspire admiration. Conversely, an exclusive focus on intention would disregard consequence and only scrutinize motivation. In typical attributional logic (Kelley 1973) and in line with the work on suspicion (Fein, Hilton, and Miller 1990), knowledge of an ulterior motive would diminish the attribution of moral motives, and to the extent that this is what matters, this should diminish moral admiration.

This is demonstrated by Newman and Cain (2014) who show that people experienced *less* admiration for others who displayed charitable behavior that also had some personal benefits than for others who did not display any charitable behavior. Apparently, when evaluating moral behavior by others, people seem to weigh intent heavier than consequences. In the context of this chapter, it suggests that on the positive side, moral admiration is likely to require the perception of moral intent, and may be quite detached from the actual consequences of good deeds.

The relationship between intent, consequences, and moral admiration is further complicated by the fact that non-philosophers often perceive consequential reasoning as non-moral. As Kreps and Monin (2011) have demonstrated, individuals see policies argued on the basis of principles as more morally motivated than those justified on the basis of maximizing welfare. Thus, although philosophers have argued that decisions based on consequences (i.e., outcomes) can be equally moralized as those based on intentions or rules, lay people often do not recognize decisions or policies based on consequential reasoning as grounded in moral reasoning. Thus, a politician who promotes cracking down on opioids because of the financial burden these constitute for society in terms of health services, decreased productivity, the cost of crime, and so on, might come across as an able and pragmatic administrator, but is less likely to be seen as morally motivated, and therefore elicit less moral admiration than a politician who takes the same measures but grounds them in a rhetoric of the evil of drugs and the purity of the heartland, with seemingly little consideration for pragmatic consequences.

It is also interesting to note in the example of opioids just discussed that the moral intent argument naturally gravitates toward a story of culprits (drug dealers, either from criminal cartels or from the pharmaceutical health-industrial complex) and victims (innocent children, or patients with debilitating pain), in line with the dyadic morality model (Gray, Schein, and Ward 2014). At the extreme, sacrifice seems to elicit moral admiration, even when the costs incurred were not chosen (i.e., victimhood). That Martin Luther King or Harvey Milk, in the American context, are admired as moral heroes makes sense because they put their lives on the line for a moral cause, knowing some of the risks. But why is Anne Frank often spoken of as if she were a moral hero? Or Helen Keller? While there is plenty to feel sorry about in their stories, and their resilience is worth admiring, it is less clear why their victimhood necessarily should elicit moral admiration. Feats of amazing benevolence can be summarily dismissed as unworthy of moral admiration if attributed to self-serving ulterior motives. Conversely, extreme abnegation leading to enormous self-sacrifice and clearly articulated moral motives inspires great moral admiration even in the absence of any tangible benefits for society, humankind, or the world as a whole. Both Western and Eastern religions provide examples of sainthood predicated on martyrdom and self-inflicted pain or discomfort with little benefits to worldly concerns. Schaumberg and Mullen (2017) have shown that suffering a cost, even if incidental (e.g., being stung by a bee while volunteering), makes the moral act seem more worthy of praise, even if there is no normative justification for it (i.e., it's not like the volunteer chose to endure it).

In summary, it is important in future work to focus on the difference between intentions and consequences in the domain of moral admiration. As some of the examples above suggest, humans may be biased towards intent when it comes to moral admiration, and not give enough credit to the consequences aspect of moral behavior, which is often where the real impact is.

Assessing Moral Admiration

At this stage it is worth paying some attention to how moral admiration is assessed in research. Although moral admiration is the nominal focus of this chapter, a somewhat different construct—which could be termed "praise" or "moral agreement"—is more typically assessed in research. Even here, we have until now confounded the two somewhat. An examination or potential differences and similarities between admiration, praise, and agreement is warranted. By "praise," we mean the type of measures generally used in the moral psychology literature to capture whether participants deem a behavior or individual to be morally worthy. This is any measure that taps into whether a behavior is moral or immoral, often by relying on vignettes with subtle variations. This is rooted in the classic philosophical tradition of moral dilemmas or the reflective equilibrium approach (Rawls 2009) in ethical reasoning, which identifies cases which fit a general ethical theory (e.g., utilitarianism) but clash with a moral intuition, suggesting that the theory may need adjustment.

Much of moral psychology sidesteps the issue of moral admiration by asking whether a character in a scenario or vignette *should* have acted in a certain way or not, or whether it would be appropriate for someone to engage in a given behavior. In the classic Kohlberg dilemmas (1969), for example, the interviewer asks, "Should Heinz have broken into the laboratory to steal the drug for his wife? Why or why not?" There is no opportunity to express admiration for Heinz even if you think he did the right thing, the focus is on deciding what the actor should do. In Greene, Sommerville, Nystrom, Darley, and Cohen's (2001) widely cited exploration of moral reasoning in the MRI scanner, participants answered questions like "Is it appropriate for you to hire this surgeon to carve out a stranger's eye in order to help restore your vision?"—again the focus seems to be on the act, and perhaps on the repugnance for the actor, but there is no room for participants to express moral admiration. Haidt, Koller, and Dias (1993) ask, after reading situations like the family eating their dead dog, "What do you think about this? Is it very wrong, a little wrong, or is it perfectly okay?" Again, "Perfectly okay" is arguably not the same as admiration. Similarly, Haidt (2001) asks about the famous sibling incest dilemma, "What do you think about that? Was it OK for them to make love?" Again, moral admiration is not part of the picture.

Even when the focus is squarely on moral character, it probably should not be equated with moral admiration. Schaumberg and Mullen (2017), for example, operationalized perceived moral character as the average of ratings on traits like honest, kind, or moral. Wiltermuth and colleagues (2010), less subtly, just asked, "How moral is [the vignette character] for acting like this?" on a scale ranging from "extremely immoral" to "extremely moral." It can be questioned whether these types of measures are related to moral admiration. In the non-moral domain if one asked participants to describe how tall or how intelligent a target seems, their answers would most likely not be coded as admiration. So it is not clear to what extent the work on perceived moral character is relevant to the psychology of moral admiration. And what would be the additional step required for admiration?

This is an important question because although one may assume that evaluating an action is equivalent to evaluating the actor, recent research suggests otherwise. In a fascinating series of studies, Uhlmann, Zhu, and Tannenbaum (2013) compared asking people about whether a decision was ethical or morally right/good vs. whether actors have good moral character, are ethical, or are morally good. They find that a choice can be praised as the right thing to do (e.g., ones that involve sacrificing one person for the good of the many), even when the person making that choice is seen as less moral than those who do not. Again, this suggests that it would be inaccurate to interpret moral approval for a course of action as necessarily implying praise, let alone moral admiration for the actor, as observers can approve of a course of action and disapprove of the actor.

What then might be the difference between moral praise and moral admiration? Moral admiration is more than the acknowledgement of the morality of the actor's actions, it requires self-relevance, as well as some acknowledgement of the admirer's own inferiority. We started this chapter by defining admiration as "acknowledgement of the superiority of another person, as well as a sense of wonder at their excellence" (Onu et al. 2016). This suggests at least two elements beyond praise to qualify as admiration: (1) a recognition that beyond being good (praise), they are superior, and (2) a sense of wonder (described earlier as elevation, see Haidt 2000). Whenever the admiration is not self-relevant, it seems that it is used merely as a figure of speech. When a person who never smoked "admires" someone quitting cigarettes, the admiration only rings true if it is self-relevant—I remember how hard it was for me to quit coffee. Admiration is a diluted version of "I wish I were you." It is upwards social comparison devoid of resentment.

In short, when investigating moral admiration, it is important to assess the right construct. Moral admiration is different from the judgement that an action is or is not moral, or even merely that someone's character is moral. It is acknowledgement of the moral superiority of the other's action (and one's own inferiority), as well as a sense of marvel at the other's excellence and a motivation to improve. It is important to include all these elements in future research on moral admiration.

CONCLUDING REMARKS

Experiencing moral admiration has the potential to change the world for the better. It is the motivation to improve oneself and one's behavior after witnessing moral excellence in someone else. Although moral admiration is often evoked by learning about moral excellence of distant others, it is more difficult to experience when proximal others show moral superiority. In these cases, several obstacles arise. Moral superiority of close others may threaten one's positive self-regard and may underline inequality between people in a domain that is highly self-relevant for most people. This raises the question of how moral admiration could or should function in egalitarian societies where all people are (or are supposed to be) equals. These obstacles therefore raise important questions: Does striving for an egalitarian society where everyone is equal actually hinder admiration of those who try to move society forward and thereby also undermine the potential positive influence of these people on others' behavior? Should people strive for small increments of moral improvement rather than radical change?

Because of the potential of moral admiration to create meaningful change, moral admiration may be a fruitful area of future research. Several areas are particularly interesting for future research, such as the different domains of moral behavior; the differences between intent and consequences of moral behavior; and how these aspects influence moral admiration. Finally, we think that it is important to study the actual construct of moral admiration, in order to gain more insight in its workings and consequences, and perhaps even answer some of the thought-provoking questions raised above.

REFERENCES

Algoe, S. B., and J. Haidt. 2009. "Witnessing Excellence in Action: The 'Other-Praising' Emotions of Elevation, Gratitude, and Admiration." *The Journal of Positive Psychology*, 4 (2): 105–27. doi:10.1080/17439760802650519.

Aquino, K., B. McFerran, and M. Laven. 2011. "Moral Identity and the Experience of Moral Elevation in Response to Acts of Uncommon Goodness." *Journal of Personality and Social Psychology* 100 (4): 703–18. doi:10.1037/a0022540.

Aquino, K., and I. I. Reed. 2002. "The Self-Importance of Moral Identity." *Journal of Personality and Social Psychology* 83 (6): 1423.

Bashir, N. Y., P. Lockwood, A. L. Chasteen, D. Nadolny, and I. Noyes. 2013. "The Ironic Impact of Activists: Negative Stereotypes Reduce Social Change Influence." *European Journal of Social Psychology* 43 (7): 614–26. doi:10.1002/ejsp.1983.

Blascovich, J., and W. B. Mendes. 2010. "Social Psychophysiology and Embodiment." In *The Handbook of Social Psychology, Vol.* 5, edited by S. T. Fiske, D. T. Gilbert, and G. Lindzey, 194–227. New York: Wiley.

Bolderdijk, J. W., C. Brouwer, and G. Cornelissen. 2018. "When Do Morally Motivated Innovators Elicit Inspiration Instead of Irritation?" *Frontiers in Psychology* 8 (2362). doi:10.3389/fpsyg.2017.02362.

Campbell, E. M., H. Liao, A. Chuang, J. Zhou, and Y. Dong. 2017. "Hot Shots and Cool Reception? An Expanded View of Social Consequences for High Performers." *Journal of Applied Psychology* 102 (5): 845–66. doi:10.1037/apl0000183.

Cramwinckel, F. M., K. Van den Bos, and E. Van Dijk. 2015. "Reactions to Morally Motivated Deviance." *Current Opinion in Psychology* 6 (December): 150–56. doi:10.1016/j.copsyc.2015.08.007.

Cramwinckel, F. M., E. van Dijk, D. T. Scheepers, and K. Van den Bos 2013. "The Threat of Moral Refusers for One's Self-Concept and the Protective Function of Physical Cleansing." *Journal of Experimental Social Psychology* 49 (6): 1049–58. doi:10.1016/j.jesp.2013.07.009.

Dunning, D. 2007. "Self-Image Motives and Consumer Behavior: How Sacrosanct Self-Beliefs Sway Preferences in the Marketplace." *Journal of Consumer Psychology* 17 (4): 237–49.

Fein, S., J. L. Hilton, and D. T. Miller. 1990. "Suspicion of Ulterior Motivation and the Correspondence Bias." *Journal of Personality and Social Psychology* 58 (5): 753.

Festinger, L. 1954. "A Theory of Social Comparison Processes." *Human Relations* 7 (117). doi:10.1177/001872675400700202.

Gray, K., C. Schein, and A. F. Ward. 2014. The Myth of Harmless Wrongs in Moral Cognition: Automatic Dyadic Completion from Sin to Suffering." *Journal of Experimental Psychology: General* 143 (4): 1600.

Greene, J. D., R. B. Sommerville, L. E. Nystrom, J. M. Darley, and J. D. Cohen. 2001. "An fMRI Investigation of Emotional Engagement in Moral Judgment." *Science* 293 (5537): 2105–8.

Haidt, J. 2000. "The Positive Emotion of Elevation." *Prevention & Treatment* 3 (3): 1–5.

Haidt, J. 2001. "The Emotional Dog and Its Rational Tail: A Social Intuitionist Approach to Moral Judgment." *Psychological Review* 108 (4): 814.

Haidt, J., S. H. Koller, and M. G. Dias. 1993. "Affect, Culture, and Morality, or Is It Wrong to Eat Your Dog?" *Journal of Personality and Social Psychology* 65 (4): 613.

Han, H., J. Kim, C. Jeong, and G. L. Cohen. 2017. "Attainable and Relevant Moral Exemplars Are More Effective Than Extraordinary Exemplars in Promoting Voluntary Service Engagement." *Frontiers in Psychology* 8 (283). doi:10.3389/fpsyg.2017.00283.

Janoff-Bulman, R., S. Sheikh, and S. Hepp. 2009. "Proscriptive versus Prescriptive Morality: Two Faces of Moral Regulation." *Journal of Personality and Social Psychology* 96 (3): 521.

Jensen, J. M., P. C. Patel, and J. L. Raver. 2014. "Is It Better to Be Average? High and Low Performance as Predictors of Employee Victimization." *Journal of Applied Psychology* 99 (2): 296–309. doi:10.1037/a0034822.

Johansson, L.-O., and H. Svedsäter. 2009. "Piece of Cake? Allocating Rewards to Third Parties When Fairness Is Costly." *Organizational Behavior and Human Decision Processes* 109 (2): 107–19. doi:10.1016/j.obhdp.2009.02.001.

Kelley, H. H. 1973. "The Processes of Causal Attribution." *American Psychologist* 28 (2): 107.

Kohlberg, L. 1969. *Stage and Sequence: The Cognitive-Developmental Approach to Socialization*. Chicago: Rand McNally.

Kreps, T. A., and B. Monin. 2011. "'Doing Well by Doing Good'? Ambivalent Moral Framing in Organizations." *Research in Organizational Behavior* 31: 99–123.

Mazar, N., O. Amir, and D. Ariely. 2008. "The Dishonesty of Honest People: A Theory of Self-Concept Maintenance." *Journal of Marketing Research* 45 (6): 633–44.

Minson, J. A., and B. Monin. 2012. "Do-Gooder Derogation: Disparaging Morally Motivated Minorities to Defuse Anticipated Reproach." *Social Psychological and Personality Science* 3 (2): 200–7. doi:10.1177/1948550611415695.

Monin, B. 2007. "Holier Than Me? Threatening Social Comparison in the Moral Domain." *Revue Internationale de Psychologie Sociale* 20 (1): 53–68.

Monin, B., and D. T. Miller. 2016. "Moral Opportunities versus Moral Tests." In *The Social Psychology of Morality*, edited by J. Forgas, P. van Lange, and L. Jussim, 56–71. New York: Routledge.

Monin, B., and A. H. Jordan. 2009. "The Dynamic Moral Self: A Social Psychological Perspective." In *Personality, Identity, and Character: Explorations in Moral Psychology*, edited by D. Narvaez and D. K. Lapsey, 341–54. New York: Cambridge University Press.

Monin, B., P. J. Sawyer, and M. J. Marquez. 2008. "The Rejection of Moral Rebels: Resenting Those Who Do the Right Thing." *Journal of Personality and Social Psychology* 95 (1): 76–93. doi:10.1037/0022-3514.95.1.76.

Newman, G. E., and D. M. Cain. 2014. "Tainted Altruism: When Doing Some Good Is Evaluated as Worse Than Doing No Good at All." *Psychological Science* 25 (3): 648–55.

O'Connor, K., and B. Monin. 2016. "When Principled Deviance Becomes Moral Threat: Testing Alternative Mechanisms for the Rejection of Moral Rebels." *Group Processes & Intergroup Relations* 19 (5): 676–693. doi:10.1177/1368430216638538.

Onu, D., T. Kessler, and J. R. Smith. 2016. "Admiration: A Conceptual Review." *Emotion Review* 8 (3): 218–30. doi: 10.1177/1754073915610438.

Parks, C. D., and A. B. Stone. 2010. "The Desire to Expel Unselfish Members from the Group. *Journal of Personality and Social Psychology*, 99 (2): 303–10. doi:10.1037/a0018403.

Rawls, J. 2009. *A Theory of Justice: Revised Edition*. Harvard University Press.

Schaumberg, R. L., and E. Mullen 2017. "From Incidental Harms to Moral Elevation: The Positive Effect of Experiencing Unintentional, Uncontrollable, and Unavoidable Harms on Perceived Moral Character." *Journal of Experimental Social Psychology* 73: 86–96. doi:10.1016/j.jesp.2017.06.016.

Schnall, S., J. Roper, and D. M. T. Fessler. 2010. "Elevation Leads to Altruistic Behavior." *Psychological Science* 21 (3): 315–20. doi:10.1177/0956797609359882.

Shaw, A., and K. R. Olson. 2012. "Children Discard a Resource to Avoid Inequity." *Journal of Experimental Psychology: General* 141 (2): 382–95. doi: 10.1037/a0025907.

Sherman, D. K., and G. L. Cohen. 2006. "The Psychology of Self-Defense: Self-Affirmation Theory." *Advances in Experimental Social Psychology* 38: 183–242.

Siegel, J. T., A. L. Thomson, and M. A. Navarro. 2014. "Experimentally Distinguishing Elevation from Gratitude: Oh, the Morality." *The Journal of Positive Psychology* 9 (5): 414–27. doi:10.1080/17439760.2014.910825.

Stouten, J., M. Van Dijke, D. M. Mayer, D. De Cremer, and M. C. Euwema. 2013. "Can a Leader Be Seen as Too Ethical? The Curvilinear Effects of Ethical Leadership." *The Leadership Quarterly* 24 (5): 680–95. doi: -10.1016/j.leaqua.2013.05.002.

Tesser, A. 1988. "Toward a Self-Evaluation Maintenance Model of Social Behavior." In *Advances in Experimental Social Psychology* (Vol. 21), 181–227. Cambridge, MA: Elsevier/Academic Press.

Thomson, A. L., J. Nakamura, J. T. Siegel, and M. Csikszentmihalyi. 2014. "Elevation and Mentoring: An Experimental Assessment of Causal Relations." *The Journal of Positive Psychology* 9 (5): 402–13. doi: -10.1080/17439760.2014.910824.

Uhlmann, E. L., L. L. Zhu, and D. Tannenbaum. 2013. "When It Takes a Bad Person to Do the Right Thing." *Cognition* 126 (2): 326–34.

Van de Ven, N. 2017. "Envy and Admiration: Emotion and Motivation Following Upward Social Comparison." *Cognition and Emotion* 31 (1): 193–200. doi: -10.1080/02699931.2015.1087972.

Van de Vyver, J., and D. Abrams. 2015. "Testing the Prosocial Effectiveness of the Prototypical Moral Emotions: Elevation Increases Benevolent Behaviors and Outrage Increases Justice Behaviors." *Journal of Experimental Social Psychology* 58 (May): 23–33. doi: 10.1016/j.jesp.2014.12.005.

Vianello, M., E. M. Galliani, and J. Haidt. 2010. "Elevation at Work: The Effects of Leaders' Moral Excellence." *The Journal of Positive Psychology* 5 (5): 390–411. doi: -10.1080/17439760.2010.516764.

Vonasch, A. J., T. Reynolds, B. M. Winegard, and R. F. Baumeister. 2018. "Death before Dishonor: Incurring Costs to Protect Moral Reputation." *Social Psychological and Personality Science* 9 (5): 604–13. doi: -10.1177/1948550617720271.

Watanabe, S. 2017. "Social Inequality Aversion in Mice: Analysis with Stress-Induced Hyperthermia and Behavioral Preference." *Learning and Motivation* 59 (August): 38–46. doi: -10.1016/j.lmot.2017.08.002.

Wellman, N., D. M. Mayer, M. Ong, and D. S. DeRue. 2016. "When Are Do-Gooders Treated Badly? Legitimate Power, Role Expectations, and Reactions to Moral Objection in Organizations." *Journal of Applied Psychology* 101 (6): 793–814. doi:10.1037/apl0000094.

Wiltermuth, S. S., B. Monin, and R. M. Chow. 2010. "The Orthogonality of Praise and Condemnation in Moral Judgment." *Social Psychological and Personality Science* 1 (4): 302–10.

Xiao, E., and C. Bicchieri. 2010. "When Equality Trumps Reciprocity." *Journal of Economic Psychology* 31 (3): 456–70. doi:10.1016/j.joep.2010.02.001.

Chapter Fourteen

How Admiring Moral Exemplars Can Ruin Your Life

The Case of Conrad's Lord Jim

Alan Thomas, Alfred Archer, and Bart Engelen

What role should admiration for moral exemplars play in the moral development of those with more ordinary levels of moral virtue? Linda Zagzebski (2017) has argued that exemplars should serve as models for emulation. We agree that exemplars have an important role to play in moral education (see Engelen et al., forthcoming). However, our aim in this chapter will be to sound a warning about the ways in which attempting to emulate exemplars can go badly wrong. While in some circumstances, attempting to imitate a moral exemplar can improve one's behaviour, in other circumstances it can constitute a distinctive form of moral error. We will illustrate this with the example of the eponymous hero of Joseph Conrad's novel *Lord Jim*, whose attempts to emulate his heroes lead to disaster. The case of Jim reveals how emulating heroes can ruin a person's life. Imagining oneself in the exemplary role of a hero may undermine one's ability to respond appropriately to ethical challenges. It leads Jim not only to ruin his life, but also to embrace his unnecessary death.[1]

Our discussion proceeds as follows. In section 1, we explain Zagzebski's account of moral development through the emulation of moral exemplars. Section 2 shows how attempting to emulate moral exemplars can ground a distinctive form of moral error. In section 3, we relate this analysis to the notions of "moral weightlifting" and "reflexive anchoring" and provide an alternative account of how moral exemplars should feature in moral reasoning.

1. ZAGZEBSKI ON EXEMPLARS, ADMIRATION, AND EMULATION

Zagzebski claims that we learn to become virtuous through imitating moral exemplars (2017, ch. 5). Exemplars set an inspiring standard by demonstrating the "upper reaches of human capability." They are not merely good people; they are excellent people. A hero is one form of exemplar who "takes great risks to achieve a moral end" (Zagzebski 2017, 1). Key to Zagzebski's (2017, 2) account is the emotion of admiration as it is through admiration that we first identify moral exemplars. Admiration helps us to identify exemplars via the properties of the person admired: "we recognize a connection between feeling admiration and seeing someone *as* admirable, as deserving of admiration" (Zagzebski 2017, 3). Admiration is, in other words, a response that is merited in virtue of some properties of the person admired.

In addition, admiration provides us with a desire to emulate those exemplars. Zagzebski (2017, 43) makes a distinction between admiration for natural talents (those that people are born with) and for acquired excellences (those that people have had to work to develop). While the latter tends to be motivating, the former is not. When we admire the natural talents of a Beethoven or a Frida Kahlo, we cannot emulate them. But if the artistic exemplar's achievements depend on hard work, then we can admire and be inspired by that work. She supports this claim by appealing to a number of psychological studies that support this link between admiration and emulation.[2] As moral and intellectual excellence is acquired rather than in-born, Zagzebski argues, we typically have a desire to emulate the person whose moral or intellectual excellence we admire.

What exactly is involved in this desire to emulate? According to Zagzebski (2017, 131), "Emulation is a form of imitation in which the emulated person is perceived as a model in some respect—a model of cooking, dancing, playing basketball, doing philosophy." Emulating someone then need not involve trying to be like them in every respect; it is more sophisticated than merely imitating them. We do not want to impersonate exemplars; rather, we try to follow in their footsteps. Zagzebski stresses that emulation involves taking an exemplar as a model in particular areas of life and relative to some specific practice or activity. She thus deliberately limits the scope of her claim: emulating is imitation only of that limited set of characteristics that enabled the admired person to do what she did.

Zagzebski concedes that this claim is not always strictly true. While she admires the character of Sir Robert Falcon Scott, she does not want to emulate him even in the limited sense of wanting to develop the qualities of character that would enable her to lead an expedition to the South Pole. Nonfictional narratives about Scott, Zagzebski (2017, 20) argues, can still motivate her to be a person of the same general kind as the exemplar one admires.

Our worry is that this immediately begins to put some strain on the idea of emulation. What is it to be the same *kind* of person as Scott, but not Scott? Perhaps we should interpret this along the lines of virtue ethics: exemplars are exemplifying bundles of interconnected virtues, which are the proper focus of people's admiration. At times, Zagzebski comes close to this: "Admiration for a person moves us to emulate the admired person *in the respect in which the person is admired*" (Zagzebski 2017, 51, emphasis added). We admire "not the acts themselves, but *whatever it is about the person that leads her to do such acts*. . . . In Western philosophy that has been called a trait of character" (Zagzebski 2017, 97). It is hard to see how such claims, which fit traditional virtue ethics perfectly, can constitute a new moral theory.

Conceding that this postulated connection between admiration and emulation is controversial, Zagzebski explains that by emulating an exemplar we can improve our behaviour, even if the end result falls far below the level of the exemplar's achievements:

> When I speak of emulating X, then, I mean taking X as my model, attempting to be more like X. I do not think of emulation in such a way that whenever A emulates X, it is possible for A to become as good as X, nor does it include A's belief that she can do so. (Zagzebski, 2017 38)

So the person who is inspired wants to be a person of the same general type of the exemplar but does not aim to be *as* excellent. You approximate the ideal set by the model in your own life and improve your behaviour.

Before setting out our warning about the use of exemplars as an educative resource—that emulating moral exemplars can actually lead to moral error—note that even Zagzebski's more nuanced account raises questions. Is emulation a "success term" (you emulate X only if you succeed in being more like X) or is trying enough? And is emulation about the process of improving (becoming more like X) or the end result (being the same kind of person)? Even when I succeed in becoming more like some moral exemplar, I can remain quite distant from my target. At the lower end of the scale of human ambition, a person who emulates a moral exemplar can remain, even when improved, a morally unimpressive person. Our main worry about the use of moral exemplars as a tool for moral improvement, however, is even stronger. We argue that emulation of moral exemplars can lead to moral error and ruin your life.

2. HOW ADMIRING MORAL EXEMPLARS CAN RUIN YOUR LIFE

Conrad's *Lord Jim* (Conrad 1900/1993) demonstrates how exemplars playing the wrong kind of role in reflection can play an ethically destructive role in a person's life. Conrad introduces the narrative's eponymous anti-hero, Jim, as an English sailor who envisages himself as a hero in waiting. Jim continually fantasizes about "his" acts of heroism:

> On the lower deck in the babel of two hundred voices he would forget himself, and beforehand live in his mind the sea-life of light literature. He saw himself saving people from sinking ships, cutting away masts in a hurricane, swimming through a surf with a line; or as a lonely castaway, barefooted and half naked, walking on uncovered reefs in search of a shellfish to stave off starvation. He confronted savages on tropical shores, quelled mutinies on the high seas, and in a small boat upon the ocean kept up the hearts of despairing men—always an example of devotion to duty, and as unflinching as a hero in a book. (Conrad 1900/1993, 5)

Early in the narrative, Jim has the opportunity to help to rescue two drowning men. However, rather than rushing to assist, Jim finds himself transfixed whilst his crewmates carry out the rescue. Jim broods while the leader of the rescue operation is treated like a hero. He consoles himself, though, with contempt for such minor acts of heroism, deeming them unworthy of his own greatness (Conrad 1900/1993, 6).

Another opportunity for heroism soon presents itself. Jim is working aboard the *Patna*, an unseaworthy ship taking pilgrims to Mecca, when the ship strikes a submerged object and begins to take on water. The crew of "Europeans," including Jim, abandon ship and make no effort to save any of its passengers. The ship, in fact, does not sink and is towed into port with no loss of life. When the crew are picked up, they face the scandal of having abandoned ship and appear before a disciplinary tribunal. Jim is disgraced and loses his professional license. When Captain Charles Marlow offers Jim the option to flee before final sentencing, Jim refuses. Aided by Marlow, he takes on jobs as a chandler's water clerk. However, every time the *Patna* scandal "catches up with him," he flees, always further "East."

Jim ends up in the isolated province of Patusan. Involved in local, colonial politics, Jim is accepted by Patusan's citizens as a trusted intermediary earning the honorary title of "Tuan"—"Lord." He is respected and finds both love and a kind of peace in Patusan: "I have got back my confidence in myself—a good name—yet sometimes I wish . . . No! I shall hold what I've got. Can't expect anything more" (Conrad 1900/1993, 254).

Jim's happiness, however, is fated not to last. In Jim's temporary absence, an adventurer, Brown, leads a gang of criminals in an assault on Patusan. On his return, Jim permits safe passage for Brown and his companions, but is caught unaware when Brown and his gang, on departing, kill several of the villagers. These include Dain Waris, son of the local chief and Jim's friend. While he could have fled, Jim scapegoats himself and presents himself to Dain Waris's father, knowing that his punishment will be death.

Throughout the novel, the explanation of Jim's conduct is his conception of how a hero ought to behave. Drawn from "light literature," Jim's fantasies see him ill-prepared to even recognize situations that call for heroism and to respond appropriately to the situations in which he finds himself. Jim views himself as the victim of bad luck: the occasion or the timing is never right. After the *Patna* incident, the depths of the demands placed on him by the ideal of the heroic lead Jim to think of himself as a total disgrace. He attempts to atone by standing trial, and accepting his formal punishment, but views himself as forever disgraced in the eyes of others. Hence his constant flight, leading to his apparent redemption in Patusan. But here, too, Jim seeks out an opportunity to redeem himself through a tragically misplaced sacrifice.

We are not alone in taking Conrad's portrait of Jim as a source of inspiration for moral philosophy. Daniel Brudney (1998) appeals to it to present a challenge to views of moral judgement that place too great an emphasis on the importance of rules and principles. Craig Taylor (2011), meanwhile, argues that there is an ambiguity at the heart of the novel in how we should assess Jim's decision to accept his death. Appreciating this ambiguity can contribute to our moral understanding by helping us see the potential blind spots and limitations of our own characters. Peter Goldie cites Jim as an example of how our understanding of people through fictional genres can flatten out our view of their characters and lead us to "expect too much of our heroes, and . . . too little of our villains" (2012, 169). Because he expects too much of himself, Jim is unable to forgive himself for failing to live up to his idea of the hero, ending up in self-reproach and self-blame. In a response to Goldie's analysis, Edward Harcourt (2016) focuses on the distinctive form of Jim's moral consciousness and his susceptibility to "Bovarysme": Jim ethically ruins his life by having literary models from "light fiction" dominate his life. His consciousness is formed by fiction, which provides scripts and ideals he simply never questions. Instead of taking "heroic imaginings" as mere starting points for practical reasoning (which Harcourt would deem appropriate), he wants to act them out in attempts to sustain his grandiose self-image.

We do not intend to argue against any of these claims. Our goal is to offer a complementary analysis of Jim's case that builds on these analyses and highlights the potentially damaging effects of attempting to emulate moral exemplars. Our diagnosis of Jim's moral errors consists of two parts: (1) Jim's focus on superficial aspects of his admired heroes and (2) the fact that he does not attend to those heroes' specific moral psychology.

First of all, Jim's admiration for heroes is indeed superficial, seeking solely to imitate those who paradigmatically fulfil the role of "the hero" and imaginatively substituting himself into heroic narratives. To use one of Bernard Williams's expressions (1985, 10–11) this is a "misdirection of ethical attention," away from occasions for virtue, to what it is to be ascribed virtuous by others. Jim is excessively concerned with the outward form of the heroic rather than with the moral character of heroes. He adopts the mannerisms and appearances that he deems fitting for men capable of the kind of heroism he sees himself performing. As a result, Jim is overly focused on the perception of his own character in the eyes of others; he is (tragically) less concerned with developing the capacity to act appropriately when occasions for virtue present themselves.

Being attracted to the superficial aspects of heroes need not always constitute an error. Zagzebski (2017, 97) notes that "we are usually drawn to [exemplars] initially because we admire something easily observable about them—typically, their acts, although it could also be something about their physical bearing or speech." Typically, however, this initial attraction is only a useful first step in the process of recognizing the virtues possessed by moral exemplars. Problems arise when our attention does not go beyond these superficial features. An appropriate response to moral exemplars needs to go beyond focusing on outward appearances.

An upshot of Jim's focus on these superficialities is his obsession with cases of spectacular heroism. Jim dreams of "saving people from sinking ships, cutting away masts in a hurricane, swimming through a surf with a line" (Conrad 1900/1993, 5). The problem is that this leads to Jim's failure to recognize that opportunities for heroism often do not present themselves in spectacular ways. Conrad makes the actual occasion on which the *Patna* is holed below the waterline as bathetic as possible: a barely distinct noise as the hull of the ship is gashed, all taking place on a bright, humid, day. Jim is completely unaware of the significance of what has occurred. Imaginarily rehearsing what heroes do in exceptional circumstances leaves him ill-prepared to recognize more mundane opportunities for heroism and to act correspondingly.

The second part of our diagnosis is that Jim fails to consider what it would actually take to become a hero. Jim wants to skyhook himself into the role of a hero without inquiring what qualities are actually exemplified by morally exemplary people and how they conceive of the circumstances calling for action. This is problematic as it turns out that heroes have distinctive ways of conceiving themselves and the situations they find themselves that are not shared by the non-heroic. We emphasize three distinctive features here and refer to empirical insights into the moral psychology of exemplars to back this up. Admirers need to acknowledge these features in their attempts to appropriately respond to the exemplars at hand.

A *first*, widely observed feature of how heroes conceive of their actions is that they do not see themselves as heroic. For example, Dutch resistance hero John Weidner helped numerous people escape the Nazis at great risk to himself. Asked whether his dedication to the resistance was "an extraordinarily good deed," he answered, "No. Absolutely not. I did my duty. That is all" (Monroe 2004, 117). Miep Gies, who helped hide Anne Frank and her family, said, "I am not a hero. . . . I was only willing to do what was asked of me and what seemed necessary at the time" (Gies and Gold 1987, 11). "Subway hero" Wesley Autrey, who risked his life to save a man who had fallen onto the tracks of the New York Subway, told the *New York Times*, "I don't feel like I did something spectacular; I just saw someone who needed help. I did what I felt was right" (Buckley 2007). While most people would regard these acts as heroic, heroes themselves typically do not. Vanessa Carbonell (2012, 231) refers to this as "a *persistent agent-observer disparity*."[3]

In contrast, Jim characterizes his actions as heroic even before he has performed them. While real heroes do not care about heroism or being seen as a hero, Jim definitely does. He cares much more about the status of a hero rather than about helping those in need. His "ethical attention" is not on the actual plight of people in need, but on opportunities for him to enact the role of a hero. To use Michael Smith's helpful distinction, his attention is not directed *de re* to actual instances of human need, but rather *de dicto* to how his response should be conceptualized (third personally) by others (Smith, 1994). This compounds Williams's distinction between an ethical awareness directed "outwards" on other people and their needs, and a third personal appraisal of one's character using characterological terms that ought to be ascribed to you *by others*. This misdirected focus explains Jim's moral errors: he cannot see the opportunities for heroism that actually present themselves and reacts incorrectly when the facts finally do impinge on his awareness. Conrad brings out the irony by making the other crew members of the *Patna* nothing other than cheats and cowards. While their response to the situation directly manifests their cowardice, Jim ends up behaving no better than they do.

The *second* distinctive feature of moral exemplars is that they view themselves as having no choice but to act as they did. In their study of those who risked their lives to rescue victims of Nazi persecution, Samuel and Pearl Oliner (1988) point out that many rescuers felt obliged, having no real choice except doing what needed to be done:

> I could not stand by and observe the daily misery that was occurring.
> It was necessary. Somebody had to do it.
> I saw the Germans shooting people in the street, and I could not sit there doing nothing.

> My husband told me that unless we helped, they would be killed. I could not stand that thought. (Oliner and Oliner 1988, 168)

As one of us has argued elsewhere (Archer, 2015), these claims are plausibly interpreted as exemplifying what Bernard Williams (1981) has called "practical necessity": one (feels one) has no option but to act in a particular way (see also Fruh 2017). According to Williams (1981, 128), practical necessities are conceptually tied to incapacities. In judging that I *must* act a particular way, I judge that I would be *incapable* of acting otherwise. Among these practical incapacities are a more limited set of what we would call "moral incapacities."[4]

> Incapacities that are themselves an expression of the moral life: the kind of incapacity that is in question when we say of someone, usually in commendation of him, that he could not act or was not capable of acting in certain ways. (Williams 1993, 59)

These experienced incapacities and necessities are, again, something distinctive about the moral psychology of heroes. In the words of Harry Frankfurt, this does not arise from some kind of deficiency (being incapacitated), strong desire (experiencing an irresistible urge or compulsion), or practical reasoning (seeing good reasons not to act differently). Instead, it is simply the case "that every apparent alternative to that course is unthinkable" (Frankfurt 1982, 263). While exemplars experience their heroic actions as moral necessities, most people would not: another first-person versus third-person asymmetry.

When the opportunity for heroism presents itself to Jim, he definitely does not experience a sense of practical or moral necessity. Instead, Jim is struck by indecision. Marlow describes Jim's decision to abandon the *Patna* as follows:

> The next minute—his last on board—was crowded with a tumult of events and sensations which beat about him like the sea upon a rock. I use the simile advisedly, because from his relation I am forced to believe he had preserved through it all a strange sense of passiveness, as though he had not acted but had suffered himself to be handled by the infernal powers who had selected him for the victim of their practical joke. (Conrad 1900/1993, 68)

As Jim himself later describes the experience to Marlow, "I was so lost, you know. It was the sort of thing one does not expect to happen to one. It was not like a fight, for instance. . . . One couldn't be sure" (Conrad 1900/1993, 81). Jim tries to justify himself by trying to show how unclear the situation was: "There was not the thickness of a sheet of paper between the right and wrong of the affair" (Conrad 1900/1993, 82). Marlow is thoroughly unimpressed, responding, "How much more did you want?" (Conrad 1900/1993, 82). The indecisiveness Jim experiences when push comes to shove could not be further removed from the experience of moral necessity.

The *third* distinctive feature of moral exemplars, which may go some way to explaining the other two, is that they tend to have made moral goals a core part of their identity. In their in-depth study of moral exemplars, Anne Colby and William Damon (1992) found that moral exemplars identified so closely with certain moral values that they saw little or no gap between doing what was needed to promote these values and doing what would promote their self-interest:

> The exemplars have done so without devaluing their own personal goals. Nor do they disregard their own fulfilment or self-development, nor, broadly construed, their own self-interests. They do not seek martyrdom. Rather than denying the self, they define it with a moral center. (Colby and Damon 1992, 300)

The contrast with Jim is, again, obvious. While he seems to imagine himself in the role of a hero, he is primarily concerned not with the moral values that make up heroes but with the role and the reputation that comes with it. Interestingly, Jim seems to be seeking martyrdom and longing for opportunities to become a martyr, while, tragically of course, not seeing and grabbing them as they present themselves.

Our claim about the close integration of the identities and moral values of exemplars is backed up by two studies conducted by Jeremy Frimer and his colleagues (Frimer et al. 2011). Their comparative study involving life review interviews of twenty-five recipients of national awards for exceptional volunteerism and a twenty-five strong demographically matched control group found that the award winners were significantly more likely to have integrated their own interests with their moral values. A similar study investigating the motivations of influential historical exemplars through a content analysis of their speeches and interviews produced comparable results (Frimer et al. 2012).[5] This part of the moral psychology of exemplars is distinctive, as most people face significantly more conflicts between their self-interests and their moral values. This integration is not something that exemplars are born with, nor is it something that happens instantly (Colby and Damon 1992, ch. 7). Instead, it is achieved through a long and gradual process of moral development, a process that Jim clearly did not undergo. His fantasizing and self-delusion disable him from doing the necessary work of moral development that actual heroes do.

3. EMULATION, IMITATION, AND MORAL WEIGHTLIFTING

So moral exemplars are exceptional in a number of ways and we should not overlook this. Jim thinks that it is enough that he wants to be heroic without engaging in an honest inquiry into whether he has the relevant virtues and character to even be capable of so doing. Jim's reaction to the *Patna* events should have been a warning sign that he lacks the capacities to be a hero. But instead of realizing his limitations, Jim persuades himself that this was not a true opportunity for heroism and reassures himself that when such an opportunity arises, he will rise to the occasion. If instead Jim would have reflected on the fact that he (apparently) lacked relevant characteristics to be morally exemplary, he would have reconsidered his attempt to emulate his heroes. Instead, he would and should have been led to consider ways in which he could become more virtuous.

One lesson to learn from Jim is that we must appreciate that moral exemplars are in many ways exceptional, effectively placing a distance between those exemplars and most ordinary individuals. Practical wisdom requires engagement in a process that we call "reflexive anchoring." When considering moral exemplars, we ought to take into account the distance between ourselves and the exemplar before deciding on the wisdom of making the exemplar's reasons our own—in the situation in which *we* find ourselves. We should not make Jim's mistake of assuming that we would be capable of performing similar acts whenever the opportunity presents itself. According to Williams, a person of less-than-ideal character, when considering the example of an ideal, ought reflectively to take into account *the degree of distance* between her current standard and the ideal standard:

> This immediately raises a problem, which is as much ethical as analytical. . . . [W]hat A has most reason to do in certain circumstances is what the *phrōnimos* would have reason to do in those circumstances. But, in considering what he has reason to do, one thing that A should take into account, if he is grown up and has some sense, are the ways in which he relevantly fails to be *phrōnimos*. . . . The homiletic tradition, not only within Christianity, is full of sensible warnings about the dangers of moral weight-lifting. (Williams 1995, 190)

Williams's point is that ethical error can result from trying to copy exemplars without reflecting on the ways in which we are not (yet) like them and in which acting like them lies beyond our reach (for now). When we have reason to believe that we are not heroic we should realize that acting heroically will not be as easy for us as it will be for genuine heroes.

We can replace the person of sound practical wisdom (the *phrōnimos*) with the hero in Williams's quote. In both cases, practical wisdom ought to take into consideration the degree of moral "stretch" for us in attempting to act on the reasons that our ideal adviser (our best self) or a hero would find it effortless to put into practice. Our ideal rational adviser is an ideal version of ourselves—not an ideal person, tout court.

Reflexive anchoring does not preclude trying to be a better person, perhaps even becoming a hero over time. Zagzebski's view is that we ought to try to make ourselves a better person by emulating an exemplar. We follow Williams, however, in stressing the importance of considering how exactly the imitation of an exemplar is supposed to figure in the ethical improvement of a person's character. We always and irrevocably start from here and with the character we have: setting ourselves the challenges that an exemplar would surmount with ease is quite often a bad piece of practical advice.

Imagine I admire Confucius. According to Zagzebski, I am inspired to try to be like him. Even granted Zagzebski's concession that I do not aim to *become* a second Confucius, I still want to be the same general kind of person as him and try to approximate his excellence of character. In our view, this thins out the idea of emulation to the point where it lacks content: to try and become a person of a Confucian type, but without Confucius's developed excellences, seems indeterminate advice unmoored from the ideal set by the exemplar.

Along Williams's lines, and based on our emphasis on reflexive anchoring, we can provide a different account. When Confucius is a source of inspiration for me, the content of the reasons that I derive from my admiration will be given not in terms of what Confucius would do in my situation, but what he would advise me to do, given that I am not him (and taking into account my starting point and distance from his own). That is, it seems to us, a defensible account of how an ideal adviser, a hero, or a *phrōnimos*, can feature in moral reasoning and development. Instead of asking "what would my admired exemplar do?" I should be asking, "What would my admired exemplar advise me to do in light of my own limitations?" Emulation no longer has a role to play in this account (Thomas 2006, 84–87).[6]

The difference between our account and Zagzebski's is reflected in her remark that it is "unlikely that we can know how far we can stretch ourselves morally without the experience of moral exemplars who show us how far human beings have gone in developing and expressing admirable human qualities" (Zagzebski 2017, 38). The problem, put succinctly, is that, depending on one's circumstances, "stretching oneself morally" may be a practically inadvisable goal. We take the example of Lord Jim to show how, in fact, moral "stretching" can be an essential prelude to specific kinds of moral error.[7]

One could object that Jim is not engaged in moral weightlifting or stretching at all. His imagined heroism fails to spur Jim into action, whereas in genuine cases of moral weightlifting, people are spurred into action but with detrimental results. A proper case of moral weightlifting would be that Jim's obsession with heroes propels him into the water, drowning himself without saving any passengers (for example, because he cannot swim).

We nevertheless insist that Jim's life story is a good case in point. After all, it is Jim's deeply rooted conviction that he can and should be as heroic as his admired exemplars that induces the feeling of shame that leads to his demise. Jim's horribly misplaced ideas about his ability to do the right thing lead him to sacrifice himself. As such, the desire to emulate his heroes is not merely insufficient to motivate Jim to moral action (Jim's indecision on the *Patna*) but ultimately leads him to do the wrong thing (meaninglessly sacrificing and ruining his life). A hero displays sensitivity to the right reasons and to the context of action; Jim's sacrifice is not morally admirable, but ethically a mistake. He has found personal redemption, personal happiness, and the admiration and trust of his peers on the *Patna*. The tragic events in which he has been involved that led up to Dain Waris's death were not, on any reasonable construal, Jim's fault. His volunteering for an unnecessary punishment at the cost of his own life is motivated solely by his mistaken understanding of his own ideals. Being unjustly killed for no good reason is not heroic.

Before concluding, let us return to the distinctive role imagination can and should play when admiring moral exemplars. In cases such as Jim's, we can distinguish between two ways in which we can put imagination to use in moral learning and discrimination (Engelen, Thomas, Archer and van de Ven, forthcoming). Richard Wollheim (1974) draws a seminal distinction between "acentral" and "central imagining." If you imagine Napoleon triumphantly entering Paris on horseback, you can represent to yourself an imagined scene containing Napoleon (acentral) or you can imagine the scene from and thus, as imaginer, take the point of view of Napoleon himself (central).

In his engagement with "light fiction," Jim fails to engage in central imagining: seeing ethical choices as framed from the perspective of the morally exemplary people themselves. Were he to centrally imagine the life of a hero, Jim would come to appreciate that any hero's virtuous responses consist in two crucial aspects. First, they are directed to what Schopenhauer (1995 [1840]: 143) poetically calls the "weal and woe" of another. Instead of acting out some social script, exemplars react to the plight of those in need. Secondly, as we have seen, in the specific psychology of morally exceptional people, the demands posed by a situation are often experienced as practically necessary. To their minds (which is the perspective central imagining requires one to take), exemplars are not being heroic but are simply doing their duty. What Jim lacks, then, is a form of reflective insight into the perspective of another (i.e., the moral exemplary). Instead, he focuses on the acentral imagination of playing the role of a hero with no appreciation of the cognitive work and the motivational necessities actually experienced by the exemplary. When Jim imagines himself in situations that demand heroism, "cutting away masts in a hurricane," he is not only focused too much on himself, playing the part of the hero, he mistakenly believes that heroism will be as effortless and straightforward to him as it is to real heroes.

4. IMPLICATIONS FOR MORAL EDUCATION

According to Zagzebski, narratives about moral exemplars ought to play a central role in moral education. Our discussion up to now suggests a note of caution: too much of a focus on narratives of moral exemplars may obscure their exceptional nature. This is particularly the case if they are conceptualized in the crude and superficial "light fiction" so adored by Jim. Such narratives run the risk of making it appear easy to act as exemplars do, which can give rise to all the problems mentioned above such as moral weightlifting. We suggest two ways to respond to these problems.

First, narratives of moral exemplars should include elements that contextualize their actions, reveal their inner thoughts and stress their exceptional character. Only then can admiration and a possible desire to emulate be informed and constrained by reflexive anchoring. Second, there ought also to be a role in education, next to narratives of moral exemplars, for narratives of moral failure. Again in order to appreciate the exceptional nature of exemplars and to encourage reflexive anchoring, moral education ought to include an awareness of the many ways in which people fail to be exemplary.[8] These narratives ought also to go beyond the shallow and superficial. *Lord Jim* itself is not about a moral exemplar but can nevertheless serve a useful role in moral education.

We can find further support for the importance of narratives of moral failure in Catherine Elgin's (1991, 199) important observation that the context in which something is presented is of crucial importance for making salient the features that we wish to make salient. Bryan Warnick (2008 44) extends this point to the topic of education through examples by pointing out that "[a] context of both strong similarity and salient difference within a group is often what makes exemplarity possible." In order to make the relevant features of moral exemplars salient, using only narratives of moral exemplars in education will not suffice. These must be contrasted with narratives of people who failed to reach exemplary levels of moral conduct. Relying exclusively on examples of moral exemplars in moral education runs the risk not only of flattening out their character but also of failing to clarify the *distinctive* features of their psychology that make their heroism possible and effortless.

5. CONCLUSION

Instead of addressing Zagzebski's ambitious claim that exemplarism is a novel, foundational contribution to meta-ethics, we have restricted ourselves to her more limited claim that the desire to emulate moral exemplars is an appropriate attitude and an important form of moral development. In addition to raising concerns about the extent to which Zagzebski can distinguish her view from virtue ethics, the main of the chapter was to sound a note of caution. The cultural scripts that educate us towards virtue and excellence also contain resources, such as Conrad's novel *Lord Jim*, that illustrate how the desire to emulate morally exemplary people can also lead to moral error and failure. Along the lines of Williams, we have stressed how attempts to emulate the exemplary should go hand in hand with and be constrained by reflexive anchoring. We concluded by explaining the implications of our cautionary note for moral education. Narratives of moral exemplars should include elements that contextualize their actions, reveal their inner thoughts and stress their exceptional character. Such narratives should be utilized alongside narratives of moral failure to raise awareness of the many ways in which people fail to be exemplary.[9]

NOTES

1. A remark on the scope of our chapter: while Zagzebski hopes to construct an entirely new moral theory based on her account of exemplars, we set this ambitious project to one side. Our goal here is to evaluate her more restricted claims about the importance of moral exemplars to our moral thinking, our admiration for them, and their prevalence in both fictional and nonfictional cultural narratives.

2. Zagzebski cites Algoe and Haidt (2009) in support of her view. See also Aquino et al. 2011, Cox 2010, Freeman et al. 2009, Immordino-Yang and Sylvan 2010, Landis et al. 2009, and Schnall et al. 2010. For an alternative way of conceptualizing the motivational profile of admiration see Archer (forthcoming).

3. See Archer and Ridge (2015) for a discussion of a puzzle these claims raise about moral heroes.

4. Williams does not use the term "moral necessity" though if practical incapacities to perform any alternatives lead to practical necessities, then moral incapacities will, in turn, lead to moral necessities. The term "moral necessity" is used by Christopher Cowley (2004).

5. See Archer (2017) for discussions of further philosophical implications of these findings.

6. It is worth noting that a number of objections have been raised against such ideal adviser accounts (see Johnson 2003 and Svensson 2010). We do not have the space to respond to such objections here.

7. Given the empirical grounding of her theory, Zagzebski acknowledges that her claim that admiration leads to emulation may not hold true for all exemplars. The example of perfect people (saints) can be de-motivating, but we can aim to recapitulate the journey of exemplars in our own lives (Zagzebski 2017, 39).

8. Berger and Alfano (2016) suggest a related use of narratives of moral failure, in informing us of the ways in which situations shape character and action.

9. This publication was made possible through the support of a grant from the Beacon Project at Wake Forrest University and the Templeton Religious Trust. The opinions expressed

in this publication are those of the authors and do not necessarily reflect the views of the Beacon Project, Wake Forrest University, or the Templeton Religious Trust.

REFERENCES

Algoe, S. B., and J. Haidt. 2009. "Witnessing Excellence in Action: The 'Other-Praising' Emotions of Elevation, Gratitude, and Admiration." *The Journal of Positive Psychology* 4 (2): 105–27.

Aquino, K., B. McFerran, and M. Laven. 2011. "Moral Identity and the Experience of Moral Elevation in Response to Acts of Uncommon Goodness." *Journal of Personality and Social Psychology* 100 (4): 703–18.

Archer, A. 2015. "Saints, Heroes and Moral Necessity." Royal Institute of Philosophy Supplement 77: 105–24.

Archer, A. 2017. "Integrity and the Value of an Integrated Self." *Journal of Value Inquiry* 51 (3): 435–54.

Archer, A. Forthcoming. "Admiration and Motivation." *Emotion Review*.

Archer, A., and M. Ridge. 2015. "The Heroism Paradox: Another Paradox of Supererogation." *Philosophical Studies* 172 (6): 1575–592.

Berger, J., and M. Alfano. 2016. "Virtue, Situationism, and the Cognitive Value of Art." *The Monist* 99 (2): 144–58.

Brudney, D. 1998. "Lord Jim and Moral Judgment: Literature and Moral Philosophy." *The Journal of Aesthetics and Art Criticism* 56 (3): 265–81.

Buckley, C. 2007. "Man Is Rescued by Stranger on Subway Tracks." *New York Times*, January 3, 2007. Accessed on January 16, 2018. http://www.nytimes.com/2007/01/03/nyregion/03life.html.

Carbonell, V. 2012. "The Ratchetting-Up Effect." *Pacific Philosophical Quarterly* 93 (2): 228–54.

Colby, A., and W. Damon. 1992. *Some Do Care: Contemporary Lives of Moral Commitment*. New York: The Free Press.

Conrad, J. 1900/1993. *Lord Jim*. Ware: Wordsworth Editions.

Cowley, C. 2004. "Moral Necessity and the Personal." *Croatian Journal of Philosophy* 4 (1): 123–38.

Cox, K. S. 2010. "Elevation Predicts Domain-Specific Volunteerism 3 Months Later." *The Journal of Positive Psychology* 5 (5): 333–41.

Elgin, C. Z. 1991. "Understanding: Art and Science." *Midwest Studies in Philosophy* 16 (1): 196–208.

Engelen, B., A. Thomas, A. Archer, and N. van de Ven. Forthcoming. "Exemplars and Nudges: Two Strategies for Moral Education." *Journal of Moral Education*. Published online at https://doi.org/10.1080/03057240.2017.1396966.

Frankfurt, H. 1982. "The Importance of What We Care About." *Synthese* 53 (2): 257–72.

Frimer, J. A., L. J. Walker, W. L. Dunlop, B. H. Lee, and A. Riches. 2011. "The Integration of Agency and Communion in Moral Personality: Evidence of Enlightened Self-Interest." *Journal of Personality and Social Psychology* 101 (1): 149–63.

Frimer, J. A., L. J. Walker, B. H. Lee, A. Riches, and W. L. Dunlop. 2012. "Hierarchical Integration of Agency and Communion: A Study of Influential Moral Figures." *Journal of Personality* 80 (4): 1117–45.

Fruh, K. 2017. "Practical Necessity and Moral Heroism." In *Oxford Studies in Agency and Responsibility: Volume 4*, 28–49. Oxford: Oxford University Press.

Gies, M., and A. L. Gold. 1987. *Anne Frank Remembered: The Story of the Woman Who Helped to Hide the Frank Family*. New York: Simon and Schuster.

Goldie, P. 2012. *The Mess Inside: Narrative, Emotion, and the Mind*. Oxford: Oxford University Press.

Harcourt, E. 2016. "The Dangers of Fiction: *Lord Jim* and Moral Perfectionism." In *Art, Mind and Narrative: Themes from the Work of Peter Goldie*, edited by Julian Dodd, 80–88. Oxford: Oxford University Press.

Immordino-Yang, M. H., and L. Sylvan. 2010. "Admiration for Virtue: Neuroscientific Perspectives On a Motivating Emotion." *Contemporary Educational Psychology* 35 (2): 110–15.

Johnson, Robert. 2003. "Virtue and Right." *Ethics* 113 (4): 810–34.

Landis, S. K., M. F. Sherman, R. L. Piedmont, M. W. Kirkhart, E. M. Rapp, and D. H. Bike. 2009. "The Relation between Elevation and Self-Reported Prosocial Behavior: Incremental Validity over the Five-Factor Model of Personality." *The Journal of Positive Psychology* 4 (1): 71–84.

Monroe, K. 2004. *The Hand of Compassion: Portraits of Moral Choice During the Holocaust.* Princeton, NJ: Princeton University Press.

Oliner, S. P., and P. M. Oliner. 1988. *The Altruistic Personality: Rescuers of Jews In Nazi Germany.* New York: Free Press.

Oliver, M. 1994. "John Weidner, Hero in Holocaust, Dies." *Los Angeles Times*, May 23, 1994. Accessed on January 16, 2018. http://articles.latimes.com/1994-05-23/news/mn-61214_1_john-weidner.

Schnall, S., J. Roper, and D. M. Fessler. 2010. "Elevation Leads to Altruistic Behavior." *Psychological Science* 21 (3): 315–20.

Schopenhauer, A. 1998 [1840]. *On the Basis of Morality*. Translated by E. F. J. Payne. Indianapolis: Hackett Publishing.

Smith, M. 1994. *The Moral Problem*. Oxford: Blackwell.

Svensson, Frans. 2010. "Virtue Ethics and the Search for an Account of Right Action." *Ethical Theory and Moral Practice* 13 (3): 255–71.

Taylor, C. 2011. "Literature, Moral Reflection and Ambiguity." *Philosophy* 86 (1): 75–93.

Thomas, Alan. 2006. *Value and Context: The Nature of Moral and Political Knowledge*. Oxford: Clarendon Press.

Warnick, B. R. 2008. *Imitation and Education: A Philosophical Inquiry into Learning by Example*. Albany, NY: The State University of New York Press.

Williams, B. 1981. "Practical Necessity." In *Moral Luck: Philosophical Papers 1973–1980*. Cambridge: Cambridge University Press.

Williams, B. 1985. *Ethics and the Limits of Philosophy*. London: Fontana.

Williams, B. 1993. "Moral Incapacity." *Proceedings of the Aristotelian Society* 93 (1): 59–70.

Williams, B. 1995. "Replies." In *World, Mind, and Ethics: Essays on the Ethical Philosophy of Bernard Williams*, edited by J. E. J. Altham and Ross Harrison, 185–224. Cambridge: Cambridge University Press.

Wollheim, R. 1974. "Imagination and Identification." In *On Art and the Mind*, 54–83. Cambridge, MA: Harvard University Press.

Zagzebski, L. T. 2017. *Exemplarist Moral Theory*. Oxford: Oxford University Press.

Index

Achilles, 135
act-focused attitudes, 36
aesthetic judgement, 131, 132
Addams, Jane, 203
admiration: appearance and, 137; aesthetic vs. moral, 40, 61, 63, 72; adoration vs. admiration, 189–193; agential, 31, 32, 34, 38, 40, 42, 121; agent-relative vs. agent-neutral, 95, 96, 99, 100, 101, 102, 103, 104, 105, 131; bodily symptoms of, 182; developmental changes in, 185–186; distance requirements of, 189–191; vs. elevation, 40, 126, 181–184, 218; equality and, 69, 70, 71; evaluation, 2, 13, 34, 46, 50, 51, 83, 96, 98, 105, 115, 122, 123, 125; fittingness, 33, 34, 35, 38, 39, 41, 42, 46, 52, 99, 101, 102, 103, 187–188, 207; for skill vs. elevation, 183–185; function, 31; grudging/reluctant, 115; ideology critique of, 161; in children, 184; just distribution of, 160–162; memory and, 134, 149; morality of, 52, 53, 61, 62, 69, 70, 71, 72, 73, 105; motivation, 3, 6, 25, 29, 30, 31, 34, 35, 50, 56, 61, 82, 87, 98, 115, 121, 122, 123, 125, 126, 190–193; non-agential, 31; object, 35, 37, 51, 80, 98, 115, 120, 121, 123, 124, 125; phenomenology of, 2, 12, 13, 14, 31, 46, 51, 98, 115; politics and, 54, 55, 56, 57, 114, 116, 125, 126, 131, 132; revolutionary, 113, 115, 116, 120, 121, 122, 123, 124, 125, 126; self-admiration, 39; social movements and, 54–55; support and, 149–162; trust and, 136, 137–138; vs. adoration, 54; vs. benign envy, 63, 67, 68, 69, 140–143, 185; vs. emulative envy, 49, 50, 51, 52, 53, 54, 55, 56, 57
affiliation, 182
alienation, 114
Algoe, Sara B., 40, 126, 190
anger, 5, 30, 35, 36, 37, 39
animal ethics, 6, 165–176
Annas, Julia, 206
Aquinas, Thomas, 20
Archer, Alfred, 3, 7, 167–168, 170, 173–175
Arendt, Hannah, 6, 18, 129, 131–133, 134, 136
Aristotle, 7, 19, 24, 55, 138, 170–171, 203, 206, 211–213
art, 86, 87, 88, 89, 96
awe, 31, 62, 66, 79, 85, 98
Augustine, 136

Bankovsky, Miriam, 55
Batson, D., 71
Baumgarten, A. G., 81
beauty, 89, 115
Bewunderung, 81, 91n9, 92n25, 106n2, 130

bewundern, 75n8, 106n2, 116
bewundernswert, 106n2
Beiser, Frederick, 85
Bell, Macalester, 2, 39
Ben-Ze'ev, Aaron, 55, 56
Berger, John, 170–171
Buddha, 184
Bhutto, Benazir, 55
Black Lives Matter, 55
blame, 1
Burke, Edmund, 80, 85

Carlyle, Thomas, 15, 19, 22, 26
Castelfranchi, Cristiano, 56
categorical imperative, 131
Cawston, Amanda, 6
Chappell, Sophie-Grace, 2
character, 129
Christ, Jesus, 16, 25
Colby, Anne, 203
cognitive, 13
Compaijen, Rob, 3
Communism, 113–114, 118
Confucius, 138, 174, 243
Conrad, Joseph, 7, 233
contempt, 29, 31, 37, 39
cool, 16
Cooney, Coleman, 173
cooperation, 182
courage, 130
Cramwinkel, Florien M., 7
creativity, 96
crisis, 129, 131

Damon, William, 203
Darley, R., 71
Darwin, Charles, 2
Dearing, R. L., 31
Descartes, René, 3, 122, 123, 124, 129–131, 138, 171
despair, 130
DeSteno, David, 34
dictatorship, 131
Duncan, Martha Grace, 115

education, 184, 186–187, 189, 211–213
emulation, 3, 4, 6, 7, 14, 25, 26, 34, 39, 40, 48, 56, 80, 82, 88, 98, 101, 104, 115, 116, 121, 126, 129, 130, 131, 138, 182, 183, 184, 208–210, 234–235, 242–244, 245
Einstein, Albert, 149
Engelen, Bart, 7
Engels, Friedrich, 117, 118, 119, 124
envy, 14, 15, 45, 46, 47, 48, 49, 50, 52, 53, 54, 55, 56, 57, 58, 67, 185, 217
epiphany, 17
Elgin, Catherin, 245
Evans, Ieshia, 55
excellence, 96, 97, 100, 101, 105, 115, 132, 182, 218
exemplars, 6, 7, 24, 25, 30, 61, 66, 67, 68, 71, 72, 73, 74, 82, 100, 101, 115, 129, 130, 133, 135, 136, 137, 138, 139, 141, 142, 143, 144n16, 166, 167, 169, 170, 171, 172, 173, 174, 175, 177n9, 177n14, 181, 185, 186, 189, 193, 201, 202, 203, 204, 205, 206, 207, 208, 208–209, 209–210, 211–212, 212–213, 213, 214n8, 214n11, 214n15, 218, 220, 221, 222, 225, 233–234, 234–246
exhortative attitudes, 29, 30, 33, 34, 39

familiarity, 131
fear, 47, 103
Fischer, Jeremy, 31
flourishing, 95, 96, 101, 105
Forrester, Mary, 2
forward-looking judgements vs. backward-looking judgements, 132
Frankfurt, Harry, 240
Frank, Anne, 226
Fricker, Miranda, 161
friendship, 13, 55, 57, 136, 170

Gaita, Raymond, 17
Gandhi, Mahatma, 54
German Enlightenment, 79
Gottman, John, 37
Grahle, André, 6
guilt, 30, 36

Haidt, Jonathan, 40, 126, 181, 202
Harmon Jones, Eddie, 51
Hegel, G. W. F., 19
Henrich, Joseph, 51
heroism, 7, 12, 19, 24, 25, 27, 80, 82, 88, 120, 125, 239

Index

Hill, Thomas, 65
Homer, 132
hope, 130, 131
human plurality, 131
Hume, David, 32, 62
humility, 15, 62, 74

ideals, 29, 30, 31, 32, 33, 34, 35, 38, 40, 41, 42, 46, 51, 54, 88, 89, 118, 165, 169, 182, 184, 185, 186, 187, 189–191, 193–194, 195, 221, 234, 235, 242
identity, 241
idols, 189
imagination, 131, 134
imitation, 242–244
immorality, 129, 131; resistance to, 129; acceptance of, 131
impartiality, 131, 134
indignation, 30, 36, 39
intention vs. consequence, 225–227
intentionality, 30
intergroup admiration, 183
intersubjectivity, 131
intimidation, 183

James, C. L. R., 20, 21, 22, 23, 27, 117
Jaspers, Karl, 135
Jefferson, Thomas, 181
Johnstone, Monty, 117

Kant, Immanuel, 16, 17, 18, 79, 80, 88, 131, 135
Kaposi, Dorottya, 123
Kauppinen, Antti, 2, 33, 37
Keller, Helen, 226
Kierkegaard, Søren, 15, 45, 50, 51, 142–143
Kim, Sung Hee, 47, 53
King Haakon VII, 132–133
King, Martin Luther, 54, 149
Koller, Aaron, 85
Kohlberg dilemmas, 227
Kristjánsson, Kristján, 54, 138, 141, 211–213

La Caze, Marguerite, 5, 6, 54, 56
L'Arche, 138
Larkin, Philip, 17
Lenin, Vladimir I., 125

Lessing, Gotthold E., 4, 79, 80, 81, 82, 83, 84
Levenson, Robert, 37
Livingstone Smith, David, 57
Located Value Promotion Account, 175
love, 5, 37, 38, 54, 57
Lord Jim, 236–241
Luxemburg, Rosa, 135

Mandela, Nelson, 32, 142, 203
Marx, Karl, 5, 113, 114, 116, 117, 118, 119, 120, 121, 124, 125, 126
Mason, Michelle, 31, 58
Matthews, Freya, 171
McConnell, Kelly, 123
McMahon, Jennifer, 169
Mendelssohn, Moses, 3, 4, 79, 80, 81, 82, 83, 84, 85, 86, 87, 88, 89
Miceli, Maria, 56
Milk, Harvey, 226
mirabilis, 130
Monin, Benoît, 7
moral status of animals, 169–172
moral weightlifting, 242–244
Morgan-Knapp, Christopher, 54
de Montaigne, Michel, 19
moral education, 4, 6, 7, 81, 82, 84, 87, 88, 89, 201–213
moral vs. intellectual virtues, 201–202
Mowat, Farley, 169

narcissism, 62
Nathan, N. M. L., 124
Nazis, 17, 41, 131, 132, 133, 239
Neu, Jerome, 54
Nicolai, Friedrich, 4, 80, 81, 83
Nietzsche, Friedrich, 4, 95, 95–96, 97, 100–101, 102, 103, 104, 105, 106
nihilism, 16, 19
Nolte, Fred, 82, 83
Nozick, Robert, 54
Nussbaum, Martha, 29, 42, 57

Obama, Barack, 55, 142
object of admiration, 29, 30
Occupy Wall Street, 55
Oliner, Samuel, 239–240
Oliner, Pearl, 239–240
ought implies can, 52

Onu, Diana, 1
openness, 16
other-praising emotions, 183

Paris Commune, 116, 117, 118, 119, 120, 121, 124, 125, 126
perfectionism, 95, 97, 105
person-focused attitudes, 36
personal growth, 183, 192–193
petitionary reasons, 153–160
phronesis, 212, 242
Plato, 17, 24
Pollok, Anne, 4
positive psychology movement, 184
practical necessity, 239–240
Protasi, Sara, 47, 57, 141
pro-scriptive vs. pre-scriptive morality
pro-social behaviour, 194
praise, praiseworthiness, 1, 37, 114, 182–183
pride, 29, 31, 32, 34, 35, 37, 38, 39

regret, 14
resentment, 104, 138, 142, 185
van der Rijt, Jan-Willem, 3
Rawls, John, 54, 64
Robertson, Simon, 4, 34
Robins, Richard, 37
Roosevelt, Eleanor, 203

sages, 24, 25
saints, 24, 25
schadenfreude, 84
Sanderse, Wouter, 211
Schiller, Friedrich, 79, 88, 89
Schindler, Ines, 1, 2, 6, 50, 51, 52, 165
Schindler, Oskar, 133, 135
Schopenhauer, Arthur, 100, 101, 102
Schmidt, Anton, 131
self-esteem, 63, 64, 65, 66, 67, 68, 69, 219–221
self-improvement, 95, 104, 105, 106
self-knowledge, 85
self-respect, 63, 64, 65, 66, 68, 69, 74
self-transcendent emotions, 183
self-threat, 217
sensus communis, 133, 135
Shaftesbury, A. A. C. (Third Earl of Shaftesbury), 80, 85

shame, 29, 31, 36, 38, 185
Shoah, 138, 213
Shoemaker, David, 31
Skorupski, John, 98, 150
Smith, Adam, 2, 3, 4, 5, 84, 98
Smith, Michael, 239
Smith, Richard H., 47, 53
Snow, Nancy, 206
Socha, Leopold, 138, 203
social comparison, 185
Socialism, 116
social norms, 130, 133
spectator vs. actor judgement, 132
spontaneity, 16
sport, 20, 21, 22, 23, 25, 26, 27
Stalinist regime, 131
Stichter, Matt, 206
sublime, 80, 85, 86
surprise, 2, 15, 16, 18, 124

Tai, Kenneth, 53
Tangney, J. P., 31, 36
taste, 132, 133, 134
Tännsjö, Torbjörn, 5
Thomas, Alan, 7
Thomas, Roger, 116
Thompson, E. P., 21
Townley, Cynthia, 170
Tracy, Jessica, 36, 37
tragedy, 81, 82, 83, 84, 86, 87, 88, 89
trait-focused attitudes, 36, 129

unattainability, 221–222
unfamiliarity, 129, 130

Value Promotion Account, 168, 173–175
Vanier, Jean, 138, 203
Varnhagen, Rahel
van de Ven, Niels, 50
virtue, 7, 32, 34, 66, 114, 115, 136, 201–213, 206
vulnerability, 15, 16

Watson, Gary, 43
Whelan, Frederick G., 114
wholehearted, 121
Williams, Bernard, 240, 242
Williams, Lisa, 34
Williams, Serena, 217

Wills, Vanessa, 5
Wilson, Alan T., 7
Wollheim, Richard, 244
Wolf, Susan, 40
Wolf, Christian, 86
wonder, 2, 6, 15, 16, 18, 26, 62, 68, 69, 71, 72, 73, 98, 116, 122, 123, 129, 130
Wordsworth, William, 174

Wunder, 130

Yousafzai, Malala, 54

Zagzebski, Linda, 3, 6, 14, 23, 24, 25, 26, 27, 38, 61, 62, 129, 131, 136–143, 166–167, 169, 170, 172, 202–203, 203–205, 233–235, 243, 246

About the Contributors

Alfred Archer is Assistant Professor of Philosophy at The Department of Philosophy and The Tilburg Center for Logic, Ethics, and Philosophy of Science at Tilburg University. His primary research is in moral philosophy, particularly supererogation (acts beyond the call of duty), and the nature ethics of admiration. He also has research interests in political philosophy, applied ethics, and philosophy of emotion. For up-to-date information about his research, visit http://alfredarcher.weebly.com/. His work for this volume was supported by the NWO (The Netherlands Organisation for Scientific Research; Grant Number 016.Veni.174.104).

Amanda Cawston is Assistant Professor of Philosophy at Tilburg University and a member of the Tilburg Center for Logic, Ethics, and Philosophy of Science. She has a wide range of interests within political philosophy and applied ethics, including the ethics of violence and non-violence, feminist philosophy, migration ethics, and topics in animal ethics. She has written on pacifism, the feminist debate on pornography, competition, and self-sacrifice. Her current research explores how mechanisms of alienation support forms of violence, and subsequently call for new forms of non-violent resistance.

Sophie-Grace Chappell is Professor of Philosophy at the Open University, UK. Her books include *Aristotle and Augustine on Freedom* (Macmillan, 1995), *Understanding Human Goods* (Edinburgh University Press, 2003), *The Inescapable Self: An Introduction to Philosophy* (Orion, 2005), *Reading Plato's Theaetetus* (Hackett, 2005), *Ethics and Experience* (Acumen, 2009), and *Knowing What to Do: Imagination, Virtue, and Platonism in Ethics* (Oxford University Press, 2014). Her main current research is about epiphanies, immediate and revelatory encounters with value, and their place in our experience and our philosophical ethics.

Florien M. Cramwinckel (PhD: 2016, Utrecht University) is Assistant Professor of Interdisciplinary Social Sciences at Utrecht University, The Netherlands. She has a background in social psychology. In her current position as an assistant professor, she focuses on the reduction of prejudice against sexual minorities. She studies measures to assess sexual orientation and gender identity prejudice and investigates the effectiveness of interventions to reduce prejudice. In her PhD research, she focused on social psychological insights into moral reactions. She investigated questions such as: how do people respond to others who take a moral stance; why is this response (often) so negative; how to reduce these negative consequences? She focused on several different areas, such as homosexuality, discrimination, and vegetarianism.

Bart Engelen is a political and social philosopher at Tilburg University (The Netherlands) and is affiliated with the Tilburg Center for Logic, Ethics, and Philosophy of Science (TiLPS). His research focuses on the borders between ethics, political philosophy (institutional design), and economics (rational choice theory). He has recently worked on issues surrounding paternalism and the role of preferences in economics but his main interest lies with the ethics of nudging. He has published papers on the legitimacy of nudging in moral education and to promote people's health. He has also addressed worries about nudges violating autonomy, rationality and transparency.

André Grahle is a Lecturer in Philosophy at LMU Munich. His PhD is from the University of St Andrews. His research areas are ethics, political philosophy, social philosophy, and moral psychology. He is currently working on questions related to the ethics testimony in contexts of migration. Another project is to turn his dissertation into a monograph. Here the focus is on ideals as conceptions of admirable ways of being, and specifically on the link between ideals and meaningfulness in life.

Antti Kauppinen is Professor of Practical Philosophy at the University of Helsinki. His research interests include philosophical moral psychology, well-being, meaning in life, and various questions regarding the foundations of normativity. In addition to a number of papers on these topics, he has co-edited the volume *Methodology and Moral Philosophy* (Routledge, 2019) with Jussi Suikkanen. He is currently writing a monograph on the role of agency in well-being.

Marguerite La Caze is Associate Professor in Philosophy at the University of Queensland. Her publications include *Ethical Restoration after Communal Violence: The Grieving and the Unrepentant* (Lexington, 2018), *Wonder and Generosity: Their Role in Ethics and Politics* (SUNY, 2013), *The Analytic Imaginary* (Cornell, 2002), *Integrity and the Fragile Self*, with Damian Cox and Michael Levine (Ashgate, 2003), the edited collection *Phenomenology and Forgiveness* (Rowman & Littlefield International, 2018), and essays on European philosophy in aesthetics; ethics, including moral psychology; and political philosophy.

Benoît Monin is the Bowen H. and Janice Arthur McCoy Professor of Ethics, Psychology, and Leadership at Stanford University, with tenures in both Psychology and the Graduate School of Business. His research interests include moral psychology, self-defensive processes, norm perception, and business ethics. He holds a PhD in psychology from Princeton University, has held visiting positions at the University of Michigan and Paris-10, and is a former associate editor of the *Journal of Experimental Social Psychology*.

Anne Pollok is a historian of philosophy (18th–20th century aesthetics and philosophy of culture), and Associate Professor of Philosophy at the University of South Carolina, Columbia/SC. In 2010 she published her book *Facetten des Menschen. Zur Anthropologie Moses Mendelssohns* (Meiner), which, together with her editions on Mendelssohn's aesthetics and his Phädon, earned her the Moses-Mendelssohn-Award in 2013. It reconstructs the most salient features of Mendelssohn's philosophy as an early form of rational anthropology, a development emerging out of Mendelssohn's engagement with his contemporaries such as Lessing, Kant, and Herder. Besides numerous publications and presentations centered around Mendelssohn's and Schiller's aesthetics, Pollok's work also focuses on the legacy of the eighteenth century in Ernst Cassirer's and Susanne Langer's Philosophy of Culture. Her recent invited talks and papers concern in particular the aesthetic and historical dimensions of symbolic formation that come to the fore in the writings of female philosophers of the late eighteenth century.

Sara Protasi is Assistant Professor of Philosophy at University of Puget Sound. She thinks, writes, and teaches about the nature and value of emotions, especially love and envy, on which she has published several articles in journals such as *European Journal of Philosophy*, *Thought*, *Philosophia*, and *Journal of the American Philosophical Association*, and in edited volumes (for pre-print drafts, see https://philpapers.org/s/Sara%20Protasi). She is currently writing a monograph on the moral psychology of envy, in which she defends a novel taxonomy of envy and examines its implications for ethics, politics, and other axiological domains. More detailed and updated information on her can be found at https://saraprotasi.weebly.com/.

Simon Robertson works mainly in ethics. Much of his research lies at the intersection of normative ethics, metaethics, and practical reason, though he also works on Nietzsche, normativity, risk, and moral psychology. He has published in each of these fields, in journals and edited collections, and is the editor of *Spheres of Reason* (OUP, 2009) and co-editor of *Nietzsche, Naturalism, and Normativity* (OUP, 2012). Currently completing a monograph critically assessing Nietzsche's ethics, he is now an independent scholar.

Ines Schindler is a Senior Researcher at the Max Planck Institute for Empirical Aesthetics in Frankfurt am Main, Germany. Her current research focus is on the development and functions of aesthetic emotions and self-transcendent or moral emotions, including the conceptualization, differentiation, and measurement of such emotions. This research is informed by her training as a lifespan developmental psychologist and subsequent interdisciplinary research on other-praising emotions, in particular admiration and adoration. She has published articles in peer-reviewed journals such as *Cognition and Emotion, Motivation and Emotion, Psychology and Aging*, and *Psychological Review*.

Alan Thomas is Professor of Philosophy and head of department at the University of York in the UK. Educated at Cambridge, Harvard, and Oxford, he is the author of the books *Value and Context* (OUP, 2006), *Thomas Nagel* (Routledge, 2008) and *Republic of Equals* (OUP, 2017). He has published numerous articles and book chapters on moral philosophy, political philosophy, and the philosophy of mind.

Jan-Willem van der Rijt is Senior Lecturer in Practical Philosophy at Umeå University. He has published on a variety of topics in moral and political theory, such as the relation between human rights and dignity, happiness as a public policy objective, retributive justice, the moral and political significance of subjective moral judgements, the evils of torture and coercion, and self-respect. Originally trained as a mathematical economist, he also has a research interest in strategic interaction and democracy. He authored *The Importance of Assent: A Theory of Coercion and Dignity* (Springer, 2012), co-edited *Wellbeing in Contemporary Society* (Springer, 2015), and published multiple papers in various international journals with differing disciplinary focus. These include *Economics and Philosophy, Erkenntnis, Law and Philosophy, The Southern Journal of Philosophy*, and *Theory and Decision*.

Vanessa Wills is a political philosopher, ethicist, educator, and activist working in Washington, DC. She is Assistant Professor of Philosophy at The George Washington University. She received her PhD in Philosophy from the University of Pittsburgh in 2011, where she wrote her dissertation on the topic "Marx and Morality." Dr. Wills received her bachelor's degree in Philosophy from Princeton University in 2002. Her areas of specialization are moral, social, and political philosophy, nineteenth-century German philosophy (especially Karl Marx), and the philosophy of race. Her research, which has been supported by grants from the Fulbright Scholar Program and the German Academic Exchange Service, is importantly informed by her study of Marx's work, and focuses on the ways in which economic and social arrangements can inhibit or promote the realization of values such as freedom, equality, and human development.

Alan T. Wilson is Lecturer in Ethics at the University of Bristol. A central focus for his research concerns the concepts of virtue and vice. This includes attempting to understand the relationships *between* virtues, both between individual virtues (such as courage, kindness, and open-mindedness) and between different types of virtue (such as moral and intellectual virtues). It is hoped that an understanding of these relationships will aid future research on strategies for the *development* of virtue (or for the avoidance of vice). His recent publications have appeared in journals including *Ethics*, *Ethical Theory and Moral Practice*, and *Metaphilosophy*.

CPSIA information can be obtained
at www.ICGtesting.com
Printed in the USA
LVHW031343101021
700056LV00006B/100